RIVER TRACKS

RIVER TRACKS

Exploring Australian Rivers

Catherine de Courcy and John Johnson

Macquarie
Regional Library

Lothian
BOOKS

Disclaimer

This book is intended as a guide only. The authors and publisher accept no responsibility or liability for accidents, breakdowns, loss of direction, delays or other inconvenience travellers may experience on these tracks.

Every effort has been made to ensure that telephone numbers, distances, directions, prices, fuel supplies and other details are correct at the time of publication. You are advised to double-check all relevant details as part of your preparation before embarking on any of these trips. Prices, especially, are likely to change.

Thomas C. Lothian Pty Ltd
132-136 Albert Road, South Melbourne, Victoria 3205

Copyright © Catherine de Courcy 2001

First published 2001

National Library of Australia
Cataloguing-in-Publication data:

de Courcy, Catherine, 1957–.
River Tracks.

Includes index.

ISBN 0 7344 0204 X.

1. Rivers – Australia. 2. Rivers – Australia – Guidebooks.
I. Johnson, John (John S.), 1947–2000.
II. Title.
919.404   551.483

Cover and text design by David Constable
Cover photograph by Peter Walton Photography
Back cover photograph by Flora Faoro
Drawings by Sheila de Courcy
Typesetting by Mandy Griffin
Printed in Australia by Griffin Press

Contents

Acknowledgements

＊＊

There are so many people and organisations we would like to thank for their assistance in completing this book that it would take forever. If we have not personally acknowledged your assistance, the very publication of this book is proof that your help was valuable and much appreciated.

We thank the many visitor centre and national parks staff along the routes for their professional assistance and courtesy in supplying information about their regions. We also thank the people we met on the way who extended us a warm welcome on our travels. Catherine would also like to acknowledge the great response she received from fishing professionals along the rivers, the staff of tackle shops and fishing tour operators.

Many thanks also to our travelling companions and supporters, Grainne Hickland, Garry Tickner, Mary de Courcy and Warren Peart. Catherine would especially like to thank her parents and sisters, particularly Anna and Bridgie, and her dear friends, Warren, Garry, Grainne, Sally Murdoch, and Ian Morrison, for their considerable help and support in completing this publication.

Introduction

In this book we have presented six great Australian river trips. Well-known holiday destinations already line the riverbanks, but often a trip along a river isn't noticed as having the potential for a terrific holiday in its own right. When you follow a river, you get a great sense of its journey from the headwaters, through the towns and settlements that have drawn life from it, and on to its end in another river, a lake or a great ocean. Along the way the river changes character, shaped by natural obstacles and man-made constructions designed to control and regulate its waters.

The rivers that we cover in this book pass through many famous towns. When you visit them as part of a total river trip, they take on a new perspective. Their links with other towns along the same river and with the countryside around them become apparent. Their geography and history come alive as you follow characteristics and features along the route. The stories of the people who have lived along the river are most fascinating when you can see these connections.

The stories of the Aboriginal people along the rivers are quite different to the stories of the Aboriginal people in the desert regions. The rich resources provided by the rivers shaped the character of these communities, and many were far more numerous and territorial than the popular image suggests. When the Europeans arrived, their resistance was marked. Today we can encounter ancient archaeological remains in some places that show life continued close to the rivers for at least 30,000 years.

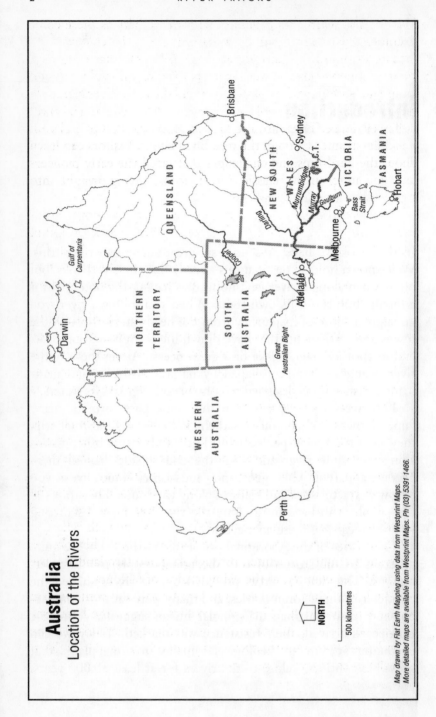

Australia
Location of the Rivers

NORTH

500 kilometres

Map drawn by Flat Earth Mapping using data from Westprint Maps.
More detailed maps are available from Westprint Maps. Ph (03) 5391 1466.

We can also learn about modern political activity as these communities strive to maintain their culture in the 21st century.

The stories of the Europeans on the rivers also have common themes. The waterways were principal routes for explorers who were quickly followed by pastoralists and drovers. River transport is now a colourful aspect of this history, with large inland wharves still in evidence. There are also modern opportunities to cruise on a paddle-steamer through the tree-lined banks. Visitors can learn about the hardships and challenges that faced the early pioneers and encounter many classic Aussie icons, giving insight into aspects of our national character.

Passing through these towns on a river trip, we don't spend much more than a day or two in one place, even in the busiest of cities. We move from elegant dining or noisy street theatre to wild bush within 24 hours. Then a few days later, we may find ourselves looking at colonial buildings and eating home-cooked food made with local produce.

We love the natural river environment, the sounds of the birds, the exotic silence and warmth of the riverbanks, the muted colours and the space in the bush camps. So you will find that each of these river trips brings you as close to that country as possible. We also love the food and the wine of the rivers, so this is an aspect we have sought out.

We have selected six different river trips and they each provide their own experience. The mighty Murray is an obvious choice. The longest river in Australia travels through three states and supports so much life and industry along the way — it is a favourite family holiday destination. We have split it into two: the first drive covers the river from its headwaters in the Great Dividing Range in New South Wales, to Wentworth where it meets its last major tributary — the Darling River. This takes us from snow country in winter, through irrigated farmland and the exotic Mallee country, to the balmy region of Mildura.

The lower Murray trip starts in Wentworth and continues on to the Murray mouth. This trip provides some of the best river driving on bitumen. At one point, the dramatic river cliffs provide us with the opportunity to drive along a good road and look down into the river valley below.

The Goulburn and the Murrumbidgee river trips are similar in character in that they both flow through towns in a way that hides the natural continuum of the rivers. Initially, when we began these two trips, we wondered what we would find and whether they were worth considering as holidays in their own right. Yet they both produced such surprises that we will forever associate the famous towns along the way primarily with the rivers. These are great holidays that provide enormous variety and terrific links.

The last two river trips reflect our great attraction to the desert regions of Australia. We selected the Darling River and the extraordinary watercourse of Cooper Creek as the fifth and sixth journeys. These holidays take you into the true desert outback of Australia and the river trips each become an adventure. The contact with the rivers is limited for various reasons. In the case of the Darling River, much of the land is private pastoral country, so access is restricted. With the Cooper, the watercourse vanishes unless it is in flood, at which point the area around it becomes impassable. But on each of these journeys, when you do get contact with the water, the experience is unique and unforgettable. In the Cooper chapter, we have concentrated on providing you with the sort of information that will support a safe trip into exotic and remote desert country.

Before we head off, we have included some general material about having successful holidays along the rivers. We hope you enjoy our stories, and your own happy and safe journeys!

Accommodation guidelines

The river tracks run through a combination of environments, from very popular tourist areas to remote wild country. Sometimes your choice of accommodation will be limited, sometimes there will be so much that it will be difficult to decide where to stay. The availability of accommodation to suit your party may influence how you pace your river trip, so here are some guidelines on what is available and what services to expect.

Along each track we have identified the general availability of accommodation in towns and settlements. Where there is a wide range, we simply tell you what variety of accommodation is available. When there is little, we include the phone numbers of specific places. Occasionally, where a place stands out because of its historical nature or its location on the riverbanks, we have included the number of that place as well. Also, since isolated camping is our favourite style of accommodation, we have identified bush camping locations along each river track.

To assist you in deciding what kind of accommodation may suit you, we have drawn on our experience and come up with some informal guidelines on the different types of accommodation available and their general price range. As part of your preparation for a trip down a river, we strongly recommend that you contact a few of the visitor information centres along the way to get lists of accommodation in the region. Some large or popular centres provide an accommodation booking service. We have mentioned these in the relevant sections.

It is important to note that during school holidays and holiday weekends, accommodation along the rivers is often heavily booked. Even places with many motels and hotels can be fully booked out. So if you plan to use conventional accommodation during the school holidays, we strongly recommend that you plan your trip carefully and make bookings in advance. In many cases you will need to book using your credit card. Be aware that if you book and don't turn up, you may be charged the full accommodation fee, or part of it, even if your room is subsequently used.

Outside of school holiday times, you could probably drive into most towns and find accommodation readily. Of course, if you do know where you want to stay, or if you prefer a specific type of accommodation, it is probably a good idea to make your reservation in advance.

MOTELS

All medium to large towns have motel accommodation. This usually means that you can park your car outside the door. The rooms are self-contained with bathrooms, and all linen and towels are provided. Generally they provide basic coffee and tea-making equipment, with breakfast available if you order it the night before. Often there are televisions in the main room, and hairdryers attached to the wall in the bathroom.

Motels vary in price but you could expect to pay between $60 and $100 for a double room. It isn't much less for a single person, and there will usually be a fee for additional people. The quality of the room will vary and we have found no way of identifying this in advance. We have had great rooms for $60 in one place, and basic rooms for $100 in another. At the peak season in popular areas, rooms may cost extra.

Family rooms in motels can be very good value if you require two separate rooms. In larger motels, it may be an extra $20–30 to get an adjoining room, or a motel suite with two rooms. However, if this is what you require, we strongly recommend that you book in advance because supply is limited.

Motels often have a limited collection of brochures about activities in the district. In medium-sized towns, they may also have a restaurant attached and we have had some terrific meals in motel restaurants.

HOTELS

Hotels provide some of the most exciting accommodation along the rivers. Often the hotels are 19th or early 20th-century buildings with history in the rooms. Some hotels have been renovated; others are basic but clean. Generally speaking, hotel rooms don't have ensuites but have shared shower and bathroom facilities. Unless the hotel is packed out, we have never found this to be a problem. Hotels usually provide all linen and towels. Some provide basic coffee- and tea-making equipment but we don't rely on this. Few provide hairdryers or televisions.

Acoustics in hotels vary. Sometimes the place will be very quiet, sometimes a dance or music session downstairs will keep on going until the early hours. Be aware of this at weekends and, if this is likely to bother you, ask the hotel manager whether there is a dance or music venue nearby that may keep you awake. Other than that, hotels tend to be very quiet even though they are often positioned on a town's main street.

Hotels usually charge per person rather than by doubles, with single rooms beginning at around $20. Prices of $35–40 per person are at the upper end of the scale. Cooked breakfasts are often included in the cost. Also, most hotels have dining rooms that serve dinner.

The great advantage of staying in hotels is that the environment is generally very friendly. More often than not, the managers of the hotel will make sure that you feel very welcome in the bar. This way it is much easier to chat with people and find out about local places, activities and fishing. If we are feeling sociable, this is unquestionably the most satisfying style of accommodation in a town.

CARAVAN PARKS

Australian caravan parks provide a wide range of accommodation. Most include powered and unpowered sites for camping or caravans, on-site caravans, cabins, and sometimes even cottages. The prices for camping sites tend to be $12–20 per night, depending on facilities. Many charge a few extra dollars per person for larger parties. Some of these campsites have great bush camping facilities where you can get access to facilities without having other parties too close to you.

On-site caravans and cabins have a greater price variation depending on the number of beds available. For large parties, the cabins are the best value. We have stayed in cabins that sleep up to twelve people. It is all pretty intimate, with bunk beds and no sound-proofing at all. Usually there is a master bedroom with a double bed, the rest of the beds are singles or pull-out sofas. The large cabins are usually self-contained, the small ones may simply have room for a bed and enough room to get in and out of it! In these cases, you would use the shared park facilities.

With caravans and cabins, you are expected to bring all of your own bedding, including linen, sleeping bags or blankets, pillows (although sometimes these are provided), and towels. However, the self-contained cabins often have reasonable kitchens with toasters, cooking facilities, kitchen utensils, cutlery and crockery. They don't usually provide hairdryers, but many do have televisions.

The cabins vary in price depending on the facilities provided in them and the number of people they can take. Cabins with only a bed could cost $25–35. Cabins that take a dozen people with two or three separate rooms, including kitchen and bathroom facilities, could cost $60–$80. However, often you are not charged per person, so these are great value for large groups.

BED AND BREAKFAST ACCOMMODATION

In Australia this is the luxury end of the market, something that may surprise European visitors who are used to B&Bs being at the budget end of the market. B&Bs are often located in fabulous, historical houses that have been beautifully restored. Or they are in cottages or purpose-built houses in great locations. The hosts go to a lot of trouble to make the place as luxurious and comfortable as possible and provide all sorts of extras.

Branch : DUBBO
Date : 2/02/2021   Time: 15:59
ID : C01175290

ITEM(S) ON LOAN   DUE DATE

The Darling : Murray Darling Basin
Commission
A0229187B   23 Feb 2021

Please retain this receipt and return
items before the due date or phone MRL
to renew them

Coolah: 6377 1910
Coonabarabran: 6842 1093
Dubbo: 6801 4510
Dunedoo: 6375 1468
Narromine: 6889 1088
Trangie: 6888 7501
Wellington: 6840 1780

THANK YOU FOR USING YOUR LOCAL
LIBRARY

Breakfasts are usually excellent and large, with cooked food, home made preserves, fruit, and great coffee or tea.

With all of the luxuries, there are several things to be aware of with B&Bs. In the most interesting historic houses or old hotels, your room may not have an ensuite. However, your hosts will make the shared bathroom facilities as comfortable as possible. Another aspect to be aware of is that sometimes where there are shared facilities, such as a dining room and drawing room, the guests are treated like houseguests and introduced to each other. This can be very pleasant if you are feeling sociable, but a bit awkward if you don't feel like making conversation with strangers over breakfast. Of course, in self-contained cottages, all of the facilities are your own and you may be lucky and get a place with a balcony overlooking the river or other scenic view.

The prices of B&Bs vary enormously, and we have been amazed that some beautiful historic buildings with grand dining rooms can be at the cheaper end of the scale. Prices tend to be per couple, rather than by the single person or family, although we did come across a few exceptions to this. The range begins at about $80 per couple, with many being in the $110–130 price range. From there on it goes up: we have heard of one or two places along the rivers that are $500 per night per couple.

BACKPACKERS' LODGE AND SHEARING SHED ACCOMMODATION

At the budget end of the market you can get a bed, and usually access to a shared kitchen, BBQ and bathroom facilities. You will need to bring your own bedding, including pillows and sleeping bag, kitchen equipment, etc.

Choosing a campsite

Most of the river tracks run through towns and pastoral country, but in each of the chapters we have identified places where you can camp in the bush. Most of these places are in national parks or state reserves that have designated camping areas. Occasionally you will need to select your own campsite, particularly in remote areas.

Bush camping is the most satisfactory way of spending a night in remote Australia. The further north you go, the warmer it gets, and you may enjoy camping under the stars rather than using a tent. The following information is designed to help you make a comfortable bush campsite.

WHAT MAKES AN IDEAL CAMPSITE?
- A clear spot with few lumps, stones or tufts of grass
- Some shade and a 'comfort wall' of low trees or high bushes
- Little or no passing traffic
- No other campers within earshot
- A waterhole for swimming and fishing.

WHAT MAKES A BAD CAMPSITE?
- Mosquitoes attracted by a waterhole or bore. Observe the number of mosquitoes about when you choose your campsite.
- A wind blowing track dust into your food and your bedding.

Do not place your camp downwind of the track — a passing truck or even a breeze could ruin your dinner.

- Excessive ant activity. Check your campsite for telltale piles of loose soil with a hole in the centre. This suggests that there are a lot of ants about, but they won't come out in force until you are asleep! Move your bed away from any suspicious mounds of loose soil, and if you are not in their path you won't even notice that they are there.
- Large gumtrees — although they look beautiful, they are dangerous to camp beneath. Eucalyptus, especially, have a reputation for dropping large branches without warning. Sadly, lives have been lost when such branches have fallen on campers resting in their shade. Camp under the smaller trees.
- Creekbeds are also deceptive. Their soft surface seems like an ideal area, and may be dry around you, but big waters from upstream can come charging through without notice. Flash floods have claimed lives also. So camp under the shade of low trees beside the dry creekbed.

A WORD OF ADVICE IN THE FACE OF NATURAL HAZARDS

Select an escape route before it is dark. In the event of a fire or a flash flood you should already know your way out. Discuss your plan with other members of your party — it only takes a couple of minutes, and will save confusion if any problems do occur that cause you to evacuate your campsite.

WHAT FIRE RESTRICTIONS OPERATE ALONG THE RIVERS?

There are certain times of the year when most localities along the riverbanks impose total fire bans. These bans will usually be between November and April. We have identified many of the bans but, if you are in doubt, check at the nearest tourist centre. When a fire ban is in place, you must not light a fire, even in designated fireplaces.

CHOOSING AN OVERNIGHT CAMP

If camping for only one night, you can make a simple camp quickly and leave with minimal fuss in the morning. Plan to make camp in the late afternoon. Look for signs of an existing track and then explore until you find a good campsite. Little traffic is likely to pass during the night on these tracks, so you can be fairly close to the road without compromising your privacy.

Your bed may simply be a tarpaulin, a mattress, a sleeping bag with a hood, and pillows. We seldom bother with a shade tent on an overnight camp unless the mosquitoes are bad.

Set up your beds and your gas cooker before it is dark. Make sure that all members of the party know where their personal torch is.

If there is no toilet nearby, dig a pit at a convenient distance, say, 100 metres from your water supply. Make sure that all of your party can get to and from it in the dark safely.

Prepare simple dinners and breakfasts. Washing dirty frying pans and Dutch ovens is a nuisance if you are tired in the evenings, or want to get away early in the morning.

Make sure you gather your rubbish in a sturdy bag. It can probably be dumped at the next major town.

Fill in your toilet pit in the morning. Also fill in and flatten your campfire and make sure the fire is completely out.

In the morning, as you break camp, drive your car about four metres away from the site and than walk back with your party to scan the ground for articles left behind, such as bottle caps and other small debris that can get lost during the night. If you set up an orderly camp and clean up thoroughly before you leave, you should not be able to identify the precise location of your campsite when you look back.

LONG CAMPS

If you are planning to stay in a campsite for at least two nights, you will have greater expectations of your campsite.

Shade from the midday sun and privacy from people passing by will be important. You may also want access to some firewood for a campfire.

Designated bush campsites will usually provide privacy and shade but generally no wood — you will have to carry this in from another source. They are likely to have a fireplace, and sometimes bush toilets.

Begin looking for a campsite in the mid-afternoon. When you select your clearing, decide on the location of the beds, the kitchen, the campfire, the dining table, the toilet pit or chemical loo, the clothesline, the rubbish bag, your petrol or kerosene dump.

Pay particular attention to the location of the campfire — in fact, it will dictate the positioning of everything else. You will want it reasonably close to the kitchen, some distance from the beds or tents, and at a very safe distance from your car and fuel store. You must make sure that it is also at a safe distance from grass, spinifex, the woodpile or anything else that may catch fire if a flame is caught in a sudden gust of wind.

Dig a small sump pit several metres from your kitchen or water supply for your waste liquids, such as soapy washing-up water and cooking oils, rather than throwing them at trees or plants. The pit doesn't need to be very deep, but it will ensure that contaminated liquids don't seep into water supplies or damage plants.

To make sure that your toilet is at a discreet distance from the camp, select the location while there is still daylight. Ensure that all of your party will be able to find it in the dark — set up a knotted string trail through the trees, if necessary.

If you leave camp during the day, make sure that everything is securely packed away in closed containers. Crows and dingoes love an empty camp. They can rip through garbage and other bags in their search for food and bright objects, making a terrible mess in the process.

When you break camp, spend time ensuring that the fire pit is filled in and the surface is flat, and that there is no charcoal lying around. Close your toilet pit, and leave that flat also. Organise all of your party to 'sweep' the camp, searching for little scraps of paper or other rubbish that may have dropped to the ground.

Fishing and fishing licences

THE FISH

Fishing is probably the most popular pastime in the world, and no more so than here in Australia. Knowledge and skills are transferred through the generations, making it a great sport for mixed age groups. The river tracks contain a myriad of delectable and not so delectable fish for the fisherperson's hook and bait. It can be a hit or miss thing unless you learn to study the fish you are hunting, find out its habitat and what it likes to eat. With that knowledge you can narrow the odds a bit.

Native fish such as the Murray cod, trout cod, yellow belly (also known as golden perch), silver perch, catfish, yabbies and Murray cray can all be found in different stretches of these waters. Introduced species such as brown trout, rainbow trout, redfin and the ubiquitous European carp are also found in many of these waters.

FISHING REGULATIONS

Although you may drop a line into the waters in most places, fishing is strictly controlled by the state fishing authorities. This is done through the licence system and regulations concerning protected fish, closed seasons, bag limits, size limits, and the use of bait and nets. Rangers patrol popular fishing locations, but mostly it is up to you to observe the detailed regulations supplied with your licence.

Strict controls are necessary to support fish stocks because of the damage that has been caused since the Europeans began to move out across the continent in the early 19th century. First the ecology of the rivers was disrupted by the removal of snags and Aboriginal stone weirs. The installation of solid weirs and locks to make the rivers navigable for river traffic, followed by heavy use of water for irrigation, further interfered with the flow and balance of the rivers.

The early use of explosives and large-scale nets were both destructive methods of collecting fish. The explosives were originally used to assist in the clearance of the snags, but the fish that floated to the surface after an explosion could fill a boat. Of course, both methods also killed off countless numbers of juvenile fish. Excess fish were used as fertilizer. Less dramatic but equally serious was the overfishing from boats and riverbanks that further reduced numbers.

In the meantime, introduced species were having an impact on native fish — the European carp was the worst of these. The carp is considered to be one of the great pests of the Australian inland

rivers and enormous work is underway to eradicate the fish. The carp stirs up silt, reduces the oxygen output of native aquatic plants, and smothers the eggs of trout and native fish. It is not even a good eating fish, being very bony and muddy. But as you are likely to catch one or two, we have included a recipe below. By the way, if you do catch one, you are prohibited from throwing it back. Recently we have been hearing along the rivers that the work of the state fishing authorities on eradicating carp is beginning to pay off, and in places their numbers may well be dropping.

This may sound like a depressing picture for keen fishing people, particularly those who remember the good old days, not 30 years ago, when fishing on the rivers yielded a good variety of fish for dinner — even a 50 kg Murray cod! However, all is not lost and it is still possible to have a terrific time sitting on a river bank, catching some fish and cooking them on an open campfire. It is just that there won't be so many of them and they won't be as large as they were in the past. So it is important to be aware of the reasons behind the strict fishing regulations so that river fishing can remain a popular pastime.

FISHING — THE PRACTICALITIES

The best fishing is usually found in the deeper water, especially in the eddies formed on bends. These are even more attractive if there are one or two snags in the water. Snags provide perfect structures for fish to hide in, strike from and move among. The river authorities are now entering into a program of placing dead trees back into the rivers. Steep banks are also good places, particularly in summer as the fish drop to the cooler water below.

Places close to inflowing water, such as tributaries or weirs, are also good options. Fish tend to position themselves off to the side of the main current flow to catch food as it floats down the water. Fishing close to the bank, rather than tossing a line too far out, is more likely to yield good eating fish in the murky water. Further out in some waters, such as the Cooper Creek waterholes, you will hook turtles and smallish yellow belly or silver perch.

Bait fishing, or dropping a line into the water with a sinker and a piece of bait, is the easiest form of fishing and the most popular along the inland rivers. Generally worms are the best bait when the water is murky, because fish go to the bottom of the water to look for feed.

Maggots are also used to attract fish by releasing them slowly from a feeder or throwing them in by hand. When a fish grabs a maggot floating past, it will continue on the trail to see if there are further maggots. Baits consisting of live mice, live frogs or live fish are illegal nowadays (although you can use certain live bait-fish in Victoria). You are usually restricted to baits such as maggots, mudeyes, yabbies, worms and grubs.

Lures are another option. These are designed to mimic bait

fish. They used to be bulky aeroplane spinners with massive treble hooks. Today they are more subtle and you can spend a fortune on lures of all sizes, hues and actions.

Fly-fishing is a technical art form that involves emulating the behaviour of insects. Fish go for insects on the surface of the water, so the objective is to attract them with artificial flies that resemble real insects (and the choice of insect for the target fish could change several times during the day). The difficulty with fly-fishing is that you have to cast an almost weightless bait to the right point in the water. This requires practice and some technical information on how it is done. Fly-fishing is traditionally used to catch trout in clear river waters, such as the Goulburn River. But now it is also being used to catch other fish that rise to the surface of the water to grab a fly. Polaroid glasses to see the trout are useful; the skilled fly-fisher can spot their prey then land the fly at exactly the right point. Most trout are released to fight another day. The odd one or two will end up in a frying pan with some butter, lemon juice, dill tips and almond shavings to become an entrée or main course.

It is important to seek local advice regarding bait, lines, sinkers and anything that can help you take a fish. Staff in fishing shops are usually very helpful sources of information. They know the local waters and pick up bits of information from other fishing folk. When the fish suddenly start to bite — perhaps when there has been a release of water from one of the dams or weirs — they know about it because the locals are at their doors early in the morning! You won't necessarily hear about the best spots, but they won't mislead you about the best baits and the best time of day to fish. So this is a really good place to begin your day's fishing.

NSW RECREATIONAL FISHING FEE

You need a receipt to show that you have paid the Recreational Fishing Fee to fish in NSW rivers and lakes, including the Darling River and both banks of the Murray. The fee can be paid at NSW Fisheries agents in the cities and in most fishing tackle outlets along the rivers in NSW. It can also be purchased by credit card via the phone on 1300 369 365. The current fee is $5 for three days, $10 for one month, $25 for one year, or $70 for three years.

Various groups and pension holders are exempt. These include people under 18 years of age, holders of Commonwealth pensioner concession cards, and some veterans who hold the Commonwealth Department of Veterans' Affairs Gold Treatment Card. Aboriginal people are also exempt from requiring a licence. A full list of exemptions is included in the NSW Fisheries brochure at outlets where the licence is sold.

When you receive your licence, you will be given a brochure containing information about freshwater fish, legal lengths and bag limits. It also provides information about closed seasons along the rivers, and on particular fish at specific times. Details about trout fishing restrictions should be noted. Fish identification charts are not included in the NSW brochure.

VICTORIAN RECREATIONAL FISHING LICENCE

This licence is required for all recreational fishing in Victoria, including freshwater fishing. The licence can be purchased from fishing tackle shops and other retail outlets along the rivers. It can also be purchased from Victorian Department of Natural Resources and Environment offices. The licence can be purchased to come into effect on a specified future date, up to one year from the actual date of its purchase. The cost is $5 for 48 hours, $10 for 28 days, or $20 for one year.

Again, several groups of people are exempt from requiring a licence to fish. These include people under 18 years of age and over 70 years of age, holders of a Victorian Seniors Card, a Veterans' Affairs Pensioner Card, some of the Commonwealth pensioner concession cards or a Veterans' Affairs Repatriation Health Card (coded TPI). For a full list, check the licence brochure in the leaflet at retail outlets.

When you receive your licence, you will get a fabulous 60-page booklet containing all sorts of detailed information about size limits, catch identification with colour illustrations, and closed seasons. It also includes illustrated information about closed and restricted waters.

A recipe for carp

The Europeans regard carp as a delicacy and it is the fish you are most likely to catch! So here is a Ukrainian recipe: Take a medium-sized fish, say 5 kg, then scale and clean it. Soak it in a light vinegar and water mix for a couple of hours and then poach in the marinade with added whole peppercorns, lots of fresh dill, a couple of bay leaves, some marjoram, coriander, pickling mix, sea salt and sliced onions. Cooking time depends on the size of the fish but a couple of hours is usually sufficient. The secret now is to let the fish cool and then place it into the fridge for 1–2 hours. The double set of rib bones and the other bones seem to calcify (a bit like canned tuna) and can be eaten with salad, lasagne-type dishes or just washed down with beer, vodka or wine. The taste brings many a fisherman back to this fish — you too may learn to love it!

Bush safety and etiquette

- When swimming, check for hidden obstructions such as dead trees, and check the depth and currents before diving into any creek or waterhole.
- Always supervise children when they are swimming. Creeks can become deep very quickly and the surface of the creekbed may be murky with suspended clay, so it is essential to stay close to children and watch teenagers closely when they are swimming.
- Swimming and alcohol don't mix — if you drink and swim, you could get yourself into serious trouble.
- Unless absolutely necessary, don't drive at night. There are too many road hazards to be safe and free of stress. Stock, kangaroos, emus and a host of other animals roam the roads after dark.
- If you are on foot and see a snake, go the other way.
- Never overtake a road train unless you are perfectly sure that the road ahead is clear.
- When approaching an oncoming road train, get off the road if at all possible.
- Do not tamper with road signs in any way or remove them as souvenirs. A missing or incorrect sign could cost someone their life.
- Leave gates as you find them.
- Leave your pets at home, especially dogs and cats.
- Don't take nets, traps or weapons into national parks.
- Take note of quarantine regulations. Carrying fresh fruit and

vegetables into vine and fruit-growing regions along the rivers is prohibited.

- Don't visit station homesteads unless you have a real emergency or are invited — this is now considered an impertinence in most areas. Station staff do not have time to entertain travellers who drop in unannounced.
- Drive very slowly when passing cattle being grazed on the 'long acre' (i.e. the side of the road).
- If you hit a stock animal with your car, you should report the matter to the station owner and, if necessary, be prepared to assist in destroying the animal if it isn't already dead.
- Do not camp next to a dam, waterhole or tank as it will frighten stock away from their water supply.
- Do not camp too close to other campers, particularly in remote regions where there are no designated campsites. Many fellow campers go to the bush to get away from noise, lights and other people — they don't want to hear you or see your camp.
- Never wash yourself or your clothes with soap or laundry powder in the rivers — you will pollute the water for stock. Take a supply of water well away from the source.
- 'Leave only your footprints and take only your memories.' All visitors to the bush and outback of Australia should adopt this motto. Remove all your rubbish — never bury it in situ.
- Burn only flammable materials — don't burn rubber or plastic.
- Use existing fire pits or fireplaces. Where allowed to make your own fire, dig a fire pit. Then bury your fire when you have finished.
- Keep fires small as wood is limited and animals live in it.
- Never cut down living trees.
- Dig latrines and toilet pits well away from water sources, and always downwind of your campsite.

- Standing trees, even if they are dead, will be the home of countless birds and animals and so should not be pulled down.

Quarantine and fruit fly exclusion zones

• •

You are not allowed to bring fresh fruit and some vegetables into the fruit fly exclusion zone in South Australia, Victoria and New South Wales. The zone covers much of the Murray River area, from west of Albury to as far as Morgan. It also includes the Goulburn north of Nagambie, and the entire Murrumbidgee Irrigation Area in south-western New South Wales. This is part of the three states' policy to control the devastating effects of fruit fly on the citrus, vine and vegetable industries in the irrigated regions.

Fruit fly can travel in egg or maggot form on fruit bought in cities. Your fruit may look perfectly healthy but these tiny creatures may be contained inside the fruit. If they get out into the environment, they can cause enormous damage to the local fruit industry. It is very expensive to control and costs jobs. The biggest danger period runs from November to April, when the warm weather ripens fresh fruit more quickly. Easter is a particularly bad time for fruit fly outbreaks.

So be aware that it is prohibited to carry fresh fruit — including stone fruit, citrus, apples and pears — into a fruit fly exclusion zone. Fruit fly also breed in some vegetables such as tomatoes, capsicums, cucumbers, chillies, zucchinis and melons. Honey products are also prohibited.

A full list of what is prohibited is available from the NSW Agriculture Department, South Australia Primary Industries and Resources Pest Eradication Unit, and the Plant Standards Centre in Footscray, Victoria. The NSW Agriculture Department has a good website listing everything that is prohibited. To check, visit <www.agri.nsw.gov.au>.

Large blue signs featuring a graphic image of 'Fang' the fruit fly have been erected on the main roads at the beginning of fruit fly exclusion zones. Bins where you can dump your fruit are provided. During busy times of the year, local authorities may set up a road block and check your vehicle for prohibited items. You may be fined for carrying items into the exclusion zone. Within the zone, there are plenty of supermarkets and fruit stalls that sell fresh local produce.

If you accidentally bring fresh fruit into a controlled area and discover it when you are unpacking your gear at a motel or a campsite, you are asked to destroy it. You can do this by sealing it in a plastic bag and leaving it in the sun for two days, cooking it, or microwaving it for five minutes. Then dispose of it in a garbage system — do not bury it in the ground.

Travelling with children

The Australian river experience is one that will remain with your children forever. It is also of great value in practical education and personal development. But the roads are long, sometimes with considerable distance between distractions. In addition, camping and bush travel have hidden dangers. Common sense and some knowledge will protect adults, but children need direction and some rules.

The following tips can be adapted for children of different ages:

ENTERTAINMENT

- Pick a route with many activities, and prepare the kids for them.
- Ask the visitor centres for a map and guide in advance, then ask older children and teenagers to prepare an itinerary for the day.
- For younger children, factor into your itinerary a playground in one of the larger towns.
- Bring music tapes and comedy audio tapes for the car; your local library may have a selection.
- Take favourite battery-powered computer games and spare batteries.
- Share any information about Aboriginal people of the region, the geography, the weather, wildlife, and explorers. Before you

leave, look at films on the region and documentaries about aspects of the rivers to excite knowledgeable interest.

- Give them the opportunity to take photos, perhaps give each child a roll of film or a disposable camera.
- If you are camping, give older children and teenagers responsibility for planning one dinner each, including designating duties on arrival into camp, overseeing the cooking, and co-ordinating serving before food gets cold.
- Invite older kids to select the campsite at your destination.

SAFETY

- Stay with children and watch them carefully when they are swimming. The water is often murky brown because of the suspended clay, and the bottom of the waterhole or creek may be muddy.
- When swimming, check for hidden obstructions such as dead trees, and check the depth and currents before diving into any creek or waterhole.
- If the kids love to spend a lot of time in the water, bring t-shirts or Zoot swimsuits to protect their shoulders and backs.
- Be careful with children around the historic wharves; the steps are usually steep and often quite high. Some parts may also be a bit loose.
- Give each child a special pair of gardening gloves to protect them from insect stings and scratches when picking up and handling wood.
- Warn children not to put their hands into hollow logs — there may be spiders or even a snake inside.
- Draw a line in the dust around open campfires and gas cookers beyond which children should not venture. You may also want to draw a line around gas lamps if you think they are a risk to young children.
- Have a supply of drinks to hand that your children enjoy, and make sure that they keep up their liquid intake. Dehydration can creep up.
- Give children a special hat, sunglasses and fun sunscreen; perhaps each child could have their own colourful bag for their

glasses and sunscreen. Although the sun is not very strong in winter, special care should be taken to make sure that young skin is always protected.

- Bring spare hats, glasses and sunscreen, although these can be replaced in outback shops.
- Discourage children from climbing trees — the bark is rough and they may put a hand or a knee on an insect, or come crashing down from a brittle branch.
- Don't allow children to wander on their own from the camp in the dark, which can be well before their bedtime in winter. The ground surface is uneven and they may lose their bearings. Give them their own small torch and go with them to the vicinity of your toilet. For older children, make sure that they learn the route to the toilet pit while it is still light.

1 The Upper Murray River

TOM GROGGIN TO WENTWORTH

The upper Murray River is a fabulous river drive that takes you from the high alpine ranges of the headwaters, down to the plains and the semi-arid regions of the Mallee. We have started the trip at Tom Groggin, or the Alpine Way, and ended where the Murray meets its last major tributary, the Darling River, in Wentworth. This river track travels through some of the most popular family holiday towns along the Murray, such as Albury, Yarrawonga and Swan Hill.

In and around the towns there is plenty of river access for picnics, fishing and bush camping. Majestic river gums line the riverbanks across the plains. The environment is tranquil, with wildlife in the trees and in the water. The state forests near Barmah and at Hattah-Kulkyne are natural environments where you can forget that you are close to busy towns or cities. Nights under the stars and slow drives along the banks of the meandering river are unforgettable experiences.

There are also great tourist attractions along here. You will be passing through the famous wine region of Rutherglen and the exciting tourist town of Echuca. You will also have an opportunity to visit the Pioneer Settlement in Swan Hill or have dinner in Stefano de Pieri's restaurant in the Grand Hotel in Mildura. You can have lunch on a paddle-steamer, or watch the boats move in and out of a Murray lock at Mildura. Each of the towns along the way has its own joys and attractions.

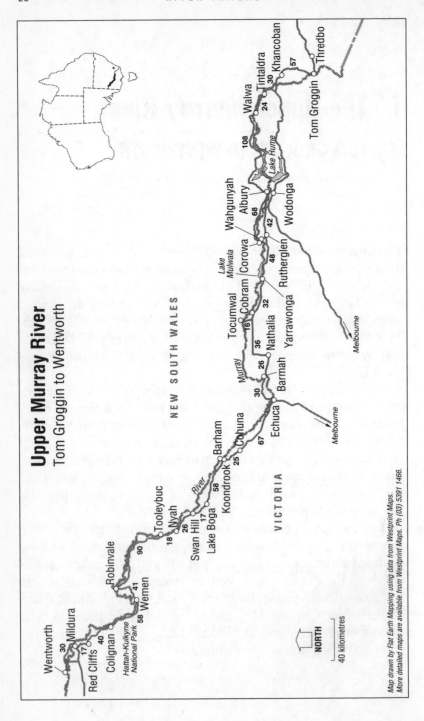

Upper Murray River
Tom Groggin to Wentworth

NEW SOUTH WALES

VICTORIA

Thredbo
57
Khancoban
30
Tintaldra
Tom Groggin
24
Walwa
108
Lake Hume
Wahgunyah
68
Albury
42
Wodonga
Corowa
48
Rutherglen
32
Cobram
Lake Mulwala
Tocumwal
16
Nathalia
36
Yarrawonga
26
Barmah
30
Echuca
67
Melbourne
Cohuna
25
Koondrook
58
Lake Boga
17
Swan Hill
26
Nyah
18
Tooleybuc
90
Robinvale
41
Wemen
58
Hattah-Kulkyne National Park
Colignan
40
Red Cliffs
17
Mildura
30
Wentworth
Barham
River
Murray
Melbourne

NORTH
40 kilometres

Map drawn by Flat Earth Mapping using data from Westprint Maps.
More detailed maps are available from Westprint Maps. Ph (03) 5391 1466.

SUMMARY

Main route

Tom Groggin — Khancoban — Albury–Wodonga — Corowa–Rutherglen — Mulwala–Yarrawonga — Echuca — Swan Hill — Hattah–Kulkyne National Park — Mildura — Wentworth

Maps

Touring Atlas of Australia, Penguin, Melbourne, 2000
Echuca–Moama Blue Guide Handy Map (Free)
Central Murray Valley State Forests, Forestry Commission of New South Wales, 1992
Swan Hill and District Blue Guide Handy Map (Free)

Passes

A New South Wales National Parks Pass is required to camp by the Murray along the Alpine Way between Tom Groggin and Khancoban. It costs $15 for a 24-hour pass. For a stay longer than 24 hours, the $80 annual pass for all NSW national parks is required. These passes are available in Khancoban or at the Snowy Region Visitor Information Centre in Jindabyne (02 6450 5600) or contact the NSW National Parks Centre for regional outlets (02 9337 2777).

Minimum number of days

The trip is approximately 900 km. It will take six days if you don't explore much.

Best time of year to visit

The Alpine Way at the headwaters of the Murray experiences snow in the winter months and may be impassable or at least require snow chains. Check at Khancoban or the Snowy Region Visitor Information Centre in Jindabyne (02 6450 5600) for road conditions. The average temperature along the Murray beyond Lake Hume is 2–14°c in winter, and 12–34°c in summer.

Accommodation and camping

There are plenty of motels, hotels, caravan parks and bush camping sites along the route. Small designated camping sites along the Murray are identified in Victoria by signposts at the head of tracks leading into the Murray. There is plenty of bush camping in the Victorian state parks.

Local information and useful telephone numbers

Albury–Wodonga Gateway Visitor Information Centre (accommodation service available)	02 6041 3875 or toll-free 1800 800 743
Corowa Information Centre	02 6033 3221
Rutherglen Visitor Information Centre	02 6032 9166
Yarrawonga–Mulwala Visitor Information Centre (accommodation service available)	03 5744 1989
Cobram Barooga Visitor Information Centre	03 5872 2132 or toll-free 1800 607 607
Tocumwal Visitor Information Centre	03 5874 2131
Echuca–Moama Visitor Information Centre (accommodation service available)	toll-free 1800 804 446
Golden Rivers Tourism, Barham	03 5453 3100
Swan Hill Visitor Information Service	toll-free 1800 625 373
Mildura Information and Booking Centre (accommodation service available)	03 5021 4424 or toll-free 1800 039 043
Wentworth Visitor Information	03 5027 3624

THE ROUTE

The Alpine Way from the headwaters to Khancoban

Our first view of the mighty Murray is at Tom Groggin campsite, 20 km west of Thredbo on the Alpine Way. The river rises in the mountains beyond this point, so this is the first place you can join it on the bitumen. It is a beautiful place where the river is wide and stony. It is also close to the site of the hut where Jack Riley, the original 'Man from Snowy River', used to live in the 19th century. Kangaroos, emus, birds and the wildlife still live on the river flats among the eucalypts. Picnic facilities have been set up along the river with fireplaces, tables and toilet facilities, making this a peaceful beginning of the river's long journey to South Australia.

From Tom Groggin, the river runs close to the sealed road as it makes its way towards Khancoban. This is a stunning drive along the Alpine Way, on a former stock route, built by the Snowy Mountains Authority in 1956. Rock covered cliffs (protected with wire mesh) line one side of the road. The other side of the road drops into a deep valley with tree-covered mountains rising out of it. In late autumn and early winter, the mist may be down over the mountains, lifting occasionally to give you a hint of the snow on the peaks.

Along the way there are several signposted short tracks that take you into the river. Grassy Flats' 4WD dry weather track is 7 km past Tom Groggin. It is a narrow, bumpy, dirt track but easily manageable when it is dry. The track is 1.4 km and leads through native forest to the river bank. The Murray seems placid here, but you can hear some rapids through the trees downstream. The trees and undergrowth are dense so there isn't an easy riverbank walk, but there is a fireplace and access to the river.

The first sign of the massive Snowy River Scheme is a sign pointing east to Geehi Lookout (10 km down the track), and Geehi Dam (25 km). There is no road access beyond that. However, if you don't want to divert at this point, keep driving for 21 km and you will see a glorious view of the great silver pipes coming down the mountain from the Alpine Way to the Scheme below.

Before that, and 32 km past Tom Groggin, we recommend that you stop at Scammell's Lookout where there are breathtaking views out to the east over the Kosciuszko National Park. Now you will get a true sense of the magnificent countryside with some of the highest mountains in Australia. In winter the peaks are covered in snow, in summer the mountain shimmers in the sunlight. An annotated photo tells you what mountains you are looking at. The highest mountain visible is Mt Townsend at 2209 metres. Mt Kosciuszko itself is not visible anywhere from the Alpine Way.

Khancoban is the first town along our upper Murray journey. It is a small holiday resort town with a surprisingly comprehensive range of tourist facilities. This once agricultural village

Tom Groggin and the Alpine Way

Tom Groggin station was named after the Aboriginal word for a water spider, tom-a-roggin. The Aboriginal people who lived in the plains of NSW gathered in the mountains in summer to hold ceremonies and harvest Bogong Moths. The moths are rich in fat and were a popular high energy food so, when the insects went to the alpine regions in summer to aestivate, the Aboriginal groups followed them. The moths were made into cakes, or smoked for preservation.

The first European to take up land around Tom Groggin was an ex-convict in 1830. Since then the station has passed through various hands and it is now notable as including the only cleared land along the Alpine Way. In 1890 Banjo Paterson was on a riding tour of Kosciuszko with some local station owners, and camped one night at Jack Riley's hut on Tom Groggin station. Riley told them the story of his famous horse ride in pursuit of a thoroughbred stallion that had gone bush. Two years later, The Man From Snowy River appeared in the *Bulletin* magazine. In response a large number of city tourists made their way up the bridle tracks to a visit the Irish-Australian bushman.

When the Snowy scheme was mooted, engineers began to survey the region in 1950; the stock route along the lower reaches of the mountains was selected as the most likely transit route through this very remote high country. Even at that the workers who lived in the construction camps along the Alpine Way in the 1950s and 1960s often found themselves bogged or snowed in. Workers who went astray were searched for quickly but given little sympathy when found. One worker, sent to find a break in the telephone connection line that had been strung from tree to tree, strayed 15 km from the line. When he was eventually found, he was given a stern lecture about the dangers of the Australian bush.

The Alpine Way remained unsealed until the early 1990s. While the Snowy Scheme teams lived up there, there was plenty of machinery to rescue bogged vehicles, but as tourism grew, the need to create an all-weather road became important. The final section was sealed in 2000.

changed dramatically during the building of the Snowy Scheme and, at its peak, 5000 people lived here. Now there are about 500 residents and all of the regional recreational services you would require. The shop in the large Khancoban Lakeside Caravan Resort is the hub of a lot of tourist activity, with Vicki and Tom Ellis coordinating white-water rafting, horse riding, canoeing and guided fishing, as well as providing accommodation from powered campsites to a luxury cabin with a spa (02 6076 9488). Across the road, the Khancoban Alpine Inn Hotel–Motel also has a range of accommodation from motel rooms to a backpackers' lodge with communal kitchens and a BBQ (02 60076 9595). You can also get good counter meals here around the blazing log fire.

One of the reasons for the popularity of Khancoban is the proximity to great trout fishing on the rivers and pondage in the vicinity. When we were there a man had just caught his first fish ever, a 1.5 kg trout — another photo for the caravan park 'Brag Board'. Vicki and Tom promote fishing for beginners, particularly women. Vicki told us that six of the eight fly-fishing national titles are held by women! For very successful fishing people, you can freeze your fish at the caravan park until you are ready to take them home. The Murray itself is in the mountains east of Khancoban but there is access via the 4WD Tiger Trail. Vicki and Tom can give you detailed information suitable for the time of year if you want to venture out that way.

KHANCOBAN TO ALBURY VIA WALWA AND LAKE HUME

From here the Murray makes its way from the rugged mountains, through pasture country into Lake Hume. There are several small, picturesque towns along the way, with basic tourist facilities including hotel accommodation. The historic town of Tintaldra is 30 km from Khancoban and is situated on the Murray banks. The mid-19th-century Tintaldra Hotel provides hotel and motel accommodation, powered caravan sites, BBQ facilities and a children's playground (02 6077 9261). You can also get a good lunch and snacks at the 1864 Tintaldra Store and Tea Rooms. Walwa is 24 km from Tintaldra and is another 19th-century town where you can stay in the single-storey hotel in rooms starting at around $25 for a single, or have a meal in the large family bistro (02 6037 1310). If you are chasing the Murray cod, this is where to start as the native fish begins around here; it is too cold further upstream.

Murray River

The Murray flows for 2530 km from the Australian Alps to Encounter Bay. It rises between Mt Pilot and Mt Forest Hill in the Great Dividing Range. From Lake Hume it flows west through a wide, grassy corridor, being fed by the rivers of Victoria that drain the northern slopes of the Great Dividing Range. It also receives water from the north through the Murrumbidgee, Lachlan and the Darling. From the Darling junction at Wentworth, the Murray meanders west to Morgan and then south to the Southern Ocean in South Australia. Great river red gums and river cliffs that glow red in the sunset are distinctive features of the Murray as it flows along the border of NSW and Victoria, and on into South Australia.

The explorers, Hamilton Hume and William Hovell named the river The Hume in 1824. Six years later Charles Sturt named it The Murray after Sir George Murray, an English statesman. In 1836 Thomas Mitchell named it the Millewa, an Aboriginal name. And the Aboriginal people in the Upper Murray regions called it the Indi. Of course Sturt's name became the official one.

Long before the Europeans arrived, the Murray River was the home of populations of relative density. The rich plant and animal resources along the river floodplain supported large Aboriginal groups such as the Wiradjuri, the Yorta Yorta and the Wadi Wadi. Evidence of life up to 30,000 years ago is contained in the river region. The Murray people were territorial and fought the pastoralists as they moved in on their land with their cattle. But even before the Europeans arrived in large numbers, many of the groups had already reduced considerably in number by the spread of introduced diseases. Yet these are also the groups that have survived the great changes, and their culture is evident along the river and in national politics.

The Murray has been jointly managed by a commission representing New South Wales, Victoria and South Australia since 1915. It is such an important water resource that joint management is essential for equitable use of the river. Today storage and man-made controls are used to regulate its flow and support extensive irrigation. It has 16 weirs, 13 locks, 5 barrages and 4 storages, the first of which is Lake Hume. The managing authority is now called the Murray–Darling Basin Commission.

The Murray is now a major recreational destination for Australians with fishing, camping and boating among the popular ways to relax along the great river.

The Murray appears periodically along this road until, almost imperceptibly, it joins one of the long arms of Lake Hume, east of Walwa. From here on, the flow of the water is managed by a combination of weirs and locks, dams and barrages.

The drive around Lake Hume is very attractive. The road on the south side of the lake is sealed and there are few trees close to the road. The land here is used for pasture, although the brown-coloured floodplains still give the landscape a wild look. On the near horizon all around you are rolling mountains. The lake and the submerged trees are visible for most of the drive. About 20 km from Walwa, in the middle of nowhere, is an Australian flag fluttering in the breeze and a historical marker below it. This is a monument to honour the birthplace of the Murray Grey, a strain of fat cattle that was registered in 1962 and has been so successful for the Australian beef industry!

You can cross Lake Hume at the Wymah Ferry and continue your journey on unsealed roads on the north side of the lake. Wymah Ferry operates on call between 6.30 am and 7.45 pm, but is closed for 45 minutes during mealtimes at 7 am, 12 noon and 6.30 pm. Alternatively, you can continue along the sealed roads on the south side of the lake and go over the bridge just before the magnificent Lake Hume Dam.

Lake Hume Dam, completed in 1936, is enormous. Unfortunately, your chances of seeing a dramatic water release are small but you can walk down to a viewing platform where you get a reasonable view of the spillway and a sense of the vast scale of the project. It is 1616 metres wide with 29 gates. From the top of the dam, and the parkland close to the carpark, you can see Lake Hume stretching back to the east. Nearby there is some original powerhouse machinery so you can try to work out the mechanics of its early operation.

Around the corner, 1 km from the dam, is the Hume Weir Trout Farm, where you are virtually guaranteed to catch a fish. The farm supplies all of the bait and tackle, they will even clean the fish for you and supply ice for you to take it home in. This is an attractive place where you can spend a full day out catching your lunch and having a BBQ in the picnic area, or else try home-made trout produce — such as smoked trout and trout paté —

from the kiosk. There is also a playground, and water features and lawns. The Farm is open from 9 am until dusk.

Lake Hume Dam

Albury–Wodonga

The pace of your journey will change as soon as you reach the twin cities of Albury–Wodonga. From here on you leave the mountains behind you and will move along the river highways from town to town. Albury–Wodonga are best known as the border towns where the Hume Highway between Sydney and Melbourne becomes a bottleneck. But if you look closely, you will see several signs that these historic towns have plenty of interest in their own right. The first indicator is the prominent sign welcoming you to Wiradjuri Country. In all of our travels around Australia, we have seen few large towns that have proclaimed traditional ownership so prominently. Then you will start to notice old buildings, large ornate brick structures like the enormous railway station, and small, low brick cottages.

The region's Gateway Information Centre is located on the east side of the Hume Highway between the two towns, and is 16 km west of the dam. There is so much to do and see at this tourist complex that it would be easy to spend an entire day here. The tourist centre itself is bulging with brochures, free tourist maps and information about activities in the region. It is open from 9 am to 5 pm, seven days a week, and operates an accommodation booking service.

The marathon swim

In November 2000, Australian marathon swimmer Tammy van Wisse began an epic swim down the Murray River in an attempt to break the record of 138 days, which was set in 1991 by Graham Middleton. She began in the cold alpine waters at Corryong, swam through floodwaters around Barmah, and on down to the warm, slightly salty waters of the Murray mouth. The 2438 km took her 106 days, swimming at speeds of 4.5–7 kph. She battled fatigue as well as the natural features of the Murray — currents, eddies, snags, logs and even poisonous snakes. At Hume Dam the water temperature in the river below the dam was only 11°c, several degrees colder than the water in the lake above it.

Her arrival at each town was quite an event as crowds of school children and local people cheered her on. She attended many receptions and dinners. In Berri the South Australian Premier, John Olsen, presented her with a medal.

Part of the objective of Tammy's extraordinary marathon swim was to highlight the health of the Murray River. One of her sponsors was the Australian Conservation Foundation and she used the publicity around the venture to highlight the salinity problems facing the river. Before she started, it was reported that, based on present trends, the Murray will begin to fail the World Health Organisations' drinking water standards within 20 years.

The Information Centre has been built beside the 1858 customs post that is now a great place to have lunch. It reminded us of an Irish country pub, with low wooden ceilings, an open fireplace, worn wooden floorboards, and a very cosy atmosphere. On top of that, the home-cooked food and coffee were top class. On the other side of the Information Centre is a modern coffee shop where you can buy wonderful home-made fudge with all sorts of rich and interesting flavours — lemon myrtle, Baileys Irish

Cream, mint and others. Around the back of the Information Centre, pottery, jewellery and other crafts are sold in a mixture of old stone and modern brick buildings.

At the southern end of the complex is another treasure for river travellers, Harvey's Native Fish Farm. This is a rare indoor native fish farm that has been set up for a family day out with extra features such as waterslides, a playground, pet animals, and a BBQ lunch area. There is also an amazing function centre that you might get a chance to peak into — this large barn-like space has a huge open fireplace and a large rusting dray in the corner. Although it is pretty rugged, you can imagine great parties being held here.

Undoubtedly one of the great attractions of Harvey's Fish Farm is the opportunity to look at some of the river fish close up. The fish tanks have been set up with windows so that when you throw some of the supplied fish feed over the wall, the fish come charging up to the window, splashing the water as they grab the pellets. You can see brown trout, rainbow trout, or yellow belly. They are also experimenting with Atlantic salmon. The tanks are labelled so that you can identify specific fish. Of course, you are also welcome to catch a fish in the pond and BBQ it for lunch, or take it home with you ready-cleaned.

Around Albury–Wodonga there is so much to do that we can only identify some places that were highlights for us. One of these is the Albury Regional Museum in Australia Park, down by the Murray. You can't miss it, there are striking Aboriginal murals around it. Travelling from the Information Centre, the turn-off into the park is shortly after the museum. The focus of the museum's display is on local Aboriginal history and Bonegilla, the immigration centre on Lake Hume. Here you can learn about the Indi or Murray River people, including the Wiradjuri who lived on the north side of the river. You can see fire-hardened wooden weapons, examine illustrations of how people made canoes and shields from the bark of trees, and read information about their clothes and ornaments. An atmospheric cave has been created in one room; here you can sit and listen to a Dreamtime story under a simulation of the night sky. The museum also displays a lot of information about the modern history of the local Aboriginal people around Albury–Wodonga.

Albury–Wodonga

The twin river cities of Albury and Wodonga grew on the site of Hume and Hovell's Murray River crossing. As usual, the explorers were followed by squatters looking for new runs for their cattle and sheep. Cattle runs were taken up in the mid-1830s and in 1839, Robert Brown — who became the first European to settle here — set up a slab hut to cater for the drovers who were increasingly using this crossing place as a camping stopover. A few years later he established a punt. In the meantime, the NSW government set up a police point here. This was one of several that the government had placed between Sydney and the new city of Melbourne. Its job was to look after travellers and also catch runaway convicts. Despite all of this movement and activity, the population of Albury in 1841 — by then gazetted — was still only seven, and Wodonga was still a cattle run.

Being almost midway between Sydney and Melbourne, Albury and Wodonga became important border towns following the proclamation of Victoria in 1851. Over the next 20 years, during which time Wodonga was gazetted, the twin towns became the break point in the telegraph between Sydney and Melbourne, a bridge was built, a customs house was built in Wodonga, and industry flourished on both sides of the river. Albury developed a paddle-steamer construction industry, Wodonga developed a major cattle market. When the railroad arrived in 1881, the towns' role as the focal point of overland communication between the great colonies developed still further.

Both towns have continued to grow and they are now centres for pastoral and agricultural industry, commerce, tourism. Their history is evident in the heritage buildings close to each of the town centres. Between them they now have a population of over 63,000 people. When the population in the hinterland is taken into consideration, this is reputedly the second largest inland concentration of people in Australia after Canberra.

The regional museum is also the centre for the Bonegilla story. Bonegilla was established as an army base in 1940, and in 1947 became the largest centre for displaced people, and later also for new migrants who responded to advertisements in Europe. There are many relics in the museum of the 320,000 people who passed through the camp, providing us with a glimpse of the strange life that post-war migrants encountered when they arrived in Australia. Folders of personal Bonegilla stories are available to browse through in the museum, and visitors are invited to add their own stories.

The cities' river history is visible on the nearby riverbank where the PS *Comberoona* is docked. Paddle-steamers began to arrive in Albury in 1855. Before the railroad arrived river transport was vital for the town — a coach ride to Sydney took 51 hours at best. For 25 years the riverboats cruised in and out of Albury, and the *Comberoona* was believed to be one of the finest. The wood-fired twin paddle-steamer provides tours on Wednesdays and at weekends, and more frequently during school holidays. If you want to be sure to arrive at a scheduled cruise time, contact the operators on 02 6041 5558, or via the Information Centre.

PS **Comberoona** *docked in Albury*

The historical buildings around Albury give the city some attractive streetscapes. If you want to look at them more closely, you can pick up a heritage trail brochure at the Information Centre. One building that we found particularly striking was the

Wiradjuri

The Wiradjuri are one of the largest Australian Aboriginal groups in terms of population and territory. Their country stretches from Albury to Hay, covering a region of 60,000 square kilometres and taking in parts of the Murray, the Macquarie, the Lachlan and the Murrumbidgee Rivers. In 1788 there were around 3000 people living in this resource-rich country, farming, hunting and gathering. They had one language, and their religious ceremonies and meetings drew great crowds. They were known for their woodcraft, which they used to make tools, dishes and shields for their own use as well as for trading.

Initially the Wiradjuri responded well to the Europeans. They greeted Governor Macquarie when he met a group of their elders near Bathurst in the Blue Mountains in 1815. Wiradjuri guides accompanied Hamilton Hume and William Hovell on their exploration along the border of Wiradjuri country from Yass into Port Phillip in 1824. Relations with the colonists began to sour when conflict arose around use of land near Bathurst. In retaliation for taking their food, the Wiradjuri killed the cattle and sheep that the Europeans had introduced to their land.

In 1823, a young warrior named Windradyne emerged to lead the Wiradjuri resistance. He trained warriors in methods of frightening the farmers off their land. The government responded, and martial law near Bathurst was declared. Windradyne was captured and displayed in chains for a month. He was later pardoned and died in 1827. During this time many Aborigines were killed as the colonists asserted their control over the land. The Wiradjuri dispersed, going to towns or friendly stations, or remaining in the bush.

As the pastoralists moved inland along the rivers, the Wiradjuri again resisted, using guerrilla tactics to frighten or sometimes kill the settlers. The settlers, supported by the police, responded with gunfire.

Disease, loss of their traditional land and resources, and battles with the Europeans decimated the Wiradjuri population. Towards the end of the 19th century, forced dispersal began and the people were moved into mission stations such as Maloga and then Cummeragunja. They lived here with other dispossessed groups, which further eroded their culture and connection with the land. Yet the Wiradjuri have survived, and they remain a powerful force in Aboriginal culture and politics.

railway station. It stands just off the east side of the Hume on the Albury side. It is a fine redbrick building with verandahs trimmed in wrought-iron lacework. It claims to have the longest platform in the southern hemisphere, which was necessary because of the different line gauges used in NSW and Victoria. Until 1962, passengers travelling between Melbourne and Sydney had to change trains here.

As you would expect, there is plenty of accommodation and places to eat. The Information Centre lists 47 places, from motels to caravan parks and backpackers' lodges. Happily, the Centre provides an accommodation booking service so you can ring them and discuss your needs. This is certainly a place where you may want to spend a few days exploring; it is both a peaceful river town and a busy city with all facilities.

ALBURY TO RUTHERGLEN

The Murray drive along the north of the river is on the Riverina Highway. You will meet the river occasionally, but mostly you will see the river red gums that line the bank. Introduced poplars and other European trees provide a contrast in colour, particularly in autumn. About 35 km from Albury, the road travels through the small town of Howlong, a 19th-century pastoral and river town. It got its name from the station, Hoolong. In 1838, John Hawdon left here with 325 animals on the first and very famous overlanding trip to South Australia. It took ten weeks and he only lost four animals on the way. Twenty years later, the town was large enough to support a ballroom and a concert hall. The town still has an historic atmosphere with several well-preserved buildings in town.

Corowa — Wahgunyah — Rutherglen

These three towns are closely linked in their history and in the way they provide services to the recreational industry of the Murray and the famous wine regions of Rutherglen. Corowa, on the northern banks of the river, is the largest of the centres with a population of around 5000 people. In the mid-19th century the

Bushrangers and Dan Morgan

Bushrangers were the scourge of the countryside in the 19th century. The term 'bushranger' emerged in 1805 to describe criminals who attacked people on the roads and then disappeared into the bush. These early bushrangers were often convicts who had escaped from assigned service or farm employment. In the mid-19th century, following the gold rushes, a new group of bushrangers emerged. Called the 'wild colonial boys', they were often the Australian-born sons of poor settlers who were not prepared to eek out a living on the land. Some of the famous bushrangers belonged to this group, including Ben Hall and Frank Gardiner. They knew the bush and the families living there, so they moved easily through the countryside, finding shelter in friendly households. They used the 'bush telegraph' to monitor police movements. They stole cash and gold from the towns' people, and horses from the squatters.

The notorious bushranger and murderer, Daniel Morgan, was one of the wild colonial boys who was active on the road between Sydney and Melbourne and around Albury. Morgan's exploits are a mixture of colourful stories and extremely violent events. On one occasion, on the run after a series of hold-ups, he met an Irish woman who brewed whisky made from potatoes and rye in a mountain gully. After hiding out with her for several weeks, he borrowed her clothes and stole a mob of cattle that was being driven through the area. He sold the cattle and returned to his camp near Wagga Wagga.

During his career, the bushranger, sometimes known as 'Mad' Dan Morgan, shot policemen and unarmed men, robbed travelers and stations, shot cattle, and burnt granaries and haystacks. In 1865, at the age of 35, he held up the homestead at Peechelba Station, on the Ovens River south of Yarrawonga. He allowed a nursemaid out to quieten a child and she sent for help. As the police arrived, a station hand shot Morgan in the neck. He died the next day, having spent his last hours conscious and surrounded by a large group of people, some of whom had been his hostages.

town flourished as a pastoral centre and major trading point when the riverboats came through, and then the railway arrived. Corowa is proud of its heritage. The numerous 19th-century buildings have been well-preserved, there are several pubs with wide balconies, the street signs are old-fashioned, and rows of sycamore and other European trees have been planted, all giving the town a very attractive atmosphere.

Like many border towns in the 19th century, Corowa supported free trade between the colonies and, in 1893, a major conference on federation was held in the town. In 1915, another important meeting was held here to establish fair usage of the Murray River. Both of these important national events are commemorated in the Federation Museum, a 1915 redbrick building originally built for the Border Brass Band. The museum is only open from 2 pm to 5 pm on Saturdays and Sundays. A guide to all of the historic buildings in Corowa is available from the Corowa Information Centre in Sanger Street.

As you drive towards the river on Sanger Street, there is a beautifully preserved two-storey building with a large verandah held up by ornate wrought-iron brackets. This is the 1860s Royal Hotel. It has recently been renovated and the pressed-tin ceilings were uncovered in the process. You can get lunch or dinner in the elegant dining room, or stay in one of the rooms. Prices start at $25 per single, or $22 per person for more than one person (02 6033 1395).

Corowa ends at the 1892 single-lane bridge over the river, with a good caravan park on the east. There is often a queue of traffic waiting to go over the bridge but you can walk across it on the thick wooden walkway, protected by heavy metal railings.

Wahgunyah begins on the south side of the bridge and, with a population of 600, it is the smallest of the three towns. The two-storey Empire Hotel was built in 1910 on the site of an 1861 pub. It now serves enormous and good quality dinners in the evenings. These are well known among locals and regular visitors, so it may be wise to book if you know you are going to be there for dinner.

Across the road from the Hotel is a short cul-de-sac leading to the Murray River and a Mass Tree. The Mass Tree is worth seeing because of its size and age. The parish priest from Beechworth celebrated the first mass in the region by this tree in 1869.

The road to Rutherglen travels through vineyards and you will see several signs along the way pointing the direction to some of the famous wineries in the region. The compact town is 9 km south of the river and has narrow streets and historic redbrick buildings. The large Visitor Information Centre is situated in an 1886 winery that was used until 1990. This is a very busy place, reflecting the popularity of the Rutherglen region as a place for an indulgent weekend of wine-tasting. An elegant restaurant, Tuileries, is also in this long building; it has both family service and silver service.

If you like tasting wine, or if you are interested in learning more about the history of one of Victoria's major industries but just want to buy pickles and other preserves, you will enjoy this region. This is red wine and fortified wine country. Famous wineries like St Leonards and All Saints are renowned for their full-bodied red wines. Stanton and Killeen, famous for port and fortified wine, is also a local vineyard. There are 17 vineyards on the Rutherglen Wine Region Touring Guide (available at the Visitor Information Centre) and these give full details of when they are open and what is special about them. Many of the wineries have set themselves up to provide more than basic wine-tasting at the cellar door.

Directions to the wineries are all well signposted and not difficult to find. Cycling tours of the wineries are also promoted; some wineries will deliver any purchases back to your accommodation in the region. You can rent bikes at the Rutherglen Visitor Information Centre.

St Leonards and All Saints are close to each other near the banks of the Murray. Both have been set up to cater for family or large groups with lunchtime restaurants and walks through the grounds. Access to the cellar door at St Leonards is via a dark shed full of large wooden casks that smell strongly of fermenting wine. It opens out into a bright cellar door and a garden beyond where they serve BBQ lunches. The cellar door at All Saints is in an unusual redbrick castle at the end of a beautiful elm tree drive. The building is based on the Castle of Mey in Caithness, Scotland. There are several historic buildings around the splendid gardens, including the dormitory where the Chinese staff used to live in the 1860s. There is also a keg factory where a cooper makes oak kegs using traditional methods involving no nails, glue or paraffin. These are both wineries where you could spend a lot of time, with something of interest for all ages.

Other wineries in the region are likely to be of more interest to serious wine-tasters, but many are set up to make it comfortable for all visitors. Stanton and Killeen is one of these, the atmosphere is very friendly and the red and fortified wines are renowned. Morris Wines, 14 km east of Rutherglen on the Mia Mia Road, is another of these and has two delicious and hard to get Amontillados.

Given its role as a major winery destination, there is plenty of accommodation and good places to eat. Between Rutherglen and Corowa, 12 km to the north, there are at least 17 motels, 4 caravan parks, and numerous luxurious and expensive B&Bs close to wineries or in fine old houses. There are also plenty of cafés, tearooms and hotels that serve meals. Several of the large wineries also serve dinner on Saturday nights. The Ball Park Holiday Retreat Caravan Park is almost under the old wooden bridge on the north side of the river, and the views up and down the Murray banks from here are stunning. They have several good ensuite cabins, as well as the usual facilities of caravan parks (02 6033 4282). It is also just a brief walk to the Empire Hotel for dinner in Wahgunyah.

Despite the range and amount of accommodation, it can be difficult to get a place to stay during one of the food and wine festival weekends here. The big festival is the Winery Walkabout, traditionally held over the Queen's Birthday weekend in June. The staff in the Rutherglen Visitor Information Centre don't provide an accommodation reservation service but they monitor room vacancies over the very busy weekends and can provide information and contact details for accommodation in the area. School holidays will also be very busy. But outside of those times, you will probably get a bed easily.

In the region there are several signposted tracks that will take you down to the banks of the Murray where you could drop in a line to fish and, in some places, camp. These include Shaw's Flat and Police Paddocks, both along the Up River Road east of Wahgunyah and signposted from the road. Follow the signs to St Leonard's vineyard and continue along the Up River Road; the camp sites are signposted from there. Further along the road, past the turn-off to Howlong, is Doolan's Bend, another favourite camping spot. There are basic facilities here, including fireplaces and tables.

Lake Moodemere on the west side of town is a beautiful and popular fishing place, although there is no camping here. Drive out towards Yarrawonga on the Murray Valley Highway and, 6 km past the Information Centre, you will see the turn-off to Lake Moodemere. Follow the signs down to the entrance of the lake area, about 1 km further down this road. This is a wild area surrounding the large lake. It is shared with water-skiers and rowers, but when there are no motors out on the lake, it is a very peaceful place. It is surrounded by old trees, several with scarring which suggests that the bark has been used to make canoes or shields.

Corowa — Wahgunyah — Rutherglen history

This region was originally part of the Wahgunyah run taken up by squatter John Foord in around 1840, just a decade after Charles Sturt charted this country. In 1856, as the law changed and Foord saw the potential for trade, he established a private town in Wahgunyah on the southern bank of the river. Wahgunyah was an inland port, transferring goods to and from Echuca. Later it was a customs point between the two colonies of Victoria and NSW. The bridge, erected in 1892, is the John Foord Bridge and is the only one along the Murray named after a person.

The region, and particularly Rutherglen, grew dramatically when gold was found in north-east Victoria in the 1850s. The population of the area grew to 30,000, the second largest goldmining region after Ballarat. Meanwhile, on the north side of the river, Corowa was flourishing with river transport, and later in the 1890s, a railway station.

Rutherglen quickly became one of the major wine-producing areas in Victoria. Wine was first grown in the region in the early 1860s. From 1875, many Victorian vineyards were destroyed by the American grapevine louse, phylloxera vastarix, and over the years the Victorian vineyards were closed down. Nevertheless, by 1890, Victoria was the main wine-producing colony in Australia, with over double the amount of land under vineyards than in NSW or South Australia.

Yarrawonga–Mulwala

It is only 48 km from Rutherglen to the next major Murray River centre. The country in between was once part of the huge run

called Yarrawonga, which was taken up by Elizabeth Hume, sister-in-law of Hamilton Hume, in 1842. The twin towns of
Yarrawonga and Mulwala now merge across the 500-metre bridge
over the Murray and Lake Mulwala. Mulwala, on the north side
of the river, is the smaller of the two centres with a population of
around 1500. Yarrawonga, on the south side, has a population of
about 3500. These are popular family holiday destinations, so
much of the focus for visitors is on activities such as sports, water-
skiing, golfing, paragliding and — of course — fishing. It is one
of the few places in Victoria where you can go paragliding (03
5744 2777). You can also take river tours or go on the Lake
Mulwala Everglade and Swamp Tour in a low boat that travels
into the lagoons around the lake (03 5744 1989).

For visitors who are following the river and its history, there
are also things to see. The main street in Yarrawonga, Belmore
Street, is an attractive street with several 19th and early 20th-
century buildings at the river end. This includes The Left Bank,
a café in an early 20th-century building with wooden floorboards,
a pressed-metal ceiling and good home-cooked food. The
Yarrawonga–Mulwala Visitor Information Centre is on Belmore
Street just beside the lake. Besides having plenty of information
on the region, it has access to the Old Yarra Mine Shaft, as well
as a small display about mining in the district. It also has some
intriguing photos of the building of the weir and the creation of
Lake Mulwala. The information centre is open from 9 am to 5
pm, seven days a week.

One of the highlights of Yarrawonga–Mulwala is the Pioneer
Museum on Melbourne Street in Mulwala. The Museum is situated in a large barn opposite the Ski Club, about 1km from the
bridge. The spacious barn is full of old farm machinery, including
a 1910 wool press set in a small display with other shearing related equipment. Tractors, old cars and other large items have been
polished and put on display. There is also the wooden frame of a
plane built in the early decades of the 20th century by Douglas
Sloane; he modelled it on the wings and flight of the wedge-tailed
eagle.

Other sections of the Museum include a clothes display, the
war room, a small picture theatre with old uncomfortable theatre
seats, the dentist's surgical instruments (which probably aren't

terribly old but look ferocious), and a nursery. Here the curators have gathered good quality items from the local community and arranged them on display with notes about the dates. The clothes collection is stunning, with garments dating back to the 1830s. They are mostly owned by the local women and the display is changed regularly. On one occasion it included antique wedding and bridesmaids' dresses. These are excellent selections ranging from ordinary and curious, to beautiful and elegant. This is one of the better museums along the rivers and is well worth visiting. It is open Wednesday–Sunday in the afternoons from 1.30 pm to 5 pm in the period between Easter and Christmas. Between Christmas and Easter it is open from 9.30 am to 1 pm, and also Sunday afternoons. It is open on public and school holidays too. There is an entrance fee of $3 for adults and 50¢ for children.

The Yarrawonga Antique Clock Museum on Lynch Street is another curiosity. This is a private collection of over 400 working clocks set out in a couple of rooms of a suburban house. It has every sort of clock you can imagine — cuckoo clocks, antique and novelty clocks — all ticking steadily and chiming occasionally. Brian and Joan Williamson have collected these clocks from all over Australia and restored them to working order. Even if clocks don't excite you, the sound of so many clocks ticking is extraordinary. The Museum is open from 10 am to 4.30 pm, Saturday to Thursday, and the entrance fee is $4.50. You may need to ring the doorbell to get into the Museum.

Of course the main feature of Yarrawonga–Mulwala is the huge lake. The 6000 hectare lake was formed in 1939 when a weir was built across the Murray to raise the water levels and support irrigation in the region. The focus of this is the weir itself off Irvine Parade, west of the Information Centre. You can drive over the narrow weir and there is also a protected walkway that is worth walking across to get a sense of the weir, the river and the lake.

A fish elevator was installed here to allow the fish to migrate upstream despite the weir. The fish swim into an elevator and are then released upstream; it is automatically controlled. The elevator is to the east of the weir and underwater so you won't see it. However, there are diagrams nearby explaining how it works. It is one of only two in Australia.

There is a nice place around on the north side of the weir for camping and enjoying the riverside but the track can be difficult — don't attempt it if it is wet. Drive over to the north side of the bridge, turn west immediately and about 100 metres down the road you will see a red dirt track leading back towards the river. The river itself is 600 metres down this track and leads to a small parking place. Down here you can hear the roar of the weir as the water rushes through a few of the great gates. Downstream from the weir and under the trees is an excellent fishing spot. Alternatively, you could stay at the Yarrawonga Caravan Park on the south side of the river near the weir, which has the usual facilities and a boat ramp (03 5744 3420).

One of the most interesting features of the area is the Aboriginal Boat Rock, 28 km north of Mulwala. This is well worth the side trip if you are interested in Aboriginal history and culture in the region. To get there, take the straight road out of town and follow the signposts in the direction of Savernake through the Mulwala Wetlands and along the railway line. About 8 km before Savernake there is a crossroads — take the left turn and travel on for 6.5 km, during which the sealed road switches to gravel. You will have to go through a gate along this track. Please ensure that you leave it as you find it; this is private property and it is important that all visitors respect this. Soon you will spot a brown sign, 100 metres from the double gate, pointing towards the Aboriginal relic. The Boat Rock is about 50 metres from the small gate, on an almost direct line to the high rock point.

The Boat Rock is part of an outcrop of granite that is covered in moss and algae. After rain, water trickles down the face of the granite rocks and gathers in an expertly positioned rock pool. The rock was excavated by local Aborigines to provide a reservoir of water during the summer months and to attract the kangaroos that gathered to drink here. The pool was constructed through the ingenious process of building fires to heat the rock, then rapidly cooling the rock to cause contraction. This had the effect of breaking the granite into small gravel-sized pieces that were extracted using primitive tools. The process was repeated over and over until the pool, approximately 2 metres deep and in the shape of a boat, was excavated. The gravel from the rock pool has been washed down over the years and is now scattered at the base of the rock. Like so many Aboriginal sites, it is not especially dramatic to look at unless you are aware of the history and process behind it.

Aboriginal boat rock, north of Yarrawonga

Back in Yarrawonga–Mulwala, there is plenty of accommodation with over 3000 beds in the area. The emphasis is on family holidays with holiday units, resorts and other places along the lake and the river. Happily, the development is sensitive to the environment and many of the buildings are low and hidden by trees. There are also 16 motels, 8 caravan parks, and several B&Bs. The region is very busy in the summer months, and packed out during the peak holiday weekends. However, the Visitor Information Centre operates a booking service to make selection easy for you. The emphasis in the restaurants is on family-style bistros.

YARRAWONGA TO ECHUCA

You can travel along the north or south of the river between these two major Murray towns. The most direct route is along the

Murray Valley Highway on the south side of the river through station country. It is 142 km this way, but there is a lot to see. There is also lots of bush camping with over 60 beach areas between Yarrawonga and Tocumwal designated by Parks Victoria as places you may camp or have picnics. To find these, either ask for information in the visitor centres close to the time you want to make camp, or simply watch the river trees and look out for the signs that point down towards the small reserves.

European exploration

Charles Sturt is credited with charting the Murray River when he shot into 'a broad and noble river' on his exploration down the Murrumbidgee in 1830. He named the Murray after Sir George Murray, an English statesman. The inland waters of the continent had puzzled the colonists, as they were aware of river flow into the hinterland. In 1824, Hamilton Hume and William Hovell (who first crossed the Murray near Yass) had provided information about the Goulburn and other north-flowing rivers. Sturt and Thomas Mitchell had charted part of the Darling and the waterways to the north of the Murray. Now Sturt brought the pieces together when he and his party rowed out into the Murray.

His party, consisting of eight men, continued their journey down the river and a month later they reached impassable obstacles near Encounter Bay. They couldn't get through to the sea where they had hoped to meet a ship that would take them back to Sydney. So, exhausted and with rations running low, the party had to row back up the river as quickly as possible. This trip is considered to be one of the most heroic episodes in Australian exploration. The group worked against the current, with only enough rations to last a month. They rowed from dawn until dusk each day, taking an hour's break at midday. When they arrived at their depot on the Murrumbidgee 23 days later, it was deserted. Now they had to continue to struggle upstream on the flooded Murrumbidgee. For another 17 days, they laboured on. Eventually they got close to a homestead and help arrived just as they exhausted their last ounce of flour. Sturt took several months to recover from this hardship, and went blind for a while. In 1838, he completed the charting of the Murray from a region around Yass to the junction of the Murrumbidgee.

The first major feature on the Murray Valley Highway is the National Trust protected pioneer's homestead, Byramine, 14 km west of Yarrawonga. This was the home of Elizabeth Hume and the main homestead of the huge Yarrawonga run. The unusual house was built in 1842 by Elizabeth Hume, sister-in-law to the explorer Hamilton Hume. It was designed to provide the family with a safe sanctuary should they be attacked by bushrangers or Aborigines. It has an octagonally shaped room in the middle of the house where the occupants could see the surrounding countryside. The other rooms — the parlour, dining room, and the bedrooms — are off the main room. The brick walls are over 30 centimetres thick. River pine was used for the floors and ceilings, as well as the wooden shutters on all of the windows, to protect the family in the event of an attack. The door handles are low to ensure that her children had easy access to the safe haven in cases of danger.

Today visitors can still get a very strong sense of the way this homestead was. The parlour and dining room are now small lunch rooms, and the bedrooms have been set up as 19th-century bedrooms with some old clothes laid out on the beds. The homestead is open from Thursday to Monday, 10 am – 4 pm. You can have an excellent country lunch in one of the original rooms, then explore the outhouses and wander through the attractive gardens. There is an entrance charge of $4 for adults and $2 for children to help maintain the historic place.

Across the road from the Byramine Homestead is the Fyffe Field winery and a very pleasant cellar door. The Diamond family vineyard produces a range of award-winning dry whites, soft reds and sweet wines that are available in very few places. You can find their wines in some restaurants but the main outlet is the cellar door as they also work on consignment. You can taste their range here and, while you are doing that, check out the pig collection! Liz Diamond has been collecting ornamental pigs for a long time, there are hundreds and hundreds of them, mostly small. They have been displayed in the outlet as conversation pieces — and to get them out of the family home! The cellar door is open from 10 am to 5 pm, every day.

Elizabeth Hume

The story of Elizabeth Hume is one of those extraordinary pioneer histories from early colonial Australia. In her early twenties, Elizabeth met John Kennedy Hume, also in his twenties. The marriage in 1825 had been delayed by his family. Elizabeth's mother had been a convict and her father was unknown. Despite all opposition, and after he agreed to protect the marriage celebrant from the wrath of his family, John married Elizabeth. By then they already had one child, so they were hardly the most conventional people of their time.

After John was murdered in 1840 by bushrangers, Elizabeth was left with eight children and pregnant with her ninth son. Her brother-in-law, Hamilton Hume, clearly long reconciled with his brother and family, set her up on this property by the Murray. She named it Byramine, an Aboriginal word. The huge run soon became known as Yarrawonga, giving its name to the modern town.

Elizabeth continued to care for her family in this house. Her eldest son was now in his teens and able to help considerably. Not a great deal is known about her life on the property over the following decades. Elizabeth died of the measles aged 61. Her eldest son and fifth daughter died before her. She was survived by her remaining six daughters and one son.

Cobram

You will pass through several river towns between Byramine Homestead and Echuca. Cobram is the first of these, 18 km from the homestead. Barooga is its corresponding town on the north side of the river and is linked to Cobram by a bridge. The Cobram district is renowned for its peaches and in January every second year it holds a 'peaches and cream' festival of music and fun. Ripe peaches feature prominently in the stalls around town. Parks Victoria have laid out a 4 km walking track along the river here that takes in Quinn's Island Wetlands Sanctuary. There are several day visitor areas where you can have a riverbank picnic, but not camp. Cobram–Barooga is another popular family holiday venue, with golfing, fishing and plenty of accommodation. The Visitor Information Centre is open from 9 am to 5 pm, seven days a week. It operates an accommodation booking service and the staff can also direct you to bush camping along the Murray in the state reserves (1800 607 607).

Tocumwal

Tocumwal is a quiet river town on the north side of the Murray. The road between Barooga and Tocumwal on the north bank travels through vine country with the trees of the Murray visible to the south. Tocumwal is another family holiday venue but there are several features here for the river traveller, notably the historic World War II aerodrome and the 19th-century town buildings.

Tocumwal was host to the biggest RAAF base in Australia during World War II and the historic aerodrome is 2 km outside town on the eastern side. The huge hangars are visible from the road as you approach it. The hangars are now full of gliders and there is a small museum with walls covered in photos of life in the 1940s, when American airmen worked with the Australians. The aerodrome is now host to several flying schools; you can go gliding out over the Murray on a 20-minute scenic trip that will cost about $75 per person (03 5874 2063).

Tocumwal was a bustling river crossing and customs post in the 1870s, with punts and ferries until the bridge was built in 1895. Its early history is still evident in some of the buildings by the wide streets of the town. The long low 1869 Tocumwal Hotel-Motel serves counter meals and has rooms from $44 for a single and $55 for a double (03 5874 2025). Next door, the Tocumwal Antiques and Gallery Tearooms is situated in a restored 1859 general store that still has an old atmosphere and is a good place for lunch or afternoon tea. Down the road, the Miniature World of Trains is a happy haven for model train enthusiasts. The redbrick building displays model railways, trains and carriages, including numerous scaled models of Australian trains. It is open from 11.30 am to 12.30 pm, and 1.30 pm to 4.30 pm, seven days a week.

Around Tocumwal, there is good access to the Murray with beaches and camping areas in bends on both sides of the river. The river eucalypt trees clearly identify the course of the river, so if you take any of the signed public roads into the river, you may find a camping spot. You can also pick up a mud-map of these places from the Tocumwal Information Centre. The Centre is open from 9 am to 5 pm, seven days a week.

BARMAH STATE FOREST

The next major diversion is the Barmah State Forest and the Dharnya Centre, which is the educational centre of the Yorta Yorta people. The small town of Barmah is 30 km from Echuca. Continue on the Murray Valley Highway until you see the turn-off to Picola, 7 km past Yalca North. Then take the Echuca–Nathalia Road into Barmah. The sealed road takes you through pasture country where you can see flocks of sulphur-crested cockatoos, small farm houses, large shire horses, and river trees in the distance. There are plenty of billabongs along the route, some with large eucalypts surrounding them. There are also flocks of birds drawn to the river region — mountain ducks with striking orange necks, spoonbills, and sulphur-crested cock-atoos.

The Barmah State Forest is one of the highlights of the Murray along here. There is a pub in Barmah where you can get counter lunches. Barmah also has a small shop, a fuel station and a caravan park. The administrative centre for the Yorta Yorta people is here with a tall canoe tree outside the door. The trunk indicates the length of the canoe that was once made from the bark.

The most useful guide to the forest is the Parks Victoria Barmah State Park and Barmah State Forest Visitor Guide, available from the Cobram–Barooga Visitor Information Centre and other information centres along the river. The map in the guide identifies the myriad of tracks around the 30,000 hectare forest area. The tracks near Barmah are easily accessible to all vehicles.

On the way into the forest itself, you will see a sawmill with an incredible pile of river red gum behind it, waiting to join the existing dune of red sawdust. The sheer size of the trunks lying here is extraordinary. Some have growths where an insect has eaten into the wood and the bark has grown around it. Wood-turners like these growths because they create interesting patterns for them to work with.

From here on, you can follow the signs and explore the forest. The Moira Lake road travels past regrowth forest and for 5.5 km,

Whitewater rafting down the Murray River in the Snowy Mountains
(PHOTO: BILL BACHMAN)

Central Murray Riverina (PHOTO: BILL BACHMAN)

Historic wharf at Morgan (PHOTO: BILL BACHMAN)

the road is sealed. From here on, the track can be rough in places and would certainly be impassable when wet. But unless you plan to go deep into the forest, every vehicle in reasonable condition would have no difficulty here when it is dry. Along the way, sign-posted tracks direct you to the river and the camping areas.

The day visitor area is 6 km from the town and is situated by a beautiful section of the river. There is a boat ramp, a designated camping ground nearby, wood fireplaces, good access to the water for fishing and a large notice reminding you that the Murray River waters here are in NSW and you must obey NSW boating and fishing regulations.

Dharnya Centre, 9 km north of Barmah, is an interpretative centre where visitors can learn more about the Yorta Yorta people and the history of the region. The displays inside include a wet-land display and a life-size display of a 'mia mia' camp, named after the style of shelter. It consists of some red gum branches tied together with kangaroo sinews. They are covered by the bark of the red gum that has been peeled off and straightened over a fire, and waterproofed with tree resin. The fireplace is positioned so that the wind blows the smoke into the mia mia to keep the occupants warm and the bugs away. Various domestic implements and the shells and bones of food from the region have been placed into this display.

Other major displays at Dharnya include a wetlands display, the bird display, stone axes and other stone implements. A small library of reference books will give you an indication of what has been written on the area. But pride of place goes to the fabulous bark canoe. The wide, flattish, dark brown canoe looks distinctly unstable. Yet it would have carried up to six people comfortably. They may have had small fires on the canoe either to cook the fish or, as was the custom, to attract fish to the surface at night where they could be speared.

There are plenty of other things to see in the centre so it is worth spending time there. The Dharnya Centre has been estab-lished as the cultural link between Yorta Yorta and visitors. The large wooden interpretative centre is well signposted and is open every day from 10.30 am to 4.00 pm, except major public holidays.

If you want to move further into the forest and drive along the Murray bank, you can follow the 4WD tracks deep into the for-

est. The tracks may be subject to flooding, so be aware of weather conditions. These wonderful forest tracks travel along some of
the 112 km of river frontage in the State Forest, and will take you
at least a day.

Back on the bitumen, the road to Echuca from Barmah will
take you out to the main Deniliquin road, through the irrigated
pastures, and in through Moama on the north side of the river.
Moama is quieter than Echuca and is a popular place for families
on holiday.

Echuca

In our experience Echuca is one of the great tourist towns of
Australia. Here it is very easy for visitors to enjoy a wide range of
relaxing or historical river-based activities, whether you are in
family groups or by yourself. Echuca is set on the Murray and
revolves around the historic port. Many of the old port buildings
have been restored and are now used for tourist-related activities.
The large Echuca–Moama Visitor Information Centre is in the
former 1877 railway engine-house, a curiosity in its own right.
You can get loads of information here about what do to and see,
and where to stay and eat in Echuca. It is easy to find the Centre
following the street signs.

Much of the activity centres on the Port of Echuca, a pedestri-
an area with a gravel road lined with wooden drains and timber
planks. There are so many attractions that it is hard to know
where to begin. There is the working blacksmith who makes fire-
side implements and candle-holders on the premises. Next door
is the working wood-turner who uses red gum to make bowls,
candle-holders, and other objects. Across the road, stuffed lions
and tigers are displayed in the public area of a kids' 'farm'; the live
farm animals are in the well-laid-out barn behind the shop. There
is an entrance fee to visit the animals ($5 for adults and less for
children) and kids can get close to them. Plonked outside on the
wharf is a huge piece of river red gum and a log-buggy beside it.
The scale is simply enormous. The buggy, pulled by bullocks, was
used to cart the logs — can you imagine trying to get that rig out
of a bog!

Further down the wharf is Sharp's Magic Movie House and

Penny Arcade. The front shop is a glittering clutter of film souvenirs of all types, but the main attraction is out at the back.
There, enthusiast Norm Sharp has gathered together scores of
penny-arcade movie machines and games. There is an example of
the coin-operated movie machine in the shop itself. For a dollar,
you can wind your way through a series of photos of Charlie
Chaplin in action. The faster you turn the handle, the smoother
the action. If you want to see more of these and play some of the
games, you can pay the entrance fee of about $11 and enter the
old-fashioned cinema and arcade at the back of the shop. A silent
movie is playing on the large screen all the time, and you sit in
old-fashioned seats to watch it. Or use the supply of large old
pennies that you get with your entrance fee to play the arcade
games and flick through old movies dating from 1896. This is a
different type of living museum; it is open daily from 9 am to 5
pm.

Back in the port, you can choose to take a ride on a Cobb &
Co. stagecoach or in a carriage around the town. You could also
join a river cruise on one of several boats that provide scheduled
trips. The *Pride of the Murray* is a large two-storey steamer with a
covered area on the lower deck. This was once a barge and the
super-structure was added in the 1970s. The steamer *Canberra* is
a smaller boat, similar in style to the *Pride of the Murray*, that
moves quickly over the water. The *Emmylou* and the *Alexander
Arbuthnot* are in a different style; passengers sit out on the decks,
and, in the case of the *Alexander Arbuthnot*, the wood used to fire
up the boat is stacked up on the deck. The steamers in Echuca
offer a range of trips — some with lunch, some with a kiosk on
board. A one-hour trip will cost around $12.50 for adults and
concession rates are also available. The *Pride of the Murray* also
has one-and-a-half-hour lunch trips where passengers can select
food from a menu prepared by the Wisteria Café. A trip on the
river is also a good opportunity to see the famous, three-storey
Echuca wharf at its best angle.

There are many other attractions here, such as the displays in
the long wooden wharf itself, and the Historical Museum, which
is in the old police station and lock-up on High Street (a block
away from the wharf) but it is only open in the afternoons.
Nearby is the National Holden Motor Museum where more than

40 historic Holden vehicles are displayed together with material on the history of the Holden in film, photographs, and memorabilia.

Echuca is also a focal point for the Goulburn and Murray river wine trails. The Murray Esplanade Cellars and the Port of Call Wine Cellar are both on the riverfront near the wharf and provide tastings for a range of wines from the river regions. They can also supply wine that might not be readily available in the cities.

There is a wide range of accommodation in Echuca, and the Information Centre offers an accommodation booking service. A few places stand out, one being the Steampacket Inn, an authentic 1860s hotel that has been renovated to accommodate 21st-century visitors. The Inn is in the Port of Echuca and has seven rooms, including a two-room family room. All have ensuites — which is unusual, given that so few interesting old places provide that facility. If you stay here ($91 for a double) you will enjoy high ceilings, tall sash windows, creaky floors, wooden walls, and individual old-fashioned furnishing in each room. Terry and Pam Banfield have created a glorious atmosphere that is within the standard motel price range. It tends to be quite busy at weekends and during peak periods, so if you want to stay here book in advance (03 5482 3411).

There are also plenty of restaurants in Echuca. Oscar W's in the historic wharf area is a great restaurant. It is known as one of Echuca's finest restaurants and has won one of Victoria's prestigious food awards — an Age 'Chef's Hat'. It is perfectly situated right on the water's edge by the wharf, and has a long frontage so you will be able to enjoy a river view. As it is open all day, you can pick your time to indulge in Devonshire tea, lunch or dinner. Inside the restaurant, the atmosphere is enhanced by a log fire in winter. There is a large open-air area that is wonderful in summer or during the day in winter. The dinner menu is dominated by fish dishes, with main courses priced around $20. To sit here and simply have a drink or a latte is a joy. You can watch the boats travel up and down the river below you and enjoy the sounds of swishing paddle-steamers and horns on the river.

Away from the wharf there is also a lot of activity. Hare Street is the main business centre with ATMs, banks and shops. High Street, running parallel to the wharf area, is a very attractive street with 19th-century buildings being used for a range of shops, including gift shops and camping shops. There are two good Italian restaurants here, Giorgio's and Fiori's, both with good reputations and both crowded at weekends. One of the more elegant (and expensive) places to stay is also along here — the River Gallery Inn, a B&B in an 1860s building that has seven rooms, each furnished and decorated in the grand style on different themes. The rooms start at $210 for a double.

Echuca is a popular fishing destination and you can join a fishing trip, or hire a boat to go out onto the water with a group like the Echuca Boat and Canoe Hire. They have a range of boats that are reasonably priced. One appealing style of boat is the BBQ boat; this takes up to ten people and has a gas BBQ on board. It is $65 for two hours, and $22 per hour after that. Smaller fishing boats are also available at $30 per hour. The canoes are cheaper still at $18 per hour. The Robertsons organise canoe trips where they will take a party up river so that you can canoe back to base with the current. They also organise canoe/camping trips where you can canoe with the current, camp under the stars, then continue canoeing the next day (03 5480 6208). This is a very pleasant way to explore the waters of the Murray, the silence of canoeing allows you to experience the peacefulness of life on the river.

ECHUCA TO SWAN HILL

The trip along the Murray Valley Highway between these major Murray towns is 158 km, and there are so many diversions that this could take you a couple of days to explore everything. Gunbower Island is a wonderful river floodplain adjacent to Cohuna, 67 km from Echuca on the south side of the river. This is the largest inland island in the world and is a state park with signed drives, bush camping, river access, bird life and all of the other joys you would expect to find in a natural river environment.

It is easy to get to the island from Cohuna, since it is well signposted. Inside the forest, however, the tracks are distinctive but the signposts are not always that clear. The chief difficulty is the distance involved; a simple round trip on the Gunbower Island Forest Drive is 38 km. You will reach the river after about 14 km

Echuca

Henry Hopwood is credited with founding the settlement that
became Echuca when he set up a punt and hotel at this busy inter-
section of the Murray and Campaspe River in 1853. A similar settlement had already been established on the NSW bank by James
Maiden in 1845. Originally known as Maiden's Punt, it is now
known as Moama. The early overlanders who drove their herds of
cattle from NSW into the newly chartered country of Victoria and
South Australia, swam their stock through the Murray around here,
so it was a logical place to establish a settlement.

The competition between the two men and their settlements was
ferocious. Hopwood won and Maiden's Punt, with its once highly
successful cattle market, sank into obscurity. By extraordinary coincidence, both Hopwood and Maiden were ex-convicts who had been
sentenced on the same day in the same court in England in 1834.
Both were in their early twenties. Maiden's death sentence had been
commuted to seven years in NSW for burglary, and Hopwood had
been given 14 years in Van Dieman's Land for possession of stolen
silk.

Hopwood marketed his settlement aggressively and Echuca flourished. This was a time when river traffic was growing and pioneer
pastoralists were moving into the land around the Murray, Darling
and Murrumbidgee Rivers. The movement of gold-miners from one
field to another brought good business to the services by the punt.
Hopwood built a hotel close to the punt and was known to alter the
times of the operation of the punt to prolong the travellers' drinking
time! He promoted the construction of the huge wharf, and lobbied
the colonial government to extend the rail line to Echuca. The railway linking the Murray to Melbourne arrived in Echuca in 1864.
The iron road-and-rail bridge was erected in 1879, confirming the
town's importance as a major inland port and transportation interchange. Hopwood died of typhoid fever in 1869, leaving a bustling
town as his legacy.

For a number of years Echuca was one of the busiest ports in
Australia, inland or coastal. Its wharf was over 1 km long, 12 metres
high, and had 3 levels. It became the focal point of transport for
passengers and goods from the Murray, Murrumbidgee and Darling
Rivers. Around the town, Echuca was a wild place and the range of
services largely reflected the interests of the wharf workers with 80
pubs and many brothels. Horse-racing in the main streets was not
unheard of, and fist fights could go on for hours. Yet at the same

time, boutiques carried the latest fashions. It was referred to as 'the Chicago of the southern hemisphere' and was once even suggested as a potential location for Australia's capital city!

Like so many other inland ports, Echuca went into decline in the 1890s when river transport diminished. Fortunately, many of the buildings in Echuca survived in reasonable condition into the 20th century and, as the trend towards river tourism grew, Echuca had many features that could be developed.

on the main track. Along the way, you will cross small wooden bridges over creeks and waterways, and travel through thick forest on the dry-weather tracks that are narrow and a bit rough in places. If you stay on the main tracks and watch your trip-meter, you can always retrace your steps if you get lost. Of course, this country is impassable when it is raining or flooded. You may camp in one of the many existing campsites along the river — these are readily found by taking a small track off the main track. You can get a map from the Visitor Information Centre in Echuca, or any of the information centres in the region. This is a lovely way to spend a day in the rich river environment.

Cohuna itself is a town on the banks of Gunbower Creek with a population of about 3000. The area is famous for its dairy produce — a concentrated protein substance made from milk, called casein, was made here for the astronauts on the Apollo space program. There are several places to stay in Cohuna including the Cohuna Hotel/Motel with both styles of accommodation (03 5456 2604), the Cohuna Motor Inn (03 5456 2972) and the Cohuna Caravan Park on the banks of Gunbower Creek. This has the usual facilities of a caravan park, including ensuite cabins (03 5456 2562).

The twin towns of Barham–Koondrook are 25 km from Cohuna. Barham is pleasantly set on the north side of the Murray with wide streets and it has at least eight motels, as well as a couple of hotels and a caravan park. Koondrook, on the south side of the river and with a population of 600, initially looks like a sleepy river town with very wide streets and no identifiable town centre. However, this was once the largest centre of the red gum forest industry. The timber was first transported to markets by river, then later by rail. It was also a trading post for paddle-steamers carrying wool from the stations.

Today, the red gum timber industry is still prominent with the large Arbuthnot Sawmill situated on a beautiful stretch of the river. The attractive smell of cut wood permeates the town. The sawmill was established in 1889 and once employed 200 men. You can take a tour of the saw mill from a walkway on weekdays from 10.30 am to 2 pm. There are several outlets around the town where you can order or buy furniture and other objects made from this beautiful timber. You can also get smaller, easy-to-carry items such as bowls, ornaments and little boxes. It is a joy to wander through these outlets looking at the fine craftwork.

Log buggy in Koondrook

A walking guide to Koondrook is available at the large red gum shop on Grigg Street on the way into Koondrook. This identifies 30 places of historical interest around the town that you might not notice otherwise.

To continue on towards Swan Hill, you can travel out to Kerang and rejoin the Murray Valley Highway, or take the side roads that travel closer to the river via Murrabit, 22 km from Koondrook, and on down to Lake Boga. This way you will stay close to the river trees, but because this is largely private property, access to the river is limited. At Murrabit there is a large picnic area on the river with an old bridge and palm trees nearby. About 3 km west of Murrabit is the lane down to Goon Punt Crossing. Keats' Cottage in the Pioneer Settlement at Swan Hill came from around here. The roads continue for 33 km on through irrigated farm country to Lake Boga and the Murray Valley Highway.

The actual lake at Lake Boga is so large that it would be easy to overlook the small township. The deep natural lake is close to the Murray Valley Highway and, long before the Europeans moved in, Aborigines gathered a reed that grew here. The roots were roasted and the fibres used for nets and fishing bags. It was also a valuable trading commodity for them.

More recently, Lake Boga gained prominence during World War II when it was selected as the RAAF base for its flying boats. This role is commemorated in the Lake Boga Flying Boat Museum at Catalina Park. The site was selected after the Japanese attacked Broome in 1941, and during the war, 416 aircraft were serviced here. The Museum has images and descriptions of all of the types of flying boats that were serviced here, as well as a short film. The Museum is open daily from 9.30 am to 4 pm, and entrance is $6 for adults or $12 for a family. If you want to try fishing in Lake Boga itself, you may catch yellow belly or redfin. This is Victorian water so a Victorian Recreational Fishing licence is required.

SWAN HILL

The city of Swan Hill, 17 km west of Lake Boga, is a major regional centre and a very popular family holiday destination (population 9300). Although the area was first settled by European pastoralists in the 1840s and the town developed in the 19th century, the historical background doesn't stand out on the city centre streetscape. Services to visitors are prominent with over 50 motels, resorts, caravan parks and B&Bs available in the region. The Swan Hill Visitor Information Service in the town centre is the best place to begin your exploration.

The outstanding feature of Swan Hill is the wonderful Pioneer

Settlement on the Marraboor River that flows into the Murray east of the Swan Hill bridge. There is so much to do and see in the settlement that you could easily spend a full day here. The settlement is a high-quality, faithful recreation of a pioneer river town, with working shops, tea-rooms, blacksmith, crafts, machine workshop and many other activities. The staff dress in historical costumes and carry on with their work. The large paddle-boat, the *Gem*, greets you. This 1876 boat was the largest passenger vessel on the river. It was sunk in 1948, salvaged, and brought here in 1963.

Beyond that, the Pioneer Settlement spreads out along the riverbank with dusty roads and boardwalks along the shopping strips. Historical buildings have been brought here and re-erected, including a redbrick church, several cottage shops, a mechanics' institute, a post office with a wide leather pad surface, a Masonic lodge and other buildings. Keats' Cottage was built in the 1860s, lived in until the early 20th century, and then used as a shearing shed before it was transferred here in 1969. Contemporary furniture has been placed in all of these buildings to give you a sense of how they might have looked in their heyday. Other activities around the settlement include street theatre, free rides in the horse-drawn carriages and cruises on the PS *Pyap*. Facilities are good, with several places to eat and relax. There is also an excellent guide book that gives you detailed information about all of the buildings and available features for sale at the Settlement entrance ($1.50).

The Pioneer Settlement is about 1 km from town on the south side of the Murray; the turn-off is signposted just before the bridge. It is open daily from 9 am to 5 pm, with a Sound and Light Tour available in the evenings. Entrance charges during the day are $16 for an adult, $8.50 for children or $41 for a family. The one hour river cruises are an additional $10 for adults, $6 for children and $26 for a family. The evening Sound and Light tour is also $10 for adults, $6 for children and $26 for a family.

The Swan Hill Regional Art Gallery, close to the Pioneer Settlement, spent 21 years in the PS *Gem* before being moved to its new building in 1987. This gallery has a small permanent collection and often hosts temporary exhibitions with an educational focus. Its permanent collection, which includes works by

Australian naïve artists, may not be on display if there are touring or temporary exhibitions here.

Back towards town there is a large, striking Moreton Bay fig tree that was planted in 1860 by Robert O'Hara Burke when the Burke and Wills expedition cavalcade moved through Swan Hill. Their visit was a major event for the small river town and all 140 residents turned out to greet them. The explorer planted this tree as a seed and it is now thought to be the largest of its type in Australia. The above-ground root structure exemplifies the high smooth ridges typical of this tree. The canopy is magnificent, although to see it properly you will have to walk back down the wide busy highway.

Roots of the Moreton Bay Fig Tree, Swan Hill

One hidden gem that we spotted was the 1922 Dun Aros Private Hospital that is now part of a junk and antique store called 'Made in the Mallee'. This is on the eastern end of Campbell Street, the main street. The unrenovated hospital rooms are filled with second-hand goods and the building probably looks much as it did when it ceased to be used as a hospital. If you want to look for other hidden historical gems of Swan Hill, pick up the excellent Swan Hill and District touring map; this contains interesting bits and pieces of historical information about features in the area.

As a major regional centre, Swan Hill has a good shopping centre and numerous places to eat. The emphasis is on bistro, family-style food, but we found another good spot in town in the Burke and Wills Motor Inn restaurant, where we had a terrific dinner one evening (03 5032 9788). The staff in the Visitor Information Service can assist you with accommodation.

Fishing is of course a popular pastime in Swan Hill. Access to the river is easy from the state parks outside town. Within the town, the caravan parks are probably the easiest places to fish from. Swan Hill is proud of its association with the Murray cod and, on Curlewis Street close to the bridge, the town has created a giant Murray cod. It is not impossible to catch a real one. A camper in the Swan Hill Riverside Caravan Park was recently reported as having pulled in a 30 kg Murray cod. The caravan park is close to the Pioneer Settlement and has camping sites on the river bank (03 5032 1494). Other fish in the river here include yellow belly, bream, the inevitable carp, yabbies and Murray crayfish. You can pick up a fishing guide at the Swan Hill Visitor Information Service; this also lists the fishing outlets where you can get bait and local information.

SWAN HILL TO MILDURA VIA HATTAH–KULKYNE NATIONAL PARK

Close to Swan Hill on the Murray Valley Highway there are several interesting places to see, notably Tyntynder Homestead and the Nyah State Forest where you can find some glorious bush campsites.

Tyntynder Homestead and Museum is 17 km west of Swan Hill and is one of the treasures of the region. Tyntynder run was first taken up by Europeans Peter and Andrew Beveridge in 1846. This was the traditional land of the Wadi Wadi people and they didn't welcome the intrusion. Andrew Beveridge was killed by Aborigines, but Peter remained on. He built a drop-log cabin and, in the 1859s, bricked up the house using sundried bricks. This is considered to be the first brick-veneer home in Australia. The cosy home changed hands and, in 1996, was purchased by the original land owners. You can visit the low brick cottage and outbuildings during school holidays from 10 am to 4 pm, or by appointment. You can also simply drive in and get a sense of the atmosphere here. When it is open, you can have lunch in the tearoom and look at the displays of Aboriginal and pioneer life — 'telling two stories, together making one future'.

Swan Hill

Swan Hill was in the traditional country of the Wemba Wemba and was first settled by Europeans in 1844, when squatters followed the passage of the explorer Major Thomas Mitchell. In 1836 Mitchell camped here and named the place after he was disturbed in his sleep by the noise of wildfowl nearby. In 1847 a punt was established. This was the only punt for about 100 km along the river, so drovers and other travellers gravitated towards the small settlement. In 1853 Francis Cadell reached here in his paddle-steamer, the *Lady Augusta*, from the mouth of the Murray. There were 12 people living in Swan Hill then. This marked the beginning of the town's role as a major inland port.

When Burke and Wills arrived here in 1860, there were 12 buildings in Swan Hill and a population of 140. Burke dismissed several members of the party, and hired Charlie Gray and two others. Gray was renowned for his knowledge of the Mallee country; he was one of the four to cross the continent some months later. He died just before the tragic party returned to Cooper Creek.

The Swan Hill punt was replaced in 1896 by the bridge. Around the same time, the government began to create blocks of land along the Murray to encourage closer settlement and farming in the region. The Mallee scrub was cleared and crops including wheat, citrus, vines and fodder crops were planted. Swan Hill is now the market centre for this part of the Riverina.

The turn-off into Nyah State Forest is 12 km from Tyntynder Homestead and this is still used by the traditional owners, the Wadi Wadi. There are Aboriginal sites here such as earthen mounds, burial sites, scar trees, as well as plants and animals that are integral parts of Aboriginal culture. For example, the Murray cod is considered to be the creator and guardian of the Murray River for this area, and the father of other aquatic creatures. The Brown Snake is the protector of the land and a totem of the Wadi Wadi people. The Aboriginal sites aren't signposted but you are asked to respect the environment and any sites you might identify.

The great stretches of bush camping and excellent river access are obvious and you should follow state park guidelines on using these. Use existing campsites and fireplaces, use fallen wood only and don't light fires on days of total fire ban. This is a popular camping place and there won't be a lot of fallen wood close to campsites; you will probably have to move away from the river to collect it. The area is prone to flooding, usually in spring. When this happens the tracks are closed off. The town of Nyah, just before the entrance to the forest, is a small river town with a pub and general store.

Back on the Murray Valley Highway towards Tooleybuc, about 8 km from Nyah, there is a signposted scarred tree on the north side of the road. This is an excellent example of a tree that has had its bark removed to make canoes, food and water containers, string and shelters. From here on you will begin to notice the classic Mallee country around you — low bushes in red soil lining the road. Much of it has been cleared for agriculture, but as you move down the Murray it will become more obvious, though you will continue see the great trees of the Murray identifying the path of the river.

Tooleybuc is 18 km from Nyah and is 2 km off the Murray Valley Highway on the north side of the river. Tooleybuc is a centre for citrus growing and there is a lovely scent over the town from the orchards in the region. The river frontage is picturesque and the narrow bridge over the river lends atmosphere to the town. The caravan park is set on the river and has ensuite cabins as well as camping sites and on-site caravans (03 5030 5025).

As you drive along the Victorian side of the Murray towards Boundary Bend and the junction of the Murrumbidgee and the Murray, irrigated farm life continues around you with the occasional hint of Mallee scrub. Just before Boundary Bend, you will see the entrance to the forest where the Murrumbidgee flows into the Murray. It is a fairly dense forest with a maze of well-defined dirt tracks leading into the junction itself. There are some signposts that give you direction but, like other forest areas, visitors have made their own tracks so this can be confusing. Again, use your own sense of direction to keep moving in towards the river and keep an eye on your trip-meter. It is about 6 km in to the point where you can see the meeting of the two great rivers through the trees. This was the point at which Sturt and his party in the whaleboat shot out into the Murray River.

Canoe trees

The river Aborigines used tree bark to make canoes and shields. For canoes, a sheet of bark up to 1 metre wide and 2 metres long were prised from the river red gums. When the shape was identified, two or three Aborigines cut around it using tomahawks while others would loosen the bark by tapping with tomahawks. Wedges were worked in, then saplings and ropes were used to slide the sheet of bark to the ground. Bark was often removed in late spring or early summer when the sap flow made this task easier. Great care was taken not to damage the tree. The bark was laid on the ground, pointed sticks were used to stop it from curling, and liquid clay was used to prevent it from cracking in the sun. Clay was also used to plug holes and gaps.

The Aborigines used the canoes for fishing at night. They would light a fire at one end of the canoe on a clay base to attract the fish. They also made fish traps; on the Murray these were made of bark, on the Darling they were made from stone.

Robinvale is 90 km beyond Tooleybuc and beside it is its twin town, Euston. These towns are popular family holiday destinations as well as being regional agricultural centres. They have taken full advantage of their beautiful positions on the river and provide a range of water-based activities. They each have a number of motels and caravan parks, and would be very busy during school holidays and peak weekends.

You can continue on to Mildura along the Sturt Highway on the north side of the river. This is 80 km and takes in Trentham Winery. The alternative route, on the Victorian side of the river via Wemen, will take you to Hattah–Kulkyne National Park and a wonderful river drive with great bush camping.

The main entrance to Hattah-Kulkyne National Park is off the Calder Highway at Hattah, 68 km south of Mildura. However, if you want to drive along the Murray river track, you can enter the park about 8 km west of Wemen on the Hattah–Robinvale Road. This will take you to the southern entrance of the park and an information sign.

Once you are in the park the beautiful wilderness area becomes apparent. This is a stunning environment with river red gums lining the Murray banks, and a mass of undergrowth between the track and the river. As you move into the park, you will come across sand dunes that are fenced off to protect them. The track is well-defined and signposted along the way, but it can be corrugated and a bit rough so expect to drive slowly regardless of what sort of vehicle you are driving. Also, this is definitely not a place to be if it is wet; you would get bogged.

Sunraysia

The Murray region known as Sunraysia got its name from an advertising campaign in 1919. The Australian Dried Fruits Association organised a competition to find a trade name for the fruit grown and dried at the Murray. It offered a prize of £50. The name that was selected was 'Sun-raised' and this was used extensively on the Association's packaging. Gradually the Murray region around Mildura became know as 'Sunraysia'.

There are two designated campsites in Hattah–Kulkyne National Park with basic facilities such as toilets, tables and fireplaces. These are close to the main entrance and information centre at the west of the park where you can pick up a Parks Victoria map to the region. There is also a moderate supply of drinking water here. The great joy of the park is that you may camp anywhere between the track and the river, and light fires in existing fireplaces. As you drive along the river track through the park, you will find lots of short tracks leading to the river and potential campsites. This is your opportunity! Drop your line into the water, boil the billy and settle back under the stars. Don't worry if your camp is close to the track, there is likely to be little traffic along here and certainly not much after dark.

The banks of the Murray along here are steep in places, which suggests that the river at this point is deep so the fishing could be good. The river's edge may be a bit muddy and you could get out of your depth quickly, so keep an eye on children. If you can't spend much time here, the 28 km drive along the river is a delight, if a bit slow. It takes some diversions around river bends that are signposted — Ki Bend, Jinker's Bend, Fireman's Bend and Retail Bend. The pleasure of driving through natural vegetation like this is immeasurable. You leave Hattah–Kulkyne about 7 km south of Colignan, a small town on the banks of the Murray.

Nangiloc, 6 km north of Coligan, is a small tidy town with a pub, food store, a caravan park and good access to the river. From there on out to Red Cliffs, the sealed road travels through endless vineyards, orchards and orange groves. On the way you could call into Lindemans Wines, a large, well set up place where you can taste a good range of wines and have a picnic in the generous grounds under the trees.

The Murray at Red Cliffs is stunning and this is the first opportunity on this trip to see the striking river cliffs that become common further downstream. To reach the river, drive along Kulkyne Way into Red Cliffs on the Calder Highway and take a look at Big Lizzie, the old train sitting in a park by the side of the highway. Then follow the signs out along Indi Avenue through the residential area of the town to the river. Out on the river there is a boardwalk and a lookout so that you can take photos of the picturesque river scene. The cliffs glow red in the sunset, but at any time of day they are glorious.

Psyche Pump, an original irrigation pump set up by the Chaffey brothers in 1891, is the next river feature worth noting. Psyche Pump was where the Chaffey brothers pumped water from King's Billabong to irrigate the land. It operated from 1891 to 1959, with steam engines doing the work. It was decommissioned and some equipment was removed, but much of it is still here. It operates occasionally, and the Mildura Visitor Centre can give you details of this.

You can drive along a very rough river track from the Red Cliffs lookout to get there, but we recommend that you take the maze of residential roads to reach the pump. From the cliffs, turn into Pumps Road, then into Cocklin Avenue. At Dewry Avenue, turn towards the river and travel back around King's Billabong until you see the signs for the pump. A map of this region is available in the Mildura Visitors' Guide, which the Mildura Visitor

Francis Cadell and the navigation of the Murray

Captain Francis Cadell (1822–1879) was the son of a Scottish shipping and coal mining magnate. After commanding one of his father's ships for five years, he arrived in South Australia and took up the South Australian government challenge of providing a river steamer service up the Murray. He first took a small party in a canvas canoe from Swan Hill to Wellington on Lake Alexandrina. Then in 1853 he took the *Lady Augusta* and a barge from Goolwa to Gannawarra, near Swan Hill, in just over three weeks. The wooden steamer had been built to his specifications in Sydney. On the way he overtook the other Murray navigation pioneer, William Randell, in the *Mary Ann*. Randell passed him in Swan Hill and continued on to Moama. On their return journeys, both carried wool back to South Australia, so beginning the use of the Murray as a river highway.

Cadell continued to navigate the inland rivers for the next six years. His steamer, the *Albury*, was the first to reach Albury under the command of G.B. Johnston; Cadell and Johnston together were the first to reach Gundagai on the Murrumbidgee and Mt Murchinson near Wilcannia on the Darling. Cadell opened a general store at what became known as Wentworth in 1856. The area was previously known as Hawdon's Ford after a drover who brought his sheep across there. But as more Europeans moved into this prime site, pressure mounted on the government to establish the settlement formally and sell the land. It was named Wentworth in 1859.

Cadell's skills as a businessman didn't match his ability to open up the waterways for transport. One company folded, then another. Over the next 20 years he took up several ventures, including supervising war traffic in New Zealand during the Maori wars, and pearling off the north-west coast of Australia. His pearling enterprise came to Australian government attention for his ill-treatment of Malay employees and kidnapping of Queensland Aborigines, and to Dutch colonial government attention for kidnapping people from the south-Asian islands. In the end his crew dealt with the situation and, after several mutinies, Cadell was murdered by his crew in 1879.

Information and Booking Centre can send you in advance, or you can pick it up at the large visitor information centres along the Murray. It is well worth the effort to find this pump, even if you are not going to continue along the track to Mildura.

The 19 km river track leaves Psyche Pump for the residential streets of Mildura. This is a lovely drive that skirts King's Billabong and meanders along the Murray past many camping and fishing opportunities towards Mildura. It is a rough track but it is signposted along the way and it brings you very close to the river. We would recommend this for people who are confident in driving along wild dirt tracks. You can't go very far wrong by staying with the river.

Mallee

Much of the land along the Murray west of Nyah was Mallee scrub that was cleared for agriculture. The word 'Mallee' is of Aboriginal origin and is used to describe country that is dominated by a small eucalypt tree that has a long underground root. The underground roots may be roughly equal in size to the trees above ground. By 1883 the term 'Mallee Country' was used when licences for this region were granted. The section of the road between Ouyen and Mildura is Mallee country in a fairly natural state with low dunes, sandy soil, and low trees and scrub.

Mallee roots may be 6–9 metres long, and were a source of water for the Aboriginal people. Mallee fowl were a good source of food because they would produce many eggs in season. Water from the Mallee roots was located by prodding the ground with a stick, then digging up the roots, chopping them into segments and draining them into a water bag made of animal skin.

Mildura

This is the major regional city with all facilities, lots of motels, restaurants, supermarkets and a population of 24,000 people. It is also an attractive place with lots to see, good picnic grounds and lovely walks along the river. The Mildura Visitors' Guide is an excellent publication to get hold of, and the large Visitor Information and Booking Centre is a good place to start. The guide includes an easy-to-follow map of the town and surrounding areas. It identifies places of interest, and walking and driving trails. Advertisements identify many of the facilities for tourists including a zoo, playgrounds, clubs, bowling, gem and opal outlets, fruit promotion centres and a fish farm offering a chance to catch yabbies. There is also a large shopping mall on the Calder Highway.

The Mildura Visitor Information and Booking Centre is part of a large complex with a small theatre, a swimming pool and lots of displays of the early history of Mildura. It includes material on the Aboriginal people of the area with maps and artefacts. There is a great display on the Mallee region that encourages kids to spot the animals. Of course, the paddle-steamers and river transport are also well covered. And there is an audio-visual display on the Chaffey brothers and their late 19th-century irrigation schemes that changed the region. The largest museum piece is a restored carriage from the turn of the century. The metre-high wheels are beautifully restored with white trims. Other smaller items of regular outback domestic use are all laid out in an uncluttered arrangement.

There are excellent opportunities in Mildura to take advantage of the river setting and have lunch or a dinner cruise on one of the paddle-steamers. The 19th-century paddle-vessel *Rothbury* offers a weekly lunch BBQ that leaves Mildura and arrives shortly afterwards at the sweeping lawns of Trentham Winery every Thursday (03 5023 2200). They also have evening cruises where you can drift up the river on the open section of the top deck, if the evening is balmy, and watch the lights of the winery and floodlit river approach. The showboat *Avoca* also offers evening cruises, and their Saturday evening dinner cruise includes a dance. So if you want to include the river in your evening out, you may enjoy this one (03 5021 1166).

Out along the river, there is plenty to see. The area around Lock 11 is a place you could spend a lot of time, particularly if there are boats going through. The lock was built in 1927 and is set in a large parkland with the weir on the other side of the lock. There are information boards about the lock — which must save the lock keeper from having to answer endless questions about the system. One Easter we watched six large riverboats fit in here before the lock gate was closed on one side and opened on the other. The lock gates close slowly with a grunt. The water then pours into the chamber and the boats rise four metres fairly quickly. Then the other gate is opened. This is interesting to look at close up but you can also get a terrific perspective of the lock in operation from the Pioneer Homestead west of the lock. From there you can see the boats rise into view before the heavy lock gates open slowly.

Lock gates opening, Mildura

Nearby, the 1887 Pioneer Homestead is certainly worth a visit. If you have done a lot of outback travel and seen many ruins, this is a chance to see what a simple, early pastoral homestead would have been like. This homestead has a log cabin section and a brick section. The log cabin has hessian-covered walls and ceilings. This was a common wall covering but you seldom get an opportunity to see it or experience the distinct smell today. Items from the past have been arranged throughout the homestead. Outside there is some farm machinery and other equipment. The whole place gives you the sense of walking into a living homestead.

On another scale, almost opposite the lock and weir parkland is Rio Vista, the grand 19th-century Chaffey house. The house was built in 1891 and is beautifully situated with views over the lawns, park and fountain down to the river. It is now part of the Mildura Arts Centre with a gallery, museum, sculpture park and restaurant. It is open during the week, but opening hours are limited on weekends and holidays with afternoon openings only. Inside, the Chaffey house is very Victorian, with dark wood panelling, marble fireplaces, a tiled floor and a wide staircase with a stained glass window on the landing. The ballroom in the basement is now an art gallery. William Chaffey lived here until his death in 1926.

Near the town centre on Langhorne Avenue is the Tulklana Kumbi Aboriginal Gallery. It sells a range of Aboriginal artefacts with many of the usual tourist items: cards, jewellery, didgeridoos and paintings. What makes the gallery stand out is the interpretative displays. The items for sale are placed in an atmospheric river setting decorated by branches from gum trees.

You can pick up an excellent Accommodation Guide at the Mildura Visitor Information and Booking Centre. This lists over 100 different places you could stay in or near Mildura. It goes as far south as Ouyen and includes Hattah–Kulkyne National Park area. The guide lists accommodation under type including backpackers', farm stays, caravan parks, hotels and motels, houseboats and paddle-steamers. It has a comprehensive range of symbols that will tell you everything from whether there is a TV in the room to whether you can take pets. It also lists costs which is very useful for planning. If you plan to stay for at least a night in Mildura, we strongly recommend that you ask the tourist bureau to send this to you in advance. They also operate an accommodation booking service.

The free Mildura Visitors' Guide has an excellent listing of restaurants in the region. The descriptions include cuisine, a price guide, licensing arrangement, whether it is a family restaurant, and whether you can eat outside. The scope ranges from the award winning Hudak's bakery that specialises in pies, to the Grand Hotel and Stefano de Pieri's famous Cantina restaurant.

Mildura is yet another place where you could spend a day or two on this river trip, there is a lot to see and do, and it is not focused in one area. The Visitors' Guide maps are essential for finding your way around the city.

The Chaffey brothers

George Chaffey (1848–1932) and his brother William (1856–1926) met Alfred Deakin, then a Victorian government minister, in California in 1885. The Canadian brothers had developed irrigation colonies there and were taken with Deakin's accounts of the availability of land in Victoria. George, an enthusiastic entrepreneur, left for Australia. He persuaded his brother to sell up their Californian business and follow him.

In 1886 the Chaffeys selected the derelict Mildura sheep station as the site of their first irrigation settlement. They were permitted to take up 100,000 hectares of land on the understanding that they would install permanent irrigation processes. They were also given land to set up an irrigation colony at Renmark and to pump as much water as they needed from the Murray. Approximately 750 km of channels were excavated and pumping stations installed. Potential buyers were brought up to Mildura to inspect the properties and by 1891, there were 3300 people living around Mildura and 1100 living at Renmark, many of them new British migrants. The Chaffeys laid out the new towns in the Californian style — wide streets lined with trees. A younger brother, Charles, was brought to Australia to manage the Renmark operation.

Initially the irrigated land yielded fruit and other crops but quickly things began to go wrong. There was loss of water from seepage, salinity damaged the trees, and yabbies bred in the warm waters of the channels and burrowed into the earthen banks causing them to collapse. In the early 1890s, Victoria was going through a recession; land prices fell causing further stress to the Chaffeys. Then the first major harvest in 1892 was lost because the river waters were so low that the paddle-steamers couldn't take the produce to market. All of this ended in a Royal Commission of inquiry and the Chaffey brothers went into liquidation. The colonial governments stepped in to support the work of irrigation in Mildura. George returned to California but William stayed on and worked hard at building a wine and dry fruit industry for the area. He was very successful and became an admired and respected member of the community. When he died, a statue of him was erected in Mildura.

MILDURA TO WENTWORTH

The final stretch of this river trip is a journey along strips of bitumen through orchards, palm trees and vineyards. Mildura and Wentworth seem to merge into one, although there is 30 km between them. Merbein and Yelta are two small towns along the way, and there are many farmhouses. So on your first visit through here, you may not be sure when you actually leave Mildura. It is a very attractive drive, particularly in the early evening as the setting sun strikes the avenue of palm trees.

We leave the Murray on this trip at Wentworth. This is the point at which the Darling River from outback New South Wales joins the Murray, and the river continues its journey through South Australia and down to the Southern Ocean. We have covered the town of Wentworth in our chapter on the Darling and we have followed the Murray down to its source in the next chapter.

2 Lower Murray River

WENTWORTH TO MENINGIE

The drive down the lower Murray River, from Wentworth to the delta, is one of the finest river drives in Australia. The road travels through semi-arid desert and irrigated vineyards before turning south at a sharp angle, with the river, in Morgan. From that point the Murray flows in a fairly straight line to Lake Alexandrina and the Murray mouth. Between Blanchetown and Walker Flat, the road is set high on the river cliffs, providing continuous and stunning views of the river valley below.

The relics of history along the Lower Murray provide many diversions along the way. The ancient traditions and culture of the Aboriginal people are accessible to visitors at several places, with the rare chance to spend the night camping and learning about ancient ways down at the Coorong in the delta region. The more recent history of inland transportation is also accessible in many lively ways, from exploring the remains of enormous, wooden inland wharves to taking a trip on an old paddle-boat.

Food and wine are great features of driving down the Murray. The bulk wine producers of the irrigated regions dominate the northern stretches of the Lower Murray. Then, just as you reach the end of your trip, you arrive at some of Australia's best-known wine producing country, the Fleurieu Peninsula and, nearby McLaren Vale. The food to look out for is the cottage-type that you would make yourself if you had the time and the skills, such as pickles, jams, mustards and sauces. It is easy to find places that provide good freshly-cooked meals along the river.

Of course, the Murray is also a famous fishing destination and

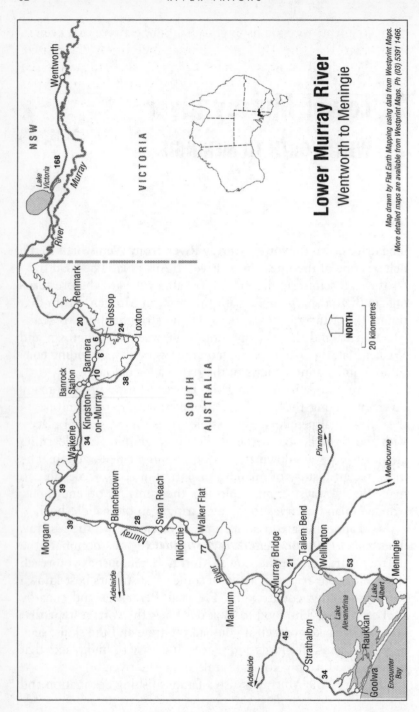

Lower Murray River
Wentworth to Meningie

Map drawn by Flat Earth Mapping using data from Westprint Maps.
More detailed maps are available from Westprint Maps. Ph (03) 5391 1466.

NORTH

20 kilometres

NSW

Wentworth

Lake Victoria

168

Murray River

VICTORIA

Renmark

20

Glossop

24

Loxton

6

6

Barmera

10

Banrock Station

38

Kingston-on-Murray

Waikerie

34

39

Morgan

39

Blanchetown

28

Swan Reach

Murray

Nildottie

77

Walker Flat

SOUTH AUSTRALIA

Pinnaroo

Melbourne

River

Mannum

Murray Bridge

21

Tailem Bend

Wellington

53

Adelaide

45

Strathalbyn

34

Lake Alexandrina

Lake Albert

Raukkan

Meningie

Goolwa

Encounter Bay

there are plenty of good fishing places. But be aware that even in the 30 years that John has been fishing in the Murray, the volume of fish has dropped dramatically. Now you will probably catch carp with some ease but if you want the tastier Murray cod or redfin, you will need local knowledge to find out what is biting and where. The scenery and atmosphere along the Murray River is magical, with the great river red gums providing shade for fishing and camping in the peaceful environment.

Main route

Wentworth — Renmark — Loxton — Morgan — Mannum — Murray Bridge — Goolwa — Meningie

Maps

Touring Atlas of Australia, Melbourne, Penguin, 2000
Riverland, Department of Environment and Natural Resources, South Australia, 1995, (this is particularly useful for navigating the region around Berri, Loxton and Kingston-on-Murray)
Mud-maps of reserves and town maps are available from tourist centres en route

Passes

NSW freshwater recreational fishing licence required for lakes and rivers to the NSW/SA border (this includes Rufus River and Lake Victoria).

Maximum distance between supplies

164 km, Wentworth to Renmark via Lake Victoria.

Minimum number of days required in dry conditions

660 km from Wentworth to Meningie; five days, if you don't spend too much time anywhere.

Best time of year to visit

The weather along the Lower Murray River weather is pleasant all year round with average daytime temperatures of 15–26°c in winter; nights are cool with average temperatures dropping to 4°c. In the summer, temperatures sometimes rise to the high 30s, but recorded average daytime temperatures are registered at 23–33°c.

Local information and useful telephone numbers

Wentworth Visitor Information	03 5027 3624
Renmark and Paringa Tourist Centre	08 8586 6704
National Parks and Wildlife, Department of Environment and Heritage, South Australia, Murraylands Regional Office Berri	08 8595 2111
Berri Tourist and Travel Centre/Bookmark Biosphere Trust, Berri	08 8582 5299
Loxton Tourism and Arts Centre	08 8584 7919
Barmera Travel Centre	08 8588 2289
Morgan Shell Roadhouse and Visitor Information Centre	08 8540 2205
Mannum Tourist Information Centre	08 8569 1303
Murray Bridge Community Information and Tourist Information Centre	08 8539 1142
Signal Point, Murray River Interpretive Centre, Goolwa	08 8555 1144
Melaleuca Centre, Meningie	08 8575 1259

THE ROUTE

Wentworth

Our journey down the lower Murray begins in Wentworth, the town at the confluence of the Darling and Murray Rivers that together form the fourth largest river system in the world. Wentworth is a small river town that once flourished because of its location on the border — first it was a customs point for travellers; in more recent years it provided Victorians with a place to gamble. Now Wentworth provides useful tourist facilities to people travelling along the Murray or up to Cooper Creek via Broken Hill.

We have discussed Wentworth in more detail in our chapter on the Darling River (see pages 268–72). The Tourist Information Centre on Darling Street, just off the Silver City Highway, is, as usual, the best place to start. The staff there are enthusiastic about the features and services in the region; they will direct you to whatever facilities you are after. They will also send you packages of information in advance if you phone them. The centre is open from 9.30 am to 4 pm during the week, and 10 am to 2 pm at weekends.

Before you leave Wentworth, visit the junction of the Darling River and the Murray River. This is to the west of the town at a park off Cadell Street. It is well signposted and easy to find. The course of the two rivers is distinctive and although they are likely to be flowing very gently, you can see where they merge. Lock 10 and the weir is visible to the west of the park, and there is a viewing platform at the junction.

WENTWORTH TO RENMARK VIA LAKE VICTORIA

There are three possible routes between Wentworth and the next major town, Renmark. The easiest, quickest but least exciting route is via the Sturt Highway on the bitumen. It is 144 km but doesn't go near the river at all. The other two tracks are longer and mostly unsealed, but will take you to the river at several points. The most interesting track is on the northern side; it takes you through semi-arid scrub plains to Lake Victoria and Rufus River. It is a long drive of 164 km, but it is worth it if you have never experienced Australian desert country before.

About 2 km to the north of Wentworth on the the Silver City Highway, turn west towards Lake Victoria and Renmark (the Silver City Highway continues to Broken Hill, 265 km north). There is 8 km of sealed road, then a section of gravel followed by another 6 km of bitumen. From there on the road is unsealed for about 100 km and is passable only in dry weather road (which is most of the time). It is reasonably maintained but like other gravel roads, has corrugations that will shake up your car if you drive too fast. Check your nuts and bolts — we lost a spotlight along this track! If there has been recent rain and the road hasn't been graded, the surface will be rough, so just slow down. During heavy rain, and for a short while after, the road will be so muddy that there is a danger of being bogged or at least of losing control of your vehicle, so don't try to drive if the track is wet.

When the weather is dry, this is a great opportunity to experience a true outback road. Many of the great desert tracks, such as the Birdsville and Oodnadatta tracks, are similar to this in texture. The outback road between Wentworth and Renmark is well signposted. The eastern section has a sandy red surface; further west, the brown clay-coloured surface takes over. The natural vegetation is low scrubby saltbush on fairly flat ground stretching to the horizon. There are few trees and no cultivation. If you are nervous about travelling out here by yourself, be assured that there seems to be enough traffic that if you get into difficulty, someone will be along sooner or later.

To fully appreciate the peacefulness of this pristine environment, bring a tarpaulin, mattresses, sleeping bags and pillows, and sleep out under the stars. It is dry and secluded enough not to need a tent.

PERRY SANDHILLS

The well-known Perry Sandhills are 4 km west of Wentworth. The turn-off down the short track to the dunes is clearly signposted. Rolling red sand hills are a rare sight in this part of Australia so we highly recommend the diversion. Perry Sandhills were once part of the Willandra Lakes System (which includes Mungo National Park). The shifting sands have banked up so deeply around one large tree that you will find yourself almost in the canopy of the tree rather than at its base. This is a favourite landscape for professional photographers.

FORT COURAGE CARAVAN AND CAMPING

Fort Courage Caravan and Camping Park is situated on the banks of the Murray, 20 km west of Wentworth where the river is wide and the trees are large and shady. The 100-acre site is owned by the Wentworth Angling Club and run by volunteers Bruce and Joyce Dunstone. They claim that the fishing here is better than average — when the fish are biting of course! There are powered and unpowered sites, each the same price at $12 for two adults, and a small fee for children.

You could also stay in one of the cottages in Fort Courage, such as the 19th-century Murray Pine Log Lodge, which was once the house of the head stockman of Moorna, a local station. The head stockman lived in this three-bedroom house, which is about 20 km from the Moorna homestead by river, or 11 km by road. It sleeps up to ten people; bring your own bedding and food. The other buildings are a double cabin with ensuite, and a three-room cottage with ten beds, a kitchen and sitting room. The charge here is $12 per adult (03 5027 3097). Communal areas in the park include two BBQs and two fireplaces — all under cover in case of rain!

You can also rely on the fishing information that Bruce and Joyce will give you. They don't provide bait or tackle, but will be able to give unskilled people some help. This is a perfect place to camp, relax and fish.

LAKE VICTORIA AND RUFUS RIVER

Lake Victoria and Rufus River are important features along this road. About 26 km west of Wentworth, a minor track meets the road. The right fork will take you to the north of Lake Victoria; the left fork, usually the better road, will take you to the south of the lake and a good fishing spot on Rufus River. It is closer to the Murray, so the trees are taller. The red sand road travels over many cattle grids and past station fences. This is the road we follow.

The Murray River is seldom visible along here, but you will get a sense of it occasionally when a creek runs from the river to the road creating nice picnic or rest spots. There is one such place 50 km west of Wentworth, where a bridge over a creek leads to a lovely picnic place where the water is clear. Despite the proximity of Lock 8, there is no access to the lock.

As you get closer to Lake Victoria, you will find good

overnight camping possibilities within 50 metres of the road among clumps of low trees. These are the sort of places where it is easy to set up a simple overnight camp. We wouldn't stay here for longer than a night, nor would we set up an elaborate camp — there isn't any good access to the river and it is close to the road.

Trouble at Rufus River

Rufus River was named after red-haired George Macleay, a member of Charles Sturt's 1830 Murray exploration party. It became a favourite stopping place for drovers after Hawdon camped there in 1836 on the first overland trip between NSW and South Australia. Given its importance as an ancient meeting place for Aborigines, it is hardly surprising that it became a flashpoint for conflict between indigenous people and the Europeans. In 1841, a large party of 3–400 Aboriginal men moved in on a droving party at the river and captured their flock of 5000 sheep while the drovers fled into the bush. Shortly afterwards, four drovers were killed on an overland trip in the same region. The South Australian government organised a retaliation party with 68 armed men. Records state that 30 Aboriginal people were killed, 10 were wounded and 4 were taken prisoner.

About 60 km west of Wentworth, the road goes over a causeway at the southern end of Lake Victoria. For the next 5 km travelling west, the road follows the high bank of Lake Victoria. The sight of the great lake shimmering under the sun is quite beautiful. In the distance you will also see sand dunes by the lake's edge. Over the decades, the levels of Lake Victoria have been manipulated by European settlers for irrigation purposes. Consequently, dead trees stand in the water. Watermarks on the trees indicate how high the water level has been here in the past.

Lake Victoria is an Aboriginal Control Heritage Site and there is no access to the lake's edge away from the road. Ancient Aboriginal cemeteries have been uncovered here; it was also the meeting place for regional Aboriginal groups. There is plenty of historical evidence, including middens, stone artefacts, ovens, burial sites and scarred trees. If you would like to visit archaeological sites, you could join one of the Harry Nanya Tours operating out of Wentworth (see pages 266, 271).

Goolwa Maritime Gallery (PHOTO: BILL BACHMAN)

Irrigating vines near Taylorville, between Morgan and Barmera
(PHOTO: BILL BACHMAN)

The Murray mouth, SA (Photo: Bill Bachman)

Lake Victoria flows into Rufus River through a regulator that controls the water levels and flow of water entering the Murray downstream. Cormorants and other birds gather close to the regulator. As with the locks further down the river, humans are not allowed to fish close to the outflow. The boundaries are clearly marked. The banks just beyond the outside limit is a popular fishing place where you can usually catch callop and carp. There are even toilets here, which will give you an indication of how popular this place is. For the companions of the fishing folk, be assured that this is a very attractive place to go for a walk or sit by the banks of the river.

Lake Victoria burial grounds

The lake was an important place for the Barkindji, as it provided food all year round — fish, wild fowl, yams, grains and animals. The Barkindji had burial sites on the southern shores of the lake but these were submerged when the water levels were raised. Then in 1994, after years of artificially high water levels, evidence of Aboriginal burial grounds became visible when the water levels were lowered. Conservation work has since been carried out on the grounds.

The extent of the burial grounds is a subject for academic debate but one estimate published puts the number of graves at 10,000. If the estimates are correct, the extent of the burial ground would be significantly different from the few dozen or perhaps 100 burial sites that are usually found at Aboriginal cemeteries. At Lake Victoria, it is suggested that some of the oldest burials at the base of the lunette, or string of dunes, are 8–9000 years old. Others are estimated to be 5–6000 years old, and some are perhaps as recent as 100 years old.

LAKE VICTORIA TO RENMARK

As you drive west, leaving the lake behind you, the road continues to travel roughly along the course of the Murray. Then, 80 km west of Wentworth, it turns north. A side track at that junction takes you into Cal Lal station, which is private property. As the road moves away from the river, the colour of the surface gently shifts from the pale sandy hue of the riverside to the rich red of Australia's interior. About 16 km north of this junction, you will arrive at a T-junction with a clear signpost indicating the direction to Renmark. (If you are travelling from the west, we recommend that you turn south towards the Murray at this point, rather than take the 85 km road to Wentworth that travels around the top of Lake Victoria).

The country between Renmark and the NSW border is part of the former Bookmark Station lease. The western section of the old station is now known as Calperum Station and is the base for the Bookmark Biosphere Trust. This is an important UNESCO initiative that supports use of land in a way that is economically viable and preserves the fragile ecology of the land — learning to 'make a living from the land without ruining it.' The eastern section of the Bookmark Station is now known as Chowilla Station, and provides excellent riverside camping sites.

Access to the campsites is down an 8 km track, the turnoff is signposted 130 km west of Wentworth. Although Chowilla Station has 46 km of Murray River frontage, the campsites are on

Bookmark Station and the biosphere reserve concept

Bookmark Station was first leased in 1864 to the Robertson brothers by their stepfather. In 1896, Bookmark was split between two of the Robertson brothers to form Calperum and Chowilla Stations. The Robertsons are still on Chowilla station; Calperum is now the base for the Bookmark Biosphere Reserve under the auspices of the United Nations.

The Biosphere Reserve concept involves the development of ecologically sustainable industries in natural environments that may be under threat. Station owners are encouraged to change their farming and agricultural techniques to methods that are easier on the environment. This requires a great commitment as, initially, the economic returns of the properties may be reduced.

Ecotourism is one of the new industries that is actively encouraged in the region. Tour operators undergo an established training program to achieve endorsement by the Bookmark Biosphere Trust.

Tours now include Bookmark by the Stars, which will introduce to you the stars at night; Renmark River Cruises, which will take you through the creeks in an open dingy; and Jolly Goodfellows Riverland that specialises in birdwatching. You can get information about these and other tours is available from the Bookmark Biosphere Trust in Berri (08 8582 5299).

the many creeks that flow through the property. There are plenty of designated campsites, each with a number and a fireplace. Signposting is minimal, but follow the dry-weather track (which was once the old coach road between Blanchetown and Wentworth) and you should have no difficulty finding a beautiful campsite. If there is any hint of rain in the air, a call to the rangers in the Murraylands Regional Office in Berri will confirm whether there may be any problem; they close the road if it is too wet. There is a fee per vehicle per night ($6), and this can be paid at the Murraylands Regional Office.

You can also stay in the historic shearers' quarters on Chowilla Station. It sleeps 25 people and has a fully equipped kitchen, BBQ, showers, toilets and other facilities to cater for large groups. As with most shearers'-quarters style accommodation, you must bring your own linen or sleeping bag. There is a minimum fee of $100 per night, with a charge of $12 per adult and $5.50 per child. Bookings are made with the Robertsons at Chowilla Station, (08 8595 8048).

Chowilla Station is an operational merino sheep station that also offers tourist services. The Robertsons conduct tours to historic sites including Aboriginal canoe trees, and the 19th century woolshed and shearers' quarters. They will also describe the modern operations of a sheep station that subscribes to Bookmark Biosphere principles. With the Department of Environment and Natural Resources, they have created a guide to the old coach road. The two-hour drive travels through the floodplain and is open to all vehicles when it is dry. They have numbered markers and a guide to help you identify evidence of Aboriginal culture, plants, trees and birds. Although Lock 6 is marked on the maps around here, there is no public access to it.

BOOKMARK INTERPRETATIVE CENTRE

There is an unusual bush structure 148 km west of Wentworth where the unsealed road meets the sealed road out of Renmark. This is the Bookmark Interpretative Centre. It consists of a series of upright sandy coloured slabs set in a circle in low scrub and bears a strange resemblance to Stonehenge. In fact, a local brochure referred to it as the 'Stonehenge Information Bay'!

From here on in to Renmark, the road travels through the vine-yards and orchards irrigated by the Murray River.

Bookmark Interpretive Centre

Renmark

Renmark is the major town in the region. Its advantageous location is emphasised by attractive lawns between the road and the water. There are BBQs, tables, toilets and the PS *Industry* docked by the Renmark Paringa Tourist Office.

Renmark was established by the Chaffey brothers as an irrigation town, and continues to support the agricultural industry of the area. There are some nice buildings dating from these early days. One of these is Olivewood, the home of one of the irrigation pioneer brothers, Charles Chaffey. The ten-room house was built in 1889 in the style of a Canadian log cabin. The 30-acre property was planted with olive trees, vines and citrus orchards on what is now the corner of 21st Street and Renmark Avenue. The path to the house is lined with magnificent palm trees.

Charles Chaffey and his family of six children lived there until 1904, when they went to Canada on holiday. While they were away, the crops failed and the property and furnishings were sold in a mortgagee sale. The property was purchased by the National Trust in 1979 and furniture was donated to re-establish its Victorian ambience. Olivewood and the small museum attached is open from Thursday to Monday, 10 am – 4 pm.

The PS *Industry* was built in 1911 and used to remove snags until it was decommissioned in 1969. It was lovingly restored by an enthusiastic team in the 1990s and is now open for inspection seven days a week. Volunteers take it out for a cruise on a number of days each year. The public are welcome to join them for a small fee, details are available from the Tourist Office. It has a simple, silent, exposed mechanism in the centre of the boat, which was common in Australian riverboats. (Unlike North American rivers, the local rivers have many bends so barges had to be towed rather than lashed to the side of the boat. Consequently, the designers couldn't put the paddle-wheels at the rear of the boats). The engine was fired by recycled or fallen wood, you can really feel the heat in the central section when it is being prepared for a trip.

Further along the river to the east, towards Paringa on Patey Drive, is picnic area with BBQs, tables, toilets and a boardwalk. Nearby is Lock 5. You can fish and relax here on the Lock 5 sand-bar, but as usual only the birds have access to the lucrative fishing ground directly beside the lock.

Much of the visible activity in Renmark is based on tourism with golf, tennis, swimming, bowling, dancing and other family facilities. There are plenty of restaurants and cafés but the emphasis is on fast food and bistro-style eating. The Tower Tavern and Lookout near the junction of Ral Ral Creek and the Murray River provides good lunches and Sunday roasts. For self-catering visitors there are several grocery stores that are open seven days a week.

In terms of accommodation, Renmark has six motels, three caravan parks, and several self-catering cottages. The Tourist Centre will give you full details and, if you are planning in advance, will send a package of information. The place that caught our eye was the heritage listed Renmark Hotel by the river. It began as a single-storey community hotel in 1897. This was a novel development at the time. Renmark was supposed to be a dry area but having a substantial percentage of men in its 900 population, sly grog shops flourished. At one stage there were 13 of them. The Renmark Hotel was set up to control the flow of alcohol and to benefit the community. It returned its net profits to the town, sponsoring parks, gardens, roads, hospitals, the riverfront and a caravan park. The Hotel, now with a large bistro attached, continues to support community endeavours, including maintaining the PS *Industry*.

RENMARK TO BERRI

There are two notable diversions along the 20 km bitumen highway between the two major river towns of Renmark and Berri: Bredl's Wonder World of Wildlife and the ferry to Lyrup.

Bredl's Wonder World of Wildlife is on the corner of Sturt Highway and 28th Street, about 6 km from Renmark Paringa Visitors Centre. It is hard to miss — its large model dinosaur looms out over the main road. Catherine, who has an academic interest in zoos, and a mild horror of small privately owned zoos, agreed to call in. John was much more enthusiastic, he loves close encounters with any animals. As it turned out, Catherine was pleasantly surprised and John was delighted. Bredl's is a good-quality private zoo, which provides plenty of opportunity for visitors to get close to the animals.

The focus in this zoo is on Australian reptiles. Blue-tongues, frill-necks, goannas and other lizards are well camouflaged in large sensitive enclosures filled with local rock and vegetation. Visitors are challenged to spot the lizards — it is not always easy! Other animals that you can get close to in this family-run zoo include a python, monkeys, kangaroos, a galah and a cockatoo. Bredl's Wonder World of Wildlife is open from 10 am to 5 pm, seven days a week. Entrance is $8 for adults and $4 for children.

The turn-off for the ferry to Lyrup is 12 km west of Renmark. Lyrup itself is a sleepy town with nice picnic lawns down by the river. The exciting bit is the free car-ferry across the Murray. If you haven't been on one of South Australia's River Murray ferries, take this side-trip, it is well worth it. The ferries across the Murray throughout South Australia all work on demand for 24 hours, are free and take about 5–10 minutes of travelling time. For most of the ferries, you are unlikely to have to wait longer than 15–20 minutes for them to arrive on your side of the river and load up. At busy times in busy places such as Mannum, we have heard of queues of cars that take a couple of hours to move across the river, but this is not common. If you are starting your trip down the Murray, you will delight in this lovely experience; if you are ending it, savour the moment.

BERRI

Berri is a small, attractive town (population 5,000) that has used its location on the Murray to develop its place as a tourist centre. Begin with a trip up the tourist lookout tower to get panoramic views of the town and beyond to the river. The lookout is in a converted water tower that was built in 1922. Water towers like this were once common along the River Murray, but most have since been demolished.

Another good vantage point from which to view the river is the pathway across the tall bridge, which was opened in 1997. A walk over the bridge in the early morning sun is delightful. You can look down on this section of the river, which is lined by willow trees dripping into the water with tall gums standing behind them. You can also look down to a dry dock on the northern bank from the western side of the bridge.

Underneath the bridge is a striking mural painted by the local community groups. It describes a Dreaming story of the Ngarrindjeri people. The story is told on a plaque with a legend describing the figures and activities in the mural.

There are two motels, a large resort motel/hotel, and the Berri Riverside Caravan Park. Tourist information around Berri is currently being managed by the Bookmark Biosphere Trust at 24 Vaughan Terrace in the town centre (although a new information centre is scheduled to be opened by 2002). The office is open from 9 am to 5 pm, Monday to Friday, and 9 am to 12 pm on Saturdays. The staff can give you a list of accommodation in the area, but they do not make bookings for you. The Murraylands Regional Office of the South Australian National Parks and Wildlife is two doors down from the Bookmark Biosphere Trust office; they are open from 8.45 am to 5 pm weekdays, and provide information about state reserves.

Local information about fishing is available from the fishing shops, including Hook, Line and Sinker (08 8582 2488), the biggest fishing shop in Berri. Around here you will catch yellow belly (also known as golden perch), Murray cod, catfish, silver perch, redfin and, of course, carp. Shrimp, which you must catch yourself, are often the best bait, but sometimes frozen prawns and tiger worms are better; both are generally available in the fishing shops.

As usual the quality of the fishing and your likelihood of catching something depends on the flow of water, which is influenced here by releases from Lake Victoria. So try the banks of the river near the town. You could also go out to Lock 4, south of the town. The fishing may be marginally better here, again depending on the flow of water. Hook, Line and Sinker supply bait, hire or sell tackle, and are generous and knowledgeable with their up-to-date local information.

BERRI TO KINGSTON-ON-MURRAY

This is a busy and exciting part of the Murray River with state parks and reserves, plenty of camping opportunities, a few towns, and several options on which road to take. The quickest way between the two towns is 27 km along the Sturt Highway. Major towns on this route are Glossop, Barmera on Lake Bonney and Cobdogla. If you follow the U-bend of the Murray, you will travel through Loxton.

From the highway, it appears that the countryside is entirely under cultivation and there is little access to natural riverland. However, there are three major natural reserves around here: Katarapko Reserve in the Murray River National Park, Moorook Game Reserve and Loch Luna Game Reserve. Access to each is not far from the Sturt Highway and we describe them separately below.

If you plan to explore this specific part of the Murray, we strongly recommend that you purchase a copy of Riverland, the map produced by the South Australian Department of Environment and Natural Resources in 1995. It is an excellent guide to the area, which has so much to offer visitors. We also suggest you pick up the free single-sheet mud-maps from the Murraylands Regional Office in Berri.

Loxton detour

The 64-km U-shaped road that follows a detour of the Murray leads to some of the quietest sections of the river in this area. The road leaves the Sturt Highway at Berri to the east, and Kingston-on-Murray to the west. You will pass the turn-off to Lock 4 about 11 km south of Berri and 13 km north of Loxton. From there it is a further 2 km down a sealed, well-marked road to the lock. The lock itself is open during the day and there is a nice picnic spot with facilities. The setting of the lock is splendid with river cliffs, weeping willows and river red gums.

The turn-off to Thiele Sandbar is 22 km south of Berri. The 2 km dirt track winds past a water tower and through wetlands and lignum. There is a popular bush campsite by the river at the end of the track. This is a truly beautiful spot. The ground is sandy and soft underneath your campbed. Campers make fires here as there is a bit of wood, but don't use much — it is home for wild animals. The sandbar opposite the camping area is undergoing a preservation order as a native wildlife sanctuary. Fishing access is excellent but according to locals, the fishing isn't great.

Loxton, on the south bank of the river, is the major town on this U-shape. It got its name from a stockman called William Loxton who built a slab hut by the river in the 1870s. The area became known as Loxton's Hut, but this was soon shortened to just Loxton. The town is proud of its historical development and has compiled a heritage walk. The walk leads down the attractive boulevard, past the main town strip to the river and the award-winning historical village. The history of Loxton isn't immediately obvious; it is a fairly plain town but with the help of the heritage walking guide, you can identify points of interest such as St Peter's Lutheran Church with its stone spire (1926).

Loxton Historical Village is on the riverbank and is a trip down memory lane for anyone over the age of 30! It displays many ordinary domestic items from the not-too-distant past. The Historical Village is a community effort that began after the original Loxton's Hut was burnt down and the community decided to rebuild it. The Village is open from 10 am every morning. It closes at 4 pm on weekdays, and 5 pm on weekends and public holidays. The entrance fee is around $8 for adults and $4 for children; there are also family and pensioner rates.

Loxton has done justice to its location on the river — it has a very peaceful picnic ground set along the bank by the red river gums and reeds. The sounds of the ducks, pigeons, galas and wood ducks gently break the silence. There are shelters, toilets, picnic and BBQ facilities by the waterside. There is also fishing access. A boardwalk across a swamp along the river takes you deep into the lush vegetation of the natural river environment.

Loxton has all standard facilities and the Loxton Tourism and Art Centre is the best place to start. Denis and his colleagues are particularly helpful and will send you a great package of information about the region, what to do and where to stay. There is one Community Motel/Hotel and the Riverfront Caravan Park. The caravan park is very spacious, with facilities and a playground set down by the river. Accommodation includes cabins with ensuites that take five to six people at about $50 for a double, with a small fee for additional people. There are also powered and unpowered sites, and powered sites with ensuites for $22. If you want to stay in a houseboat, or a farm, contact the Tourism and Arts Centre for details.

KATARAPKO RESERVE

Katarapko Reserve provides access to the land inside the U-bend of the Murray. The entrance to the park is off Katarapko Crescent, about 15 km south of Berri. Take the Sturt Highway west out of Berri and, after 4 km, take the Lower Winkie Road; after a couple of sharp bends, it becomes Katarapko Crescent. Just inside the entrance to the reserve there is an information board. A graded road leads to designated campsites along Katarapko Creek. These are all identified and most have fireplaces.

As you move deeper into the reserve towards the south, the campsites become more isolated and the track becomes rougher.

When it is dry, a standard 2WD sedan should have no difficulty in driving down it slowly. The road is closed when wet weather hits the area.

The track to the north of the information board leads to camping spots west of Lock 4. There is a stone weir south of the causeway camping area; it was probably built by the people who lived on the sheep station on Katarapko Island to give them access to the mainland.

Camping permits in the Katarapko Reserve cost $6 per vehicle per night, and visitors should make an attempt to buy a permit from Murraylands Regional Office (where you can also get an excellent map). There is no booking system for camping sites, but it only becomes busy at two or three peak times in the year, usually school holiday weekends. Although there are fireplaces in most campsites, no fires are allowed between November and April inclusive. The signage on the tracks isn't great but it is a relatively small area and is patrolled by rangers periodically, so you shouldn't have much difficulty in finding your way in and out.

GLOSSOP

This is the sort of small township on the Sturt Highway that we would tend to drive through, but in this case, the Winmante Arts Centre is a good reason to stop here. The Arts Centre is on the north side of the road near the centre of Glossop and is run by local Ngarrindjeri people. We were very impressed by the combination of the displays that outline the history of the Aboriginal people here, and the quality of the reasonably priced Aboriginal artefacts on sale in the gallery. Some of the items are by local artists, including woven and wooden objects for which the Ngarrendjeri people are renowned. There are other traditional Aboriginal artefacts from around the country. These include beautifully painted emu eggs and dot paintings, as well as western-style paintings. The Centre is open on weekdays, and Sundays from 10 am to 4 pm.

Glossop is also the home of Berri Wine, which has a cellar door outlet on the main street. This is a well laid out cellar door with a wide range of wines on sale. Berri is a bulk wine producer but there are several nice wines to taste, including a good cellar door port.

LOCH LUNA AND MOOROOK GAME RESERVES

These two Murray wetland reserves are located to the north and south of the Sturt Highway between Cobdogla and Kingston-on-Murray, and are signposted from the main roads. The signposted entrance to Loch Luna Game Reserve is from Cobdogla. The entrance to Moorook is 3.5 km along the Moorook–Loxton Road off the Sturt Highway, just east of Kingston-on-Murray.

The reserves are rich natural environments. Permanent and semi-permanent water supports the features of a river wetland, including bird life, animals, reptiles, river red gums, scrub, sand dunes and Mallee vegetation. Loch Luna Reserve, which is National Heritage listed, is one of the few nesting areas in the world for the white-breasted sea eagle, and the rare regent parrot.

There is plenty of bush camping in these game reserves. At the southern end of Loch Luna, near the Sturt Highway, there are several large campsites that may be a bit noisy because they are close to highway traffic. However, this may not bother you on an overnight camp. More isolated campsites are accessible from Cobdogla along a dry-weather track. The signposting through the reserve is minimal, so just follow the track until you see a fireplace and signs of a clearing.

Entrance to the Moorook Game Reserve is 3.5 km south of the Sturt highway on the road south to Loxton. A good track leads out to plenty of bush campsites along the river, most with fireplaces.

Both reserves are managed by the Department of Environment and Heritage. Small fires are permitted in the fireplaces from May to October, but banned in summer. There is a permit fee of $6 per vehicle per night to use these camps. As game reserves, waterfowl hunters may shoot here at specific times of the year. However, the activity is very strictly controlled. Rangers patrol the areas, particularly during peak periods. There is no booking system, but most of the time there is no difficulty getting a campsite here. Permits and free mud-maps are available from the Murraylands Regional Office.

If the environment is one you would like to spend time in without camping, you could stay at the Loch Luna Ecostay that is adjacent to the Loch Luna Reserve. Chris and Carol Ball provide different ways to explore the reserve including canoe and horseback. This is a particularly interesting example of the Bookmark Biosphere concept. Loch Luna Ecostay is a small privately owned operation that is committed to the principles of ecologically sustainable use of the land. The Balls used to run cattle and sheep on the huge Loch Luna property. In 1985 the section that is now Loch Luna Game Reserve was acquired by the South Australian government and the sheep were removed; the regrowth there dates from that period. In the 1990s, the couple investigated the biosphere option and took a major economic gamble in switching from cattle to grape-growing. They have watched the Mallee scrub regrow in their property since then.

Chris and Carol Ball also run a self-catering lodge and a self-catering cottage for travellers. Both are twin-share and reasonably priced at $85–105 for two, with an option for breakfast provisions at $10, (08 8588 7210). Loch Luna Ecostay is located close to the peaceful wetlands and mallee environment. Although it is self-catering, Carol said that most visitors take the option of going to one of the nearby eateries, such as the historic 1859 Overland Corner Hotel, where the walls are up to half a metre thick and the red gum floor looks like slate.

BARMERA

About 13 km east of Kingston-on-Murray is Barmera on Lake Bonney. This is a major tourist town set on the lake and one of the best places to see a sunset along the Murray. Yachts bobbing gently in the water add to the atmosphere. In the background is the substantial Barmera Lakes Resort Motel with views out over the shallow lake.

The town is set up for tourists with plenty of river activities and associated facilities, including the fully operational drive-in cinema. Here you can get out the camp chairs, set up a small picnic and watch the latest releases in the open air. The Barmera Drive-In Cinema operates every weekend and over long weekends and holidays. Its movie schedule is advertised in the *Murray*

Pioneer, but anyone in Barmera will probably advise you as to what is on when you are passing through. This is a pleasant and slightly different way to spend an evening on your travels and, if it is not something you have experienced before or for a long time, we highly recommend it.

Barmera is very proud of its association with country music. It is the host of an annual Riverland Music Country Festival, a huge event that takes place every June. It was established by a musician called Rocky Page, who died a number of years ago. Rocky's Country Music Hall of Fame was created in his memory. This features memorabilia collected by Page himself during his long career, as well as handprints and other memorabilia donated to the museum by the many stars who have worked with Page or who have featured in the festival over the years. This is definitely for aficionados of country music.

Life on the rivers

Snaggers and woodcutters were employed along the length of the river to supply the wood to keep the boats fired up. The crews of steamers also passed time by preparing wood stocks when they were snagged in the river for a period. Trees, young and old, were cleared along the river course to provide fuel for the hungry steamers. They had to ensure that the wood was the correct size for each steamer, as they didn't all have the same sized fire boxes. The snaggers' job was to keep the river free of fallen trees above and below the waterline. Fallen trees snagged steamers and were therefore a major hazard, as they pierced the hulls of boats, causing leaks.

Steamboat crews had to use whatever materials were available to mend problems. On one occasion the *Emerald* successfully breached a major leak caused by a submerged tree with a large container of flour. As detailed information about snags and other hazards became available, they were added to the river charts. These were on lengthy scrolls, about 25 metres long, wrapped around a pair of rollers that allowed easy use in confined spaces.

KINGSTON-ON-MURRAY TO MORGAN

As the Murray meanders through the country lined by river trees and scrub, the Sturt Highway on the south side of the river travels through irrigated, agricultural land where orchards and vines dominate. At Waikerie, 34 km west of Kingston-on-Murray, the Highway turns south-west, skipping the elbow of the river at Morgan, but we strongly recommend that you continue to follow the river to the historic inland port.

One major diversion along here is Banrock Station, long famous for its bulk wine, and now for its relationship with the river wetlands on the property. Banrock Station is 8 km from Kingston-on-Murray, and has 12 km of river frontage as well as some delicate wetlands area. The wetlands are referred to in their brochures as 'the maternity hospitals of our environment'! In real terms this means that the Banrock management is taking significant steps to protect the ecosystem on the vast station. They plant native vegetation, support animal breeding and prevent water stagnation. They have even installed barriers to keep out the dreaded European carp. Banrock Station also contributes a percentage from each sale of wine to Landcare Australia.

In 2001, Banrock Station opened a network of boardwalks and wetland walking trails. The total trail is 7 km long and, if you were to do the entire walk, it would take two to three hours. The wooden boardwalk takes you through stunning scenery and into bird-viewing hides where you can watch up to 150 species of birds. Signs will tell you about the cultural and ecological history of this beautiful environment.

The cellar door outlet and restaurant is called the Wine and Wetland Centre, and looks down onto the Banrock wetlands. An environmental walking trail of 2.5 km goes through the wetlands and mallee scrub. Banrock Station is open from 10 am to 5 pm, seven days a week.

The view from the lookout platform, 26 km west of Banrock Station at Waikerie, is quite different. Here the river cliffs are striking, particularly at sunrise or sunset. The scenery from the northern river bank, which you can reach via the Waikerie Ferry, is particularly striking. The lookout platform has been built beside a 19th-century chimney that was once part of the irrigation system.

Waikerie has some tourist facililities including the Waikerie Caravan Park (08 8541 2651) and the well-signposted Kirriemuir Motel and Cabins (08 8541 2488). For something different, you can go gliding with the Waikerie Gliding Club, which provides 20 minute scenic flights all year around (08 8541 2644). The staff in the tourist shop, the Orange Tree, can provide accommodation and other tourist contacts in Waikerie. You can't miss the Orange Tree, it is on the Sturt Highway and has an enormous green ball with oranges dotted around it on the roof! Incidentally, the Orange Tree boasts the largest range of non-alcoholic wines in the region (08 85441 2332).

In the centre of town, the Rain Moth Gallery is located in the historic Irrigation Department Building, built circa 1915. It displays local art and visiting exhibitions. Its supporters are also developing an interpretative centre focusing on an irrigation channel. These were once common sights along the Murray, but today this channel is one of the few that is being given museum treatment so that future generations can see it.

Ramco and Cadell are two small towns between Waikerie and Morgan. The view from Ramco takes in submerged red river gums, the river valley and the horizon beyond. There are several man-made lagoons designed to control salinity — hence the partially submerged trees with blackened stumps emerging from the water. Cadell, 11 km east of Morgan, was named after the river boat pioneer, Francis Cadell.

Access to Morgan is via another of the Murray ferries. It takes off from the Morgan Conservation Park, a wetlands park on the east side of the river. The creation of the park assists in the preservation of the fragile scrub-covered sandy ground in its natural state. It is a gently attractive area. You can camp here along the river free of charge. There are no facilities at all, but it is a great opportunity to enjoy the bush.

Morgan

The historic inland port of Morgan is at the point where the river changes direction almost at a right angle; from here it flows south in a relatively straight line to the mouth. In fact, the town was once known as 'the Great Elbow'. When the country around this part of the river was opened after Charles Sturt charted the Murray, the Elbow became a popular stopping point for overlanders moving stock into the new colony of South Australia. Morgan boomed after the arrival of the railroad in 1878. This provided a rail link from the stations along the Darling and Murray Rivers through Morgan to Adelaide. Morgan was so successful as an interchange between river and rail that several river ports to the south of it suffered as a result. However, as the importance of river transport declined, so did Morgan.

One of the most exciting features of Morgan is the large wharf set in a great cliff face. The platform sits so high over the water now that the paddle-steamer, the *Murray Princess*, cannot use it. However, part of the wharf has been made safe so you can climb down the steep steps and stand underneath the great mass of wooden beams. Some of the beams are loose, so you can see the enormous steel bolts sticking out that still hold the wharf together.

Locomotive at Morgan

There is a museum in the old railway buildings near the wharf. Here many relics of Morgan's history are on display. Photos, documents, models and other items salvaged from the old days are laid out in an interesting clutter. The museum requests a small donation to keep it going.

Accommodation and dining in Morgan includes the Morgan Riverside Caravan Park on the riverbank on the south side of town. It has a range of accommodation options including ensuite cabins, basic cabins and caravans (08 8540 2207). There are two hotels with rooms, the Commercial (08 8540 2107) and the Terminus (08 8540 2006), where you can get accommodation and meals. The Colonial Motel is on Federal Street on the north side of town (08 8540 2277). Further information is available from the helpful staff in the Morgan Shell Roadhouse, which operates as an informal visitor information centre. They sell bait and basic fish-

Aboriginal life on the River Murray

It is believed that this area along the river was densely populated by Aboriginal people when the Europeans moved in. The river was a rich resource running through less fertile country. The local people had a strong sense of territory and used their strength to protect their resources. Yet many of them had already suffered from the rapid spread of disease through their close settlements even before the explorers and settlers made it in person to the rivers. So there is a question mark over the precise number of people who lived on the river. When the Europeans began to trespass on their traditional resources, there were a number of serious attacks on settlers, notably near Rufus River east of Renmark where four overlanders were killed.

One of the South Australian government's more peaceful responses was to establish a settlement called Moorundie, now south of Blanchetown. They appointed the explorer, Edward Eyre, as the protector in 1841. Eyre had established good relations with some of the Murray people, who had helped him on one of his expeditions. It was hoped that the river people would move to the settlement. Buildings on the property included Eyre's own house, a reed house, barracks, and a police station.

But the Aboriginal people were reluctant to settle here and didn't stay around for long. Eyre lived at Moorundie for three years before returning to England. The Moorundie ration depot continued until 1856 when responsibility was transferred to central government.

ing tackle, and can tell you what is being caught at the time. Generally it is yellow belly, Murray cod and of course carp; there are some redfin but not so many as there once were. The Shell Roadhouse is open from 7.30 am to 8.30 pm, seven days a week (08 8540 2205).

MORGAN TO BLANCHETOWN

There are two ways of travelling between Morgan and Blanchetown. The longer way is to return to Waikerie and then back on to the Sturt Highway. This is 81 km and we would only suggest that you take it if it is raining heavily and the shorter unsealed road is impassable.

The shorter route is 39 km and follows the course of the river. Around 26 km of this is along an unsealed road. When the road is dry, it is generally smooth and well maintained. It is an attractive drive as the road travels through the river flats, with the cliffs of the Murray visible in the distance. There is access to the river at Pelican Point, a signposted turn-off 27 km north of Blanchetown.

Roonka Riverfront Cottages are nestled in along the river, 33 km south of Morgan. The 1.5 km track down to the cottages is signposted on the river-side of the road. The five self-contained cottages are set in the bush near the river and are ideal for families looking for a relaxing holiday set in beautiful country away from cities and crowds. They have excellent river access, a sandy beach, a tennis court, lawns and a heavenly atmosphere. The cottages sleep six to eight people, and cost around $70–85, depending on size. The costs are a bit higher in the peak season. If you plan to stop over along this stretch of the river, we highly recommend that you contact Paul and Victoria von Bertouch to stay here (08 85 40 5189) .

When you travel along this route, you will be close to Roonka Station, the location of significant ancient Aboriginal cemeteries. The Roonka cemeteries are not open to the public, but if you attend a tour with an Aboriginal guide in the Ngaut Ngaut Conservation Park (which we have described below), you will hear Dreaming stories and other history of the people who have lived along the Murray since ancient times.

Roonka

Ancient Aboriginal cemeteries are one of the features of the Murray. The cemetery at Roonka is one of the largest and most extensively excavated of the cemeteries along the Murray. This is an archaeological site on a river flat and dunes near Blanchetown. It is estimated that the lowest layer of the excavation, with hearths and shells, is up to 20,000 years old. The middle layer, up to 8,000 years old, has evidence of being a cemetery. The findings also show evidence of the initiation ceremony of tooth avulsion in the middle period. The recent layer, which is estimated to be up to 6,000 years old, has the remains of a cemetery, shaft burials, campsites and other everyday items buried with the people. Other ornaments that have been excavated here include a headband of wallaby teeth, a shell pendant and a necklace of reptile vertebrae, and remains of skin cloaks.

BLANCHETOWN

Blanchetown is a small river town set on the west side of the river. It was surveyed in 1855. An attractive new bridge joins the two banks of the river, replacing the twin ferries that once crossed at this point. The Blanchetown Hotel was built in 1858 and the original thatch (under the tin roof), the rafters and the sandstone walls are still part of the bar and lounge. A mural of a river scene was painted in the 1920s. The hotel serves lunch and dinner, and runs a mini-bus service to the three local caravan parks.

The main attraction of Blanchetown is the lock and weir system. Completed in 1922, it was the first to be built along the Murray. The lock and weir stands exposed by the bank of the river; a pleasant parkland runs down to the river, providing an excellent viewing platform from which to watch the activity — if there is any. If you are very lucky, you will see Australia's largest inland water paddle-wheeler, PS *Murray Princess*, moving through the lock. The three-storey boat has a huge paddle wheel at the stern and, at 67 metres in length, it is so large that it wouldn't fit into the lock in Mildura! The *Murray Princess* is based in Mannum and is used mostly for cruises between Mannum and Morgan. A weekend cruise goes as far as Nildottie. A five-day jaunt goes to Morgan and back. Phone 08 8569 2511 for details.

Realistically, you are much more likely to see a few small

leisure craft going through the lock. You will also see the great flocks of pelicans gather near the outflow, helping themselves to carp and other fish that gather near the lock wall. Human fishing enthusiasts are kept outside a 150 metre fishing limit. Fishing beyond that near Blanchetown is easy with good access; worms and other bait are available in the shops in town, or at the caravan parks. Around here you will catch carp, yellow belly and sometimes catfish, which need to be thrown back.

There are several caravan parks in Blanchetown. The Blanchetown Caravan Park has powered and unpowered sites, BBQ and dishwashing facilities, and some motel-standard ensuite cabins that sleep from two to six people. It costs $58 for two adults and $4 per child under 14 (0500 505 073). The Blanchetown Riverside Caravan Park is five minutes from the hotel and is set on the waterfront with lawns and trees. They have powered and unpowered sites, a camp kitchen, a BBQ, a private beach and a pontoon. They also have ensuite cabins that take between two and six people and cost $48–91 (08 8540 5070).

BLANCHETOWN TO MANNUM

This is a beautiful drive on a smooth, new road that moves from one side of the river to the other. It will take you along the top of the river cliffs where you can look down into the river valley; then it will take you down to the river flats, across the river on a ferry, past sheep, rocky fields and abandoned houses. It is probably one of the finest river drives in Australia, largely because the river is in a well-defined valley that is up to 40 metres deep and is visible for much of the time.

There is a series of small towns along this stretch of the river: Swan Reach, Nildottie and Walker Flat. Each has basic facilities for tourists. Swan Reach, 28 km south of Blanchetown, has a 19th-century hotel with a variety of rooms, each decorated to provide an old-world atmosphere; none has an ensuite. Prices range from $35 for a single room to $55 for a double, with breakfast (08 8570 2003).

There are many Aboriginal cultural relics in this area of the Murray that are accessible to the public in the company of local guides. The Punyelroo Caves are south of Swan Reach on the east side of the river; these are open to the public without a guide. Further on is the Ngaut Ngaut Conservation Park where there is a boardwalk along the cliff face that will lead you to archaeological diggings and rock carvings. These are not signposted because there is no general public access to the Aboriginal engravings. Sadly, too much damage has been done in the past; engravings have been defaced and even hunks of rock removed from the cliff surface.

However, Richard Hunter, the custodian, and his team of guides are happy to give groups a trip to the caves and the rock

The locks and weirs of the Lower Murray

When the European settlers first began to use the Murray for transport, it was navigable as far as Blanchetown. North of that navigation depended on the river flow. This made it difficult to maintain a reliable river transportation system. Floods and droughts could strand loaded barges for months and prevent inland produce from reaching its markets. In 1912 the South Australian government commissioned Captain E.N. Johnston, an American engineer, to design locks and weirs that would make the Murray permanently navigable. The result was a barrier stretching across the wide river and a lock chamber that opens on request. His designs were used for 11 of the 13 locks and weirs on the Murray between 1922 and 1937.

In 1922 the first lock and weir were built at Blanchetown. The weir stretched across the breadth of the river, while the lock system on the western side of the river provided boats with a system that would pass them through the barrier in about 15 minutes. The lock system was a standard design believed to have been first designed by Leonardo da Vinci in Europe in the 15th century, and similar in style to an 8th-century Chinese lock.

By the time the locks were built, the role of the river in transportation had been reduced considerably. The rail lines and roads were proving to be more reliable modes of transport and were rapidly superseding the river. Consequently, the original plan of having 26 locks and weirs on the Murray was abandoned.

Today the locks and weirs support a growing leisure industry on the river with houseboats and other recreational vehicles queuing up at busy times to move through the locks. The Murray River is now permanently navigable from the mouth to Nangiloc, upstream of Mildura. East of that it is navigable during periods of high flow.

engravings that you will never forget. They will lead you along the boardwalk through the locked gates to the engravings and tell you Dreamtime stories of ancient Aboriginal life along the river. The guides take groups with a minimum of ten, charging a fee of $5 per person. Contact Richard at 08 8570 1202 to arrange a group tour or see if you can join another group.

Walker Flat, 14 km south of Nildottie, is a tiny hamlet with fuel facilities, a general store and what appear to be lots of holiday shacks. There is also an Aboriginal canoe tree. There is great access to the river here and it isn't as busy as Mannum. The ferry across the river operates 24 hours a day. There are no caravan parks or hotels providing accommodation here.

Between Walker Flat and Mannum the road travels low along the west side of the river where thick vegetation lines the bank of the river. As you move south and away from the river, you will see fields of rocks. Some have been shifted by farmers to form dry rock walls in the time-honoured tradition of the Irish and others. There is also the occasional abandoned farmhouse made from the easily worked sandstone.

Mannum

This is a very popular tourist town set on the side of a steep river cliff where the Murray is wide and stunning to look at. This is an easy town for our kind of travelling, with plenty of distractions within walking distance in the centre of town — old buildings, interesting shops, good coffee and cakes, and an old pub. Mannum grew up around William Randell's enterprises on the waterside in the 1850s. The main street is an attractive collection of old sandstone buildings, old functional buildings and modern buildings. Behind the shops on the west side of the road, several narrow staircases run up the side of the cliff towards houses. Happily, the community has provided benches at the top of the steps so that you can recover your puff and enjoy the fabulous views.

Back down on the main street, all sorts of interesting shops have taken over the old buildings without destroying the old-fashioned interiors. These are worth exploring, particularly if you enjoy second-hand shops.

Problems suffered by the river

The Murray provides at least half of South Australia's water supply and also supports massive irrigation farming along the route. But using the river for transport, farming, leisure activities and water supply has had a huge impact on the quality of the river.

In the past, the people working for the paddle-steamers cleared the riverbanks of anything that would snag a boat. They removed a lot of the natural vegetation from the riverbank. Then the locks were installed, interrupting the natural flow of the water. The water became stale, the fish wouldn't breed without river flow and blue-green algae grew. Blue-green algae is a natural vegetation along the river but it can become a problem in the summer months when it blooms and forms a scum on the surface of the water. This also results in toxins that affect humans as well as animals.

Salinity is another source of water degradation. There is natural salinity in the land and as natural vegetation is cleared, the salt levels are increased. The barrages at the Coorong prevent sea water from getting into the lakes and the Murray. In the past, sea water could affect the fresh water up to 250 km upstream of the Murray mouth during periods of low river flow when the river was most susceptible to salt water intrusion. The barrages were completed in 1940 and now contain the water levels, ensuring that the fresh water remains about 1 metre above sea level.

Nowadays, the large number of holiday shacks also pollute the river. When holiday shack pollution is compounded with drainage water from farms, the levels of bacteria and other problems increase. This becomes very costly to filter out to make the water useful for domestic purposes. Further development on the floodplain between Mannum and Morgan has now been stopped to protect the river.

Across the road from the Pretoria Hotel are two large white wrought-iron gates sitting in a carpark. These commemorate an interesting first for Mannum. In 1899, David Shearer demonstrated what was probably Australia's first drivable steam-driven car. He had been working on it since 1885. The machine that the public saw 14 years later was an 8-seater that completed a 160 km journey cruising at 24 km/hr on the flat roads of the area. You can see samples of Shearer's historic machinery at the 'Olde Days and Olde Ways' Museum in Mannum. You can also stay in Shearer's original cottage, which is behind the Mannum Heritage Centre. Rod Williams, who developed the centre, has recently renovated the cottage and it is now available as a particularly classy B&B ($120 for a double).

The large paddle-steamer, PS *Marion*, is docked beside the Information Centre at the northern end of town. The river boat was built in Milang in 1897 and worked the river for many years. It began life as a barge before being converted to carry cargo and passengers. When it was purchased by the National Trust in 1963, it was working as a boarding-house in Berri. It has been fully restored by dedicated enthusiasts and you can explore the boat for a small fee. The PS *Marion* occasionally does cruises, ranging from one hour to a whole weekend, with gourmet food and local wines. However, these cruises aren't scheduled and if it is something you are keen on, contact the Information Centre to check details.

Wheelhouse of the PS Marion, Mannum

Accommodation in Mannum is fairly limited and includes the large Mannum Motel and Restaurant (08 8569 1808). There is also the Mannum Caravan Park which has self-contained cabins (BYO linen), powered and unpowered sites, and a bunkhouse (08 8569 1402). The Mannum Holiday Village has self-contained cabins, and there are 6 B&Bs that take 4–12 guests at normal high B&B rates. The Tourist Information Centre will send you a guide to accommodation in Mannum if you call them. However, they don't operate an accommodation service so you must contact the services directly. Mannum is so popular that Easter bookings must be made up to a year in advance!

Murray Bridge

Murray Bridge is the largest town in the region, with a population of 16,000, and a very busy business centre. The Murray Bridge Community Information and Tourist Information Centre is part of the Local Government Centre on South Terrace, parallel to Bridge Street. This is the best place to start either by visiting or ringing in advance to have a comprehensive package of information sent out to you.

Several riverboats provide scheduled short trips and work from the wharf on the southern side of the Murray near the town centre. The *Princess Andrea* usually goes out at about 1.30 pm every day, unless it has been booked for a charter. The *Barrangul* goes out at 2 pm on most days unless, again, it has been chartered. It is probably best to contact the Tourist Information Centre for details or ring the cruise companies to see if their schedules suit your timing.

Along the well-kept shore there are the usual signs of the railway and manufacturing industry that were once so closely connected to the river. There is also a pleasant recreational area for visitors including a backpackers' hostel, a pub, café, restaurant and a children's playground.

Undoubtedly the highlight for us is the hilarious Murray Monster. This has been here for a long time and still delights children and adults! No description will fully describe the experience. The mythical monster sits in a watery pit in a stone-covered cave by the water's edge. A sign nearby relates the Aboriginal myth of the bunyip, believed by Europeans to be a real animal until the late 19th century. This modern bunyip sits under the murky water and you can just make out its brightly coloured eyes. Another sign invites you to put in a dollar to see the bunyip rise out of the water three times. It's irresistible. When you put your dollar into the slot, the water bubbles and a huge, luridly painted creature emerges from the water — its ferocious red and white eyes first, then a large gaping mouth with white fangs and a blue lizard tongue. An enormous green paw emerges next. The sound effects that accompany the entire performance are the deep growly noises you would expect in an old-fashioned ghost ride! The monster returns to the water after a brief pause, then reappears twice more. It is an excellent dollar's worth of entertainment!

If you are interested in the history of Murray Bridge, you can follow a guided walk around the town. Murray Bridge began as a crossing for the overlanders; they swam their stock across the river near here, so reducing the overall travel time between Victoria and South Australia. In 1879, the bridge over the Murray was complete and the settlement flourished. The town's importance was consolidated when the rail bridge was built seven years later.

Today, the guided walk will take you to places associated with the bridges and the town's development. This includes the old 1886 railway station, an odd round house that was built in 1874 for the overseer of the bridge works, the facade of the 1924 picture theatre and the smallest cathedral in Australia — the petite St John the Baptist Pro-Cathedral on Swanport Road that was built in 1887. The simple bishop's throne is on the altar, hence the title of 'cathedral' for this modest church. According to the guide the historic walk should take you an hour, but that is only if you don't stop anywhere!

Murray Bridge has plenty of accommodation and restaurants. There are seven standard hotels and motels, as well as five caravan parks, several B&Bs, and a backpackers' lodge. One of the hotels is the 1920s Balcony Guest House. This place used to be known as the Beehive Corner and the verandah once continued along Bridge Street. Now it has everything from a luxury room with a four-poster bed to backpackers' lodgings; prices range from $30 to $77 for the luxurious room (08 8531 1411). A list of accommodation, with costs, is available from the Murray Bridge Information Centre. The Centre will also send you a list of places to eat. Most of them are of the take-away variety, but there is also the Amorosa Restaurant that specialises in Italian cuisine, the Oriental Garden Chinese restaurant and several club bistros.

In terms of fishing, there are no services specifically devoted to taking visitors fishing. However, bait is available in many of the roadhouses, and tackle is available is several camping shops in town. Conversation with the staff in these shops will give you information about what fish are around in the slow-moving river.

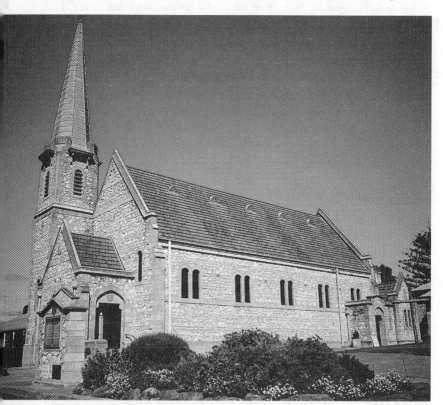

St John the Baptist Pro-Cathedral, Murray Bridge

MURRAY BRIDGE TO GOOLWA

We are now approaching the sprawling delta region of the Murray. The road along the Murray continues to Tailem Bend where the Mallee Highway meets the Duke Highway between Adelaide and Melbourne. There are many places to explore around Lake Alexandrina so, on this trip, we shall take you first into the wine country on the west side of the Lake, down to the Murray mouth, then around via the ferry at Wellington, to Meningie, the Coorong, and a modern centre of Ngarrindjeri culture. There is so much to do here that we could have spent our entire holiday here. With the diversity of activity, as well as great food and wine, it is now a worthy end to one of the great river trips.

Goolwa

Goolwa, the major town and tourist centre of the Murray mouth, is 79 km from Murray Bridge. Signal Point, the large and friendly tourist centre, is the place to start, either by phoning in advance for information on accommodation and other facilities, or by dropping in.

Within the Signal Point tourist centre, there is a museum and continuous showing of several videos on the Murray, including Aboriginal Dreaming, Paddle-Steamers and The Golden Years of Goolwa. On a wet day, you may enjoy relaxing in this small cinema and finding out about the area. There is also a wetlands display, a 3-D model of the Murray stretched out across the floor and a display of fishing on the river.

Outside, on the great wooden beams of the wharf, there is a wonderful wine bar and restaurant called Hector's on the Wharf. It is an ideal base from which to look at the rest of the town. After a long day's driving, we watched the hustle of activity around the wharf from there — the Hindmarsh Island ferry coming and going under the shadow of the high bridge, the old cockle train, and the return of the *Spirit of the Coorong* from the Murray mouth. Monica and her staff serve excellent fresh fish and chips, and choosing from a wide range of good local wines was very difficult.

The picturesque cockle train from Goolwa to Victor Harbour provides rides periodically on Sundays and during school holidays. It runs along the wharf in Goolwa, picking up and dropping off travellers at the old railway station. Sometimes the steam train is used for these tourist runs; other times the diesel engine is used.

Ngarrindjeri

The Murray delta is Ngarrindjeri country. Prior to the arrival of Europeans there were estimated to be about 3000 people in this area. The land was rich, beautiful and fertile with long stretches of water. The Ngarrindjeri had a distinct language and a sophisticated culture and society. They were a powerful stable nation comprising a federation of 18 groups. Their cookery was well known, as was their love of music, the arts and sport. Their complex language was recorded by the missionary George Taplin. They built large, strong semi-permanent houses. Their range of food was so great that 20 items of food were forbidden to the young men. These particular foods were easy to acquire and so were to be left for older, frailer people.

Strict laws helped to maintain the social order. Their laws were practical and designed to maintain harmony with the land. They were supported by religious and spiritual beliefs to ensure continuity of tradition and security of the elders' role. Young men had to pass through initiation rites that were physically and mentally challenging. The women were obliged to marry outside their particular group but within the nation.

When the Europeans moved into the area, the Ngarrindjeri were prepared to adapt as they realised that the colonists were not going to go away. They were keen to send their children to school at Raukkan to learn English and other skills that would give them an income in the new order. However, many of the traditional customs vanished in the following decades.

Young people who were drawn into the missionary circle led by George Taplin found themselves in dreadful conflict. They were now trying to oblige two powerful masters, their traditional elders and their European teacher. When several of his brightest students died after they had pledged themselves to his work, Taplin noted in sorrow that 'Bad health always succeeds the desire for religious knowledge and the manifesting of pious feelings.' He put it down to conflict with old superstitions and the negative reaction of the elders who wanted to ensure that their strong young men maintained their traditional ways. But as the young people lived through each superstition, such as not eating particular foods for fear that they would go grey, the traditional power receded.

The Aboriginal people got seasonal work on the stations in the area, such as wool washing and shearing. But this was subject to the availability of European workers. In the early years, Aboriginal labour was welcomed by the new settlers. Later on, as the settlers had large families and more Europeans moved into the area, the Aboriginal people and their labour were no longer required.

Raukkan mission station became a focus for the Ngarrindjeri as the government encouraged them to settle there. Discriminatory laws made life difficult for the people throughout the 20th century, but many moved to Adelaide and assimilated into European society. Although they fought a losing battle against European colonisation, the Ngarrindjeri did not vanish. Camp Coorong is now a successful centre for education on Ngarrindjeri culture. Raukkan was transferred to Ngarrindjeri control in 1974.

The journey takes half an hour turning inland to Middleton, then back along the coast to Victor Harbour. This was the original historic train line that once promised prosperity to Goolwa by making it a central point in the Murray River transport.

To the east of the Hindmarsh Island bridge is the Goolwa Maritime Gallery created by Chris and Judy Crabtree. This is the best treasure trove of historic relics associated with river transport that we saw along the Murray. It includes an original roller that was used to control lengthy charts in the cramped conditions on the boats. The old brick building was once a foundry, the original dirt floor of the foundry is still visible.

Outside on the water, the Crabtrees have set up two river ships. The *Captain Sturt* is a salmon-coloured steel barge that was part of the British World War II transport fleet. After the war it was brought out to Australia as deck cargo for use on the Murray. It is a rugged, functional barge that smells of oil and doesn't look as if it would have been particularly comfortable. In contrast, the *Leo*, the 1882 sugar cane tug-boat behind it, looks much more comfortable, perhaps because it has been so elegantly furnished.

Although much of the activity in Goolwa centres on the wharf, there are also plenty of curious and interesting places to see around the town. The Bow Fronted Shop on Goolwa Terrace dates from the 1850s. Down the road the Goolwa Hotel on Cadell Street has the mast, figurehead and staircase of the Irish ship, the *Mozambique*, that was wrecked in 1854. The local council has produced an excellent walking guide with a clear map that takes you to over 30 places of historic interest in Goolwa. In order to explore it properly, you would need a couple of days, but even pottering around for a day will give you a feel for what an early colonial port may have been like. The guide is available from Signal Point.

A trip out to the Coorong and Murray mouth marks the end of a trip down the Murray. There are several scheduled trips that will take you to the Coorong from Goolwa. On the *Spirit of the Coorong*, you can take a 6-hour trip in a spacious boat that takes 50 passengers. Lunch and afternoon tea are included in the cost of around $60 per adult. The trip has three stop-off points: the Murray mouth, a boardwalk across the Coorong dunes, and an Aboriginal midden with a fresh water soak. In the course of the boat ride, you will go through the lock at the barrage, this is an interesting experience in its own right!

Other trips available include a shorter trip on the MV *Aroona*, a large boat that takes 140 people and only just fits into the lock. This costs about $50 per adult. Pensioner and child rates apply. We recommend that you ring Signal Point, get as much information as you can about available trips, and make a decision based on what you feel like undertaking.

Dominating the skyline around the wharf is the controversial new bridge to Hindmarsh Island. The high bridge is designed to allow yachts to sail underneath. There are several places to stay on the 15 km long island including Narnu Farm, where kids are encouraged to get close to farm animals. There are some lovely walks and a spectacular view from Trig Point at the end of Randell Road on the eastern side of the island.

There is plenty of accommodation in and around Goolwa, but not many places to camp. We suggest that you seek the advice of the staff in the Signal Point tourist centre. The place that attracted our attention was the floating hotel, PS *Murray River Queen*. The boat offers accommodation at a range of prices — from $15 for a single to $115 for the Stateroom with ensuite and a private lounge. The low prices surprised us until we saw the rooms. Everything on the river-boat is on a small scale and the sound proofing isn't terrific. But then this is one of the very few opportunities for visitors to sleep on an old-fashioned riverboat on the Murray River.

Sternwheel of PS Murray Princess (PHOTO: BILL BACHMAN)

Murrumbidgee River west of Canberra (PHOTO: CATHERINE DE COURCY)

Murrumbidgee Beach, central Wagga Wagga (PHOTO: CATHERINE DE COURCY)

The Hindmarsh Island affair

The bridge between Goolwa and Hindmarsh Island caused enormous controversy in the 1990s when the Ngarrindjeri were forced to relate secrets in order to impress upon developers that the bridge was intrusive to their sacred sites. The problem began in 1989 when Wendy and Tom Chapman applied for approval to develop a marina on Hindmarsh Island on land they had owned for a number of years. The marina involved a large lagoon and over 150 land allotments. Approval of the second stage of the development was contingent on a bridge being built between Goolwa and Hindmarsh Island to replace the ferry and support the additional traffic anticipated by this large development.

Environmentalists were the first to protest about the development and the pressure it would put on the small island and the delta infrastructure. Then the Ngarrindjeri women raised concerns that the bridge would violate places of secret women's business and damage sacred sites. The women prepared a report, as a result of which the Federal Labour government banned construction of the bridge for a 25-year period. The report was for women's eyes only but ended up in the office of Liberal MP, Ian McLachlan. The women were devastated by the betrayal of their secrets.

Over the next year or so the story became a national issue with claim and counter-claim. In 1995, the controversy ended up in a Royal Commission, the result of which allowed the project to continue. Although the Ngarrindjeri people took the case to the High Court, they eventually lost and the bridge was completed in October 2000. Tom Treverrow of Camp Coorong, an elder of the Ngarrindjeri, was quoted as saying, 'This is a very sad day for us. We do not see it as a bridge of progress but as a bridge of destruction.'

GOOLWA TO MENINGIE VIA WELLINGTON AND RAUKKAN

This is a most attractive drive (of 177 km) around Lake Alexandrina and Lake Albert, which together form one of the largest freshwater lakes in Australia. The road passes through undulating country, past black box gums and red river gums, and past a fine example of an Aboriginal canoe tree. The canoe tree is 9 km north of Goolwa and is signposted. It is definitely worth a look to get an idea of how Aboriginal people along the rivers removed the bark of a tree to make sturdy canoes. Close to the town you will see the cockle train yards where the old trains are now sitting in storage.

As you travel around the lakes there are several small towns, including the English-looking town of Finess, and the lake towns of Milang, Clayton and Wellington. On the road between Milang and Langhorne Creek you will see a sign warning you of turtles on the road! This was a first for Catherine, but John has seen turtles the size of dinner plates on this road. The promise of seeing a cute turtle prompted us to drive more slowly, but even if you are in a hurry, be careful — they are protected.

About 21 km past Wellington along the bitumen road is the turn-off to Raukkan. This 20 km road is unsealed but well maintained. It will take you to the 1839 station of Poltalloch, 10 km west from the bitumen road between Wellington and Meningie.

It is the most idyllic setting, with magnificent views over Lake Albert and the Poltalloch lighthouse. This is a private 19th-century farm village with 22 buildings; its shearing shed is on the register of the National Trust. A variety of accommodation is provided in these buildings, including former staff cottages with wood fires and verandahs. Prices begin at $95 for two. The village is only open to visitors by appointment (08 8574 0088).

At the end of the track is the last of the Murray ferries at Narrung, 2 km from the historic settlement of Raukkan, now an Aboriginal Land Trust area. The tiny coastal village of Narrung has a World War I memorial plantation.

Raukkan is 3 km south of Narrung in an Aboriginal Land Trust area. It is a dry area — no alcohol may be brought in here. This was the site of an ancient Njarrandjeri camp and the place chosen by George Taplin for his mission in 1859. The evidence of the mission is all around you, particularly in the church and the small cottages. The Point McLeay Church, with its tiny bell tower, was built of local sandstone and brick in 1869. It still functions as a community church. Several large plaques commemorate the work of Taplin and other missionaries. Neat 19th-century missionary cottages line the streets. Today, kids play football and basketball in the large communal grassed area. This is a quiet, alcohol-free Aboriginal town and the local community don't object to tourists dropping in to have a look at the church, which is featured on the Australian $50 note. Please respect the privacy of the people who live here and don't act in any intrusive way.

From there, the 39 km drive around Albert Lake to Meningie is beautiful. The water's edge is skirted by reeds and in many places comes quite close to the road. The bird life is evident even as you drive along. The country is a mixture of windswept lake district and green farm pastures. Long sprinklers with five, six or even seven arms sit ready for use in the fields. The speed limit is 110 km/hr but the road is fairly winding and not really suited to that speed. Occasionally you will see salt lakes near the road with their characteristic pink hue. A further 12 km from Raukkan is the turn-off to Long Point, 4 km down the track in Coorong National Park.

Meningie

The small, neat town of Meningie is the focal point of the eastern banks of the Murray delta. It is set on the shores of Lake Albert. The banks of the lake have been set up in the attractive style that is typical of Murray River towns. Wide, well-kept lawns separate the road from the lake. Trees provide shade but don't impede the view. There are BBQs, tables, chairs, toilets and a designated swimming spot.

Around the town there are old sandstone buildings that are characteristic of early Murray delta colonial settlements. Coorong Cottage Industries have set up a permanent market of local crafts in the elegant old council chambers. They also have a pleasant café with good coffee and cakes.

Overall, Meningie seems to be set up for holiday-makers who like quiet river-based holidays. There is the Meningie Lake Albert Caravan Park with self-contained cabins (08 8575 1411), the Lake Albert Motel in town (08 8575 1077), and the Waterfront Motel about 1 km north of town where the dining room looks directly out onto the lake (08 8575 1152). The Melaleuca Centre provides visitor information. It is open from 9 am to 5 pm, Monday to Friday, and 10.30 am to 2.30 pm at weekends.

George Taplin and Raukkan

In 1859, a young English man called George Taplin was appointed by the Aborigines' Friends Association to work with Aboriginal people in South Australia. The Aborigines' Friends Association was one of those organisations that was concerned about the impact of European colonisation on indigenous people. George Taplin, then 29, was to build a mission and school around Goolwa to help the Ngarrindjeri people integrate with the colonists. He kept a detailed diary that recorded information about the trials encountered by the Aboriginal people and the missionaries who were trying to assist them.

Taplin chose the ancient camp ground at Raukkan to establish the mission and school. He worked well with the local people. Children lived in dormitories at Raukkan but their parents were never far away. They supported their children in learning English and other skills that would allow them to take their place in the new order that was facing them. At the same time, the children were expected to speak their own language at home.

Taplin was keen that the Ngarrindjeri should generate their own incomes through exploiting their traditional resources and skills. Fishing was one of the key activities but unfortunately attempts at establishing an industry failed due to the greed and cheating activities of some Europeans. The colonial settlers and drifters stole commercial amounts of fish from the local storage catchments; on one occasion two men beat up a rival who was going to give the Ngarrindjeri a better price for their fish.

Taplin tried to protect the Ngarrindjeri from the alcohol that was freely available to the whalers and other settlers. This was often difficult: at one time even the local policeman sold alcohol illegally.

Even at a white-collar level, people were prepared to cheat the Aboriginal people. When the extraordinary Mrs Smith of Dunesk decided to donate money to be used for Aboriginal people in South Australia, some Adelaide-based lawyers tried to divert the money for insurance funds for colonial missionaries! Mrs Smith was Lady Henrietta Smith, a Scottish woman who donated considerable amounts of money for the express purpose of assisting indigenous people both spiritually and materially. Her desires were explicit and the Ngarrindjeri people were one of the groups that she focused on. Both Mrs Smith and Taplin fought hard to have her wishes adhered to; she knew what was going on but the law wasn't strong enough to protect her interests from these unscrupulous lawyers. Even after she died, the £300 per year that she had bequeathed to the Raukkan Mission was diluted. In the end Taplin settled for £100 per annum and gave up on the rest.

Raukkan remained under Aborigines' Friends Association control until 1916 when it was transferred to Government control. In 1974, it was returned to Ngarrindjeri control.

CAMP COORONG

We came across a reference to Camp Coorong in a modest brochure and found a gem. Camp Coorong is the Cultural Tourism and Educational Centre that introduces the Ngarrindjeri culture to tourists, school and community groups. Although the camp is set up primarily to accommodate school and community groups, a phone call confirmed that passing visitors are welcome to visit, or even stay.

Tom and Ellen Trevorrow have been running the camp since 1987 and have a remarkable and vital way of passing their ancient culture on to visitors. Tom is a raconteur who has important stories to tell. Over the past 140 years, his family avoided or was excluded from white missionary culture. Consequently, he has a great knowledge of his people's culture, traditions and stories. Camp Coorong is 10 km south-east of Meningie and as you drive along the Princes Highway, the white dunes of the Coorong are visible in the distance to the south, past the coastal salt flats.

If you book into a residential course at Camp Coorong, you can see basket-weaving, for which the Ngarrindjeri were renowned. You may be brought out to the Coorong to see plants with medicinal properties. Tom organises night-time camps and, around a campfire he tells ancient Dreaming stories and what they mean to his people. It is an exhilarating experience that makes the mysteries of Aboriginal life so real and accessible.

Camp Coorong can provide accommodation for visitors who are not part of a group. There are bush camping sites, with no facilities, available for a small fee, and camping with access to facilities for a slightly higher fee. Cabins at $45 per night are sometimes available for families and passing tourists. However, because the camp is geared towards groups, we suggest you ring and discuss what accommodation might be available on the day you are passing through. You can also take the opportunity to find out if there are any activities that you can join on the day you are visiting.

Regardless of whether you plan to stay there or not, Camp Coorong is worth visiting. There is an excellent display of Aboriginal artefacts, as well as other artefacts from around the world in the museum. One piece of work that Tom showed us was a woven mat; it had been sent around the world to other cultures who had added their own woven pieces to it. Now it is back in Coorong. The museum is being expanded to increase the amount of display space. Outside on the museum wall, there is a mural of the Coorong as it once looked. Painted by Marianne Ellul in 2000, it will be the first image that will draw you into Camp Coorong. Camp Coorong is open from 9 am to 5 pm, Monday to Friday, and there is always someone there who will welcome you (08 8575 1557).

3 The Murrumbidgee River

COOMA TO BOUNDARY BEND

The Murrumbidgee track is a trip that will take you along the second longest river in NSW, from the settled regions of the state, through Canberra, by several famous country towns, and on out to the plains of south-western NSW. Despite the amount of settlement and the dominance of private ownership along the riverbanks, the Murrumbidgee is never very far from the road and there is good riverbank access.

The natural features of the Murrumbidgee River are apparent from the earliest stage of the trip. The wide river valley runs close to the Monaro Highway and its western extent is identified by the dark tree-covered Clear Range. West of Canberra there is a beautiful drive through the low mountain ranges. Then, as the river turns west near Yass, it passes through one river town after another and becomes more directly accessible. Here there is a chance to camp, picnic or fish in a great Australian river, shaded by giant river red gums, with only the sound of corellas and other native wildlife in the air.

As a holiday, a drive along the Murrumbidgee is likely to surprise most Australians because it flows through towns that have other more prominent associations. Yass and Gundagai are commonly linked with the Hume Highway between Sydney and Melbourne; Wagga Wagga is, among other things a university city; and Narrandera, Hay and Balranald are known as major pastoral centres. But when these towns are linked through their relationship with the Murrumbidgee, their character as river settlements becomes more distinctive. Together they have strong his-

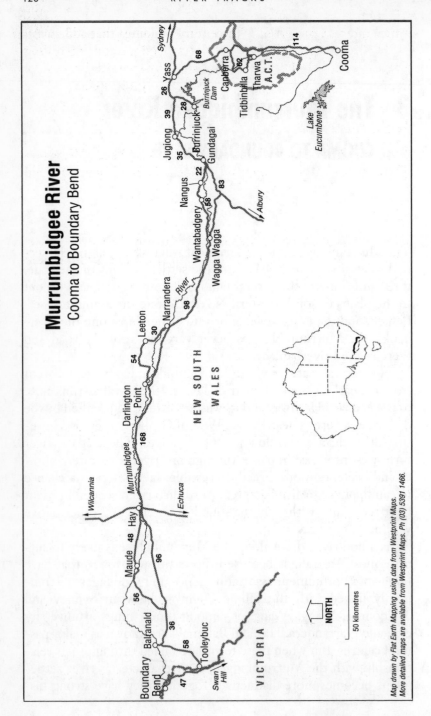

Murrumbidgee River
Cooma to Boundary Bend

Map drawn by Flat Earth Mapping using data from Westprint Maps.
More detailed maps are available from Westprint Maps. Ph (03) 5391 1466.

torical interest, preserved 19th-century buildings that add charm to the streetscapes, plenty of places to explore and interesting places to stay. Add the 20th-century purpose-built city of Canberra to the journey and this becomes a great holiday.

Main route

Cooma — Canberra — Yass — Gundagai — Wagga Wagga — Narrandera — Hay — Balranald — Tooleybuc — Boundary Bend

Maps

Touring Atlas of Australia, Melbourne, Penguin, 2000
Capital Country, Cartoscope tourist map, 2001 (free from tourist outlets)

Passes and licences

A NSW Freshwater Recreational Fishing Licence is required to fish in the Murrumbidgee.

Minimum number of days required in dry conditions

956 km from Cooma to Boundary Bend; six days for a quick visit only.

Best time of year to visit

Along the lower regions of the Murrumbidgee River, winter temperatures vary from 1–14°c, and 14–35°c in summer.

Warning

If you are coming in along the Snowy Highway from the headwaters of the Murrumbidgee, there may be snow on the road in the winter months. The optional side trips on dirt tracks will be inaccessible after rain. Maps in some of the forest areas along the lower Murrumbidgee are not very clear about river access for bush camping.

Accommodation and camping

There are hotels, motels and caravan parks at frequent intervals along the Murrumbidgee. Because many of the towns have preserved their historic buildings, it is often possible to stay in 19th-century hotels. Most of these are still traditional hotels costing $25–40 per person, with breakfast but without ensuites. A few of them have been turned into B&Bs at the expensive end of the price scale. A few tourist centres offer accommodation booking services, the most valuable of these is in Canberra where there is a huge range of accommodation. Outside school holidays and holiday weekends, standard accommodation should not be difficult to acquire along the Murrumbidgee.

Bush camping opportunities are also fairly good along the Murrumbidgee, although it is much better near the lower reaches of the river. We have identified places where you can camp in relative isolation if you wish.

Local information and useful telephone numbers

Cooma Visitors' Centre (includes accommodation service)	toll-free 1800 636 525
Canberra Visitors' Centre accommodation booking service	02 6205 0044 toll-free 1800 100 660
Yass Shire Visitor Information Centre	02 6226 2557
Gundagai Visitor Information Centre	02 6944 0250
Wagga Wagga Visitor Information Centre	02 6926 9621
Narrandera Tourist Information Centre	02 6959 1766
Hay Visitors' Centre	02 6993 4045
Balranald Tourist Information Centre	03 5020 1599

THE ROUTE

Cooma

The Murrumbidgee River rises in the Great Dividing Range north of Kiandra and flows into Tantangara Reservoir. From there it travels through a deep valley surrounded by high mountains, then south through low undulating hills. Melting snow and creeks from the mountain peaks feed the river as it makes its way towards Cooma on the Monaro Highway. Just north of Cooma the Murrumbidgee does a U-turn and begins its journey northwest towards its junction with the Murray in south-western NSW. We begin our river journey here.

The town of Cooma has two main roles: it services the tourists travelling to and from the Australian Alps and the famous ski slopes at Thredbo and Perisher, and is also a service town for the Snowy River Hydro-Electric Scheme. As the first town on this Murrumbidgee track, Cooma provides an early indication of the historic nature of the river towns. Pastoralists first moved into the district around Cooma in the late 1820s. By 1849 the village had been laid out and its name taken from the Aboriginal word 'Coombah', meaning 'open country' or 'Big Lake'. A historic 6 km walk has been set out around Cooma and this will take you past many of the 19th-century buildings and down the town's oldest street — Lambie Street.

The large number of older stone or brick houses that remain as private residences give Cooma much of its charm. The houses are unassuming, and are partially concealed on wide tree-lined streets. Their exteriors look like they have been carefully preserved over the years and, without fuss or ceremony, still serve their original function.

Several buildings stand out, notably the 1888 Court House on Vale Street, which is set majestically at the head of sweeping lawns. Beside the Court House is the decommissioned gaol. You can get a tour of the historic gaol from a prison warder from Monday to Friday, but his availability is dependent on his other duties. Tickets are sold at the Visitors' Centre, so the staff there can let you know if a tour is being held while you are in Cooma.

On Lambie Street, the 1854 Raglan Gallery and Cultural Centre is now open to visitors from Wednesday to Sunday, from 10 am to 4 pm. The long, low historic inn displays the work of local artists and crafts people. The Royal Hotel (1858), at the southern end of the Street, is a two-storey corner pub that is particularly striking from the outside, with a magnificent verandah

Murrumbidgee, the river

At 2160 km, the Murrumbidgee is the second longest river in NSW, after the Murray. About 50 km north of Kiandra, it rises in the Great Dividing Range to 1600m above sea level. As it flows down towards Cooma, it is fed by many creeks carrying the melting winter snow from the high mountain peaks. From Cooma, it flows through rolling hills and treeless plains until it arrives at Burrinjuck Dam. As it flows downstream to Gundagai, the path of the river becomes more obvious from the road as the river red gums begin to make an appearance. By the time it reaches Narrandera, the river red gums are an ongoing feature of the river.

No single explorer is given credit for charting the Murrumbidgee. Sections of the river in the southern plains of NSW were crossed in the 1820s by explorers such as Charles Throsby, and Hume and Hovell. In 1829, Charles Sturt explored country around the river from a point close to what is now Jugiong, and out as far as the Hay plains. In 1830, he put a whaleboat into the river near what is now Maude. A week later his boat entered the Murray and from there he made his epic voyage down the Murray River.

Today the Murrumbidgee passes through several big dams upstream, and weirs lower downstream. The major man-made obstacles for the Murrumbidgee are the Burrinjuck Dam and the Berembed Weir. Burrinjuck Dam was built in the 1920s to harness the water of the river so that it could be used effectively for irrigation further inland.

At Berembed Weir near Grong Grong, between Wagga Wagga and Narrandera, the waters of the Murrumbidgee are distributed to the properties in the Murrumbidgee Irrigation Areas. The water is released through a lengthy network of channels to farms that have purchased the water. This process began in 1912 when citrus farms were first established in south-west NSW. Settlers were encouraged to venture out here and farm small holdings. Indeed the government was so keen to promote the area that they paid Henry Lawson a small fee to live here and write verse praising the enterprise. By the 1920s, the MIA (Murrumbidgee Irrigation Area) was flourishing and the abundance of water was considered sufficient to build up thirsty rice farms. Rice has remained an important crop in the district.

The Murrumbidgee flows into the Murray at a point that is difficult to access and remains relatively untouched.

built in 1900. You can stay here — single rooms are priced from $25. The low ceilings and wooden dado contribute to the 19th-century atmosphere inside.

On Jindabyne Street, also on the historical walk, there is an unusual-looking monument. This is the Southern Cloud Memorial Park, a memorial to a three-engine Arvo Fokker plane that vanished in the mountains in 1931, taking eight lives with it. The wreckage was found 27 years later when a Snowy Scheme worker came upon it. Parts of the aircraft, including the wooden propeller, have been placed behind a grid in a white monument as a permanent memorial to early aviators.

Cooma is the home of the Snowy River Hydro-Electric Authority. For those interested in the massive engineering achievement that saw tunnels built through mountains and vast silver pipelines snake their way over the mountains, you can visit the Snowy Mountains Scheme Information Centre. The Information Centre is open every day: Monday to Friday, 8 am – 5 pm; weekends and public holidays, 8 am – 1 pm. The displays cover all aspects of this Scheme, from the technical operation of the generating stations to the historical aspects of this extraordinary project. There is a metal relief of the Snowy Scheme on the street beside the Cooma Visitors Centre. This is a graphic depiction of the terrain that the engineers and an army of 100,000 workers from 30 countries had to deal with to complete its construction.

Cooma's service role to the Snowy Scheme and to visitors travelling to the mountains is evident in the wealth of accommodation and restaurants. There are 2 caravan parks, 12 motels, 4 hotels and several B&Bs. Some cater for family groups. Happily the Visitors' Centre operates an accommodation booking service, so they can make arrangements to suit your needs. The Centre is open seven days a week: from 7 am to 5 pm during the ski season, and 9 am to 5 pm throughout the rest of the year.

By the way, we have never seen so many restaurants serving pancakes in one small area. We went to M&M's East End Café on Sharp Street, and the home-cooked food and pancakes were excellent.

Snowy River Scheme

In 1884,suggestions were first made about diverting some of the abundant water resources of the Snowy Mountains — and specifically the Snowy River — into the Murrumbidgee. The Snowy River rises on Mt Kosciuszko and flows out to sea near Orbost in Victoria. The Snowy River Valley did not require irrigation so valuable water resources were flowing out into the sea. In the meantime, irrigation had prompted extensive development of agricultural industry along the Murray and Murrumbidgee valleys, and there was a desperate need for more summer water out there.

Preliminary surveys were made in the 1920s, and an organisation to promote the concept was formed in 1936. Groups with regional interests lobbied government, but none looked at an integrated scheme that would use the Snowy waters with maximum efficiency. Then, in 1949, after much politicking, Prime Minister Ben Chiffley announced the establishment of the Snowy Mountains Hydro-Electric Authority.

The Snowy River Scheme became one of Australia's major feats of civil engineering as 140 km of tunnels were bored through the mountains, 16 dams were made, and pumping stations, power stations, aquaducts, and other features of the network were built in difficult terrain. Over 100,000 workers from 30 countries took 25 years to complete construction.

As well as adding to the folklore of Australia, the Snowy River Scheme now feeds a portion of its water to irrigate agricultural land in NSW, Victoria and South Australia. It also supplies electricity to the states during times of peak power load or at times of emergency.

Figures alone can't fully explain the extraordinary nature of the work involved in the Scheme. The display in the Snowy Mountains Scheme Information Centre in Cooma is presented in a way that will give you a sense of the dimensions of the job. There are photos, diagrams and videos that explain the Scheme and provide some insight into the historical development. The staff are happy to explain things in non-technical terms.

COOMA TO CANBERRA

The river drive between Cooma and Canberra is different from any of the other river drives described in this book. You see the river only occasionally, but as you drive north you will be aware that you are driving up the Murrumbidgee corridor. You won't see a line of great river red gums or other trees marking out the riverbank, but all along the busy Monaro Highway you will notice that you are driving almost parallel to a high mountain ridge several kilometres to the west. The dark tree-covered mountains are in sharp contrast to the treeless pasture country between the base of the mountains and the road. The Murrumbidgee River course is in this wide corridor.

You can travel out to the Murrumbidgee U-turn, 9 km north of the Cooma Visitor Centre. Take Smith Street, then Mittagang Road out of Cooma, pass through the suburbs of the town and soon you will be in bald, rolling pastureland. The bridge over the Murrumbidgee is signposted, so you can't mistake it. Its proximity to the Cooma Water Treatment Plant that processes town's water supply means that swimming here is not permitted. However, you can drop a line into the water off the banks at this attractive and peaceful location. There is a pleasant clearing by the treatment plant with picnic tables, a BBQ and toilets under the shade of the trees. There is no chance of bush camping here.

If you cross the Murrumbidgee and continue driving up the road through the pasture, you will come to Billilingra Road after 11 km. This road eventually joins the Monaro Highway 25 km north of Cooma. Otherwise it is necessary to return to Cooma and follow the signs out to the Monaro Highway and on to Canberra.

The Murrumbidgee joins the Monaro Highway briefly 19 km north of town, but there is a lot of traffic along this road and it is not easy to stop here. There is fabulous river contact along the western reaches of Canberra, but we shall take you out on that drive following our visit to the city.

Canberra

After you have been to one or two major attractions in Canberra, you will be left in no doubt that you are in the nation's capital. For overseas tourists — and possibly for Australians also — Canberra tends to have a rather grey image and is often left off the tourist itinerary. However, as part of the research for this book, Catherine visited Canberra for the first time and was sorry that she didn't have more time to spend there. What is most attractive about this city is the integrated way in which the features and landscape have been designed to blend into each other. And as the trees mature over time, the beauty of the city will grow.

Of course, what brings most tourists to Canberra are the iconic national institutions that have been created here, including the War Memorial, the National Gallery, the National Museum of Australia, the National Library, the Australian Archives, and so on. It is also the centre for embassies and huge numbers of public servants.

In order to get a full sense of the city and its role in Australia, we strongly recommend that you begin your exploration of Canberra at the National Capital Exhibition on Regatta Point. This excellent exhibition describes the making of Canberra and includes information on everything from the philosophy behind the building of a capital city, to design features such as the choice of trees. This information will contribute significantly to your appreciation of the city. So when audiovisual presentations seem to have very strong nationalist overtones, or you are faced with yet more images of well-known Australians, or you wonder at scores of houses in the suburbs with identically coloured roofs, you will be able to consider them in the context of the city as the focal point for Australian identity.

The Canberra Visitors' Centre is on Northbourne Street in the leafy suburb of Dickson. The staff here are very helpful and friendly, and can provide you with all sorts of information about what is going on in Canberra. You can get free maps of tours around the city and the staff can advise you of special events to look out for. There is a small coffee shop in the Visitors' Centre where you can take time out to digest all of the information. The Centre is open from 9 am to 5 pm, Monday to Friday; and 9 am to 4 pm on Saturdays and Sundays.

In our own exploration, we covered the major permanent institutions. On the way back to town from Dickson, the War Memorial is the major national institution on the north side of Lake Burley Griffin. This is a magnificent and reverential homage to the Australians who fought and died in war. The drive up Anzac Parade is the first taste of the scale on which this memorial has been created. The wide parade is lined by trees, and cars are not allowed to park by the side of the road so there is nothing to clutter the vista up and down the parade. Memorials to those who fought and died in the different conflicts have been built along the Parade; these seem to have been designed as peaceful places suitable for private remembrance.

The War Memorial on the top of the hill is on a grand scale. The names of all of those who died in battle are listed in metal on the walls. In the centre is the Eternal Flame, and behind it the main Hall of Memory and the Tomb of the Unknown Soldier. The many staff are warm and helpful. Often visitors go there to get information about family members, and the staff couldn't be more supportive. They have access to databases of information about all of those who served. The view from the steps of the War Memorial, down Anzac Parade, across the lake and back up to the two parliament houses, is one of the most striking urban vistas in Australia. The War Memorial is open from 10 am to 5 pm, every day of the week. Admission is free but donations are welcomed.

The new National Museum is also on the north side of the lake. It is set on Acton Peninsula and was opened in March 2001. The angular, brightly coloured building stands out on the water-side. The entrance hall is spacious with a souvenir shop and café. Give yourself plenty of time to explore this museum. There are so many audio visual displays running at the same time that if you try to move through the place in a hurry, you will become confused and possibly irritated. The Aboriginal display is well worth visiting. Traditional tools, equipment and art are displayed with contemporary stories of Aboriginal life. The exhibit looks to the future as well as back into history. The 'Tangled Land' display features a large 'buff car', used to catch buffalo in the northern territory, as well as a kaleidoscope of well researched topics relating to the land. The bombardment of sound, confusion of the passages through the displays, and the dim lights made the occasional glimpse out over the tranquility and order of Lake Burley Griffin a relief to tired senses. The Museum is open from 9 am to 5 pm every day. Entrance is free and the guide to the Museum will be important to help you navigate your way around the building.

The National Library and the National Gallery are both on the south side of the lake within sight of Parliament House. The Library has a grand foyer with a café and substantial shop. It also has small exhibitions. This is the place to pay homage if you are an Australian or a librarian, before you meander down by the lake to the National Gallery about 1 km away.

Fishing at Lake Burley Griffin

The Gallery's permanent collection includes several icons of Australian art, including works by Sidney Nolan depicting Ned Kelly. The entrance to the galleries is through the long shop, a design feature unfortunately quite common in large galleries around the world. At the end of this obstacle course, new acquisitions hang for comment and reference. If you are lucky there may be a high profile and controversial exhibition on display — the fuss caused by the $8 million painting, *After Cézanne* by Lucien Freud, was as diverting as the painting itself. The Gallery's permanent collection is well documented and its temporary exhibitions are well advertised. Its early colonial art collection is well worth visiting if you are interested in the early history of the country. The Gallery is open from 10 am to 5 pm every day. Entry is free and you can pick up a guide to the Gallery when you arrive.

For us, one of the highlights of a trip to Canberra was a visit to Old Parliament House. This elegant building was used as the seat of parliament from 1927 until 1988, by which stage it was bursting at the seams. You can now wander through the parliamentary chambers and down the corridors of power to the former Prime Minister's office. There are plenty of enthusiastic guides there to give you informative chatty tours through the complex. At the rear of the building, through the courtyard, is Backbenches Café and Bar, an essential part of the visit. The former parliamentary restaurant has large wooden tables and chairs, and the buzz of conversation is probably reminiscent of its days as the hub of national politics. The menu includes good lunch and snack food. Old Parliament House is open from 9 am to 5 pm every day. There is a $2 entry charge for adults.

On the lawn between Old Parliament House and the lake is the Aboriginal Embassy, a settlement of huts with caravans under the trees. There is also a camp with traditional red and yellow poles set out on the lawn. This is a major protest site for the Australian Aboriginal people and it is very eloquent. Visitors are welcome to go into the Embassy, although there may be no one there.

Rising out of the lawns behind Old Parliament House is the contemporary parliament building. This is open to visitors from 9 am every day and free guided tours commence every 30 minutes. Parliamentary question time begins in the House of Representatives and in the Senate at 2 pm every day the house is sitting. You may sit in on these sessions, but you must book first by calling 02 6277 4889.

As a specially designed 20th-century city, there is one major advantage for the tourist — Canberra is relatively easy to drive around and fairly compact, with wide streets and lots of roundabouts. This doesn't mean that you are necessarily going to arrive at the place you want to get to the first time around, as the signage is not always continuous, it doesn't give you enough notice to change lanes and is sometimes hidden by trees. On the other hand, if you do overshoot your turn-off (as we did many times!), it is very easy to get back onto the right track quickly, without stress and without creating a traffic hazard — you just take the next turning and return to the original route. There also tends to be plenty of parking near the major visitor attractions. So overall, for a driving holiday, Canberra has to rank as one of the easiest cities for strangers to get around.

Canberra has every variety of accommodation available and the Canberra Visitor Centre has an accommodation booking service called Canberra Getaways. As Canberra is definitely one of the places that is worth staying in for a couple of days, we strongly recommend that you chat to the staff in the Visitor Centre and source a couple of places in Canberra before you leave home.

One of the things that will strike you about Canberra is the beauty of the landscape, and the way the city and its suburbs blend into it. Integration with the local environment was central to the original design of the city by Walter Burley Griffin, an American landscape architect. By the 1950s, about 1.5 million trees had been planted on the formerly treeless plains. In addition, strict planning regulations ensure that the surrounding hilltops are free from building. When you see early images of the bare countryside around the city site, you will appreciate the extraordinary achievement of the planting program. Now, when you travel out to join the Murrumbidgee south-west of Canberra, you will notice that banks of houses creeping up the sides of the hills all have similar coloured roofs — muted greens, rusty reds and beiges. At first the uniformity looks strange, particularly the brick-red lake frontage by Lake Tuggeranong. But as the trees grow, these suburbs will no doubt blend beautifully with the mountainside.

THE MURRUMBIDGEE IN ACT

The Murrumbidgee River drive to the west of Canberra is a side-trip full of surprises. It includes a river swimming pool, a historic cottage, the old hill town of Tharwa, the nature reserve at Tidbinbilla, the Canberra Deep Space Station, bush camping at Cotter Dam and Mt Stromlo Observatory. Lake Burley Griffin, designed to create a water axis to complement the land axis, is on Molonglo River, which feeds into the Murrumbidgee at Uriarra Crossing north of Cotter Dam. The Canberra Visitor

Information Centre has a leaflet on the drive that includes a simple map of the area; it is known as tourist drive number five.

The ACT Murrumbidgee drive begins by following the signs from the Capital Hill to Tuggeranong Parkway, one of the major arterial roads leading out of the city. At traffic lights about 16 km later, turn right into Sulwood Drive and follow the sign to

Creating Canberra

The proposal to create a purpose-built national capital was first agreed upon during the negotiations between the colonies as part of the lead up to federation in 1901. Forty sites were considered and the selection of the 2358 sq km expanse of limestone plains in NSW was made after intensive politicking. It was vested in the Commonwealth in 1911.

Following an international competition for a plan for the new city, the design of Chicago-born architect, Walter Burley Griffin, was selected. Griffin's plan revolved around the use of the natural landscape to create a spacious city in the irregular amphitheatre of the site. The focal point is Capital Hill, and all main avenues radiate from that. The two parliament buildings are now on the slopes of Capital Hill. From here, the city and its suburbs extend outwards.

Work on the infrastructure began before World War I, but no great progress was made until the 1920s. There was still opposition to the concept of the 'bush capital' and there was constant criticism of the money being spent on it. But the Commonwealth Government was keen to make cost savings and move public service operations to their permanent home as quickly as possible. Residential housing, shopping centres and other facilities were built and by 1927, the parliament was ready to move into its new home from its temporary location in Melbourne. Now Canberra has a population of over 300,000 and extends for nearly 30 km from north to south.

The landscape of Canberra was central to Griffin's design. North American firs and birches, Mediterranean cypresses, English oaks, elms and beeches were planted alongside Australian natives to provide the mix of colours that is particularly striking in autumn. The layout of the city was designed as a 'Y' shape to allow the natural landscape to remain part of the city. Planning is carefully controlled so that the relationship with the landscape is maintained.

Lake Burley Griffin, part of the original plan, wasn't formed until 1964. It is 9 km long, 4 metres deep and keen fisherfolk can catch carp, yellow belly and redfin in this peaceful waterway.

Kambah Pool. The pool, about 6 km from Sulwood Drive, is a popular Murrumbidgee swimming pool for Canberrans. This is a lovely place, with banks of rocks that you can clamber over when the water level is low. There is perfect swimming access and plenty of places to prop up a rod. There are toilets here and several BBQ huts.

Back on Tuggeranong Parkway, continue travelling south via the uniformly coloured suburbs. The wide river corridor is to the west beyond the suburbs. Lanyon historic cottage is 30 km south of the city, on Tharwa Drive, surrounded by trees. This was one of nine large grazing properties that was in the territory when it was acquired by the Commonwealth Government in 1911 from NSW. Lanyon is still a working property but the old homestead and outhouses are open from 10 am to 4 pm, Tuesday through to Sunday.

Continuing down Tharwa Drive, you will rejoin the Murrumbidgee River 4 km further south. The 1895 bridge is the oldest surviving bridge of this style. It has four wooden spans and still supports the traffic. It was designed by Percy Allan of the Department of Works, NSW, and when it was built, it at last provided an all-weather link between the Sydney–Cooma railway and the grazing pasture land of the Murrumbidgee. High up on the side of one of the supports, and well above the bank and picnic ground, there is a line identifying the 1991 flood level. Unless you are there when the river is in full flood, it is difficult to imagine the scene when the water flows at this depth.

Tharwa was one of only two small settlements in the territory in 1911 and it still retains a village atmosphere with an old general store as the focal point of the town. Off the main tourist road, 3 km south of the town, there is the entrance to Namadgi National Park and Visitor Centre along with a display centre highlighting the features of the local environment. You can get information about the 4WD tracks and camping in the park from here. There are Aboriginal sites in the park, which the rangers in the Centre can tell you about. The Centre is open from 9 am to 4.30 pm, Monday to Friday (02 6207 2900).

Back in the Murrumbidgee corridor, the sealed road travels north towards Tidbinbilla Nature Reserve. About 5 km past Tharwa is a scenic lookout over the river valley, and back to the

low-spread southern suburbs of Canberra. Now you can really see
the value of the softly coloured roofs. A little beyond this is the
turn-off to Point Hut Road, a sealed road that takes you down
into the river valley to a low causeway. This is closed if the river
is up. There is a carpark on the western side of the causeway.

As the road approaches Tidbinbilla, 17 km from Tharwa, there
are lovely views of the mountains to the north. You can also see
the Murrumbidgee corridor to the east. At the Tidbinbilla Nature
Reserve you can get close to native animals as well as take a break
in the café. Along this entire drive, you are likely to see wild kangaroos and emus. At dusk, drive carefully as the animals may well
cross the road in your path.

The highlight of this drive is 2 km past Tidbinbilla — the
Canberra Deep Space Station. As you drive around a bend and
over a crest, an array of large dishes reaching out to the stars suddenly appear. This is a magical view. The white dishes are nestled
in the hills and lit up by lights at dusk. It is a very dramatic and
quite unexpected sight. Even if you don't want to visit the station's
information centre and look at displays of spacecraft, space food,
and a piece of the moon, do drive out to the crest for a look, it is
a rare sight. The Canberra Deep Space Centre is open from 9 am
to 5 pm every day, and admission is free.

The track around the Murrumbidgee returns to nature after
this unusual experience. Cotter Dam is a beautiful place and very
popular at busy times of the year. There are walks, picnic areas, a
playground, toilets, an old wooden bridge, plenty of bush camping, wildlife and the scent of the pine forest around it. There is
also a hotel. This is a good fishing place with several weirs on the
bends of the Cotter River, which feeds into the Murrumbidgee.
The Brindabella Road, just over the bridge, leads to Uriarra
Crossing, 13 km to the north. This is where the Molonglo River
meets the Murrumbidgee.

On the way back into town, there is another space experience
with Mt Stromlo Observatory, 8 km past the bridge near Cotter
Dam. From here, follow the signs back into the centre of
Canberra, take Northbourne Avenue past the Information
Centre, and follow the signs to Yass to continue on the
Murrumbidgee track.

CANBERRA TO YASS

This is wine country and there are several cool climate wineries with cellar doors along the route. The small settlement of Murrumbateman is the centre of the wine district. There are eight wineries and many more vineyards in the area. In Murrumbateman itself you can stay in the hotel/motel and have meals in the pub under a 19th-century shearing shed roof. The general structure of the hotel is recent, but the roof is the original and once belonged to a shearing shed. Farm implements have been attached to the rafters. The ornate handles on the pub doors are not original to the pub.

The wineries that have cellar doors are all clearly signposted in the region. They are more suited to wine lovers who want to check out local wines, rather than family parties who are looking for diversion. The Visitor Information Centre in Yass sells local wines but you can't taste them there.

As you approach Yass, follow the signposts to leave the Hume Highway and drive into town. The highway travels over rolling plains and through sparse agricultural country, broken only by isolated rows of trees. There is no sign of the Murrumbidgee in the distance from this section of the road because its course is not yet lined by large river trees.

Yass

The Yass district was first settled by Europeans in 1821, and the first town site established in 1837. Its relatively old history is reflected in the look of the town (now with a population of 9100). Yass used to be a town on the Hume Highway, then in 1994 it became a town bypassed by the highway. Since then the council has promoted its history and the historical elegance of the town with wrought-iron verandahs, large colonial buildings, and heritage street furniture. The calm historical feeling of the town would probably surprise any travellers who now take the time out on the trip between Sydney and Melbourne.

The streetscape on the main road, Comur Street, features numerous ornate 19th-century buildings, such as the majestic courthouse (1880), the railway station behind it (which boasts the shortest platform in Australia), the National Bank (1873), and opposite it — the Royal Hotel (1849). The Globe on Rossi Street is a grand 1847 building that was owned by an ex-convict when it was a hotel. It is now run as a B&B (with basic rates of $110 for a double, phone 02 6226 3680).

Streetscape in Yass

These are the buildings that stand out but there are many other smaller cottages and private residences that look like they date from the later decades of the 19th century. As in Cooma, most of these are residential stone or brick cottages with veran-dahs, and they contribute to the historical atmosphere of the town. There are also several 19th-century hotels, mostly on the north side of Comur Street. These are all two-storey buildings with low balconies, low ceilings, and tiles halfway up the walls on the outside. They all provide accommodation, meals and — of course — drinks. There are several guides available in the Visitor Information Centre.

Cooma Cottage, 4 kms east of Yass, is one of the town's oldest buildings and is now the focus of historic displays on the region. Cooma Cottage was built in 1835 and later became the home of the explorer Hamilton Hume. It is a small, single-storey colonial building that has been restored to house a museum with displays about colonial station life, Hume the explorer and pastoralist, and other information displays. It is open from Thursday to Monday, 10 am to 4 pm, and there is an entrance charge of $4 for adults, with child and concession charges at $2. Hamilton Hume Museum, next to the Information Centre, is only open at weekends from 10 am to 4 pm, or by appointment. It includes a display of historic photos of Yass.

There are nine motels, six hotels and one caravan park in the immediate vicinity of Yass. There are also several caravan parks along Burrinjuck Dam. The old hotels — the Club House and the Commercial — provide rooms at around $25 for a single. If you want to plan your stay in Yass, contact the Visitor Information Centre for information about your options. There are also plenty of restaurants, cafés and bistros. We had an excellent home-cooked lunch in The Eatery, sitting out in the sun admiring the row of country pubs across the road.

BURRINJUCK DAM

There are several access points to the Burrinjuck Lake near Yass, including two picnic places and two beautifully positioned caravan parks. The lake was formed from the Murrumbidgee River following the construction of the Burrinjuck Dam. To reach these places take Dog Trap Road west out of Yass and follow the signposts for each feature. To reach the picnic spots, continue along the road through pasture land for 20 km to Taemas Bridge. As you drop into the valley, you will get some great views down into the river and to the bald mountains beyond. However, if there isn't much water in the river, this is not the most exciting place to be as the river bed is wide, the banks muddy, and most of the land around here is private. Locals prefer to go to Beabolo, a picnic place signposted off the main road to the bridge, 13 km from Yass. This unsealed 11 km track travels through station country, over grids and through gates, but it is a public road and you are welcome to use it. The picnic spot by the river is delightful with shade, a stony bank and good access to the river. There is no camping here and fires are not permitted.

The turn-off to the two caravan parks on Lake Burrinjuck is clearly signposted 5 km from Yass. The Good Hope Tourist Resort (02 6227 1234) has ensuite cabins, powered and unpowered sites, a BBQ, river access, a launching ramp, and good fishing. In the lake, you will catch yellow belly, redfin, trout, Murray cod and carp. An enormous 44 kg carp was once caught in the lake but it would only have been good for a photo! Hume Park, around the corner, also has a range of accommodation as well as an attractive brick house built in the 1920s as a guest house (02 6227 1235). The owners have turned a section into a shop and are living in the rest of the house. This was the location of the camp made by Hume and Hovell on their expedition in 1824. They spent time here as they worked out how to get their party, supplies and animals across the flooded Murrumbidgee, then 40 metres wide and flowing at an estimated five knots.

Both of these caravan parks on Burrinjuck Dam rely on good water levels to support their enterprises, at least during the busy season in spring, summer and Easter. But for some years, the water levels in the dam have not provided a level of consistency to make it easy for these parks to operate. One owner told us that they could have a reasonable water level in the dam one day, and a few days later it might look as if a plug had been pulled. Nevertheless, the fishing is still reasonable. You can hire small fishing boats at each of the caravan parks; the owners will also give you advice on what is biting and where. During the busy period, they can supply bait also. Regardless of the water level, the location is beautiful and peaceful, with lovely walks in the region and calm lake views.

YASS TO GUNDAGAI

The major features on the road to Gundagai from Yass is the Burrinjuck dam wall and one of the best caravan parks we have visited in Australia. The road out to the dam wall is 26 km past Yass on the Hume Highway, and it is a further 28 km to the dam. The turn-off is clearly identified and the road is sealed all the way. It travels through native forest and as you get closer to the dam you will see some wonderful views out over the water. But there is no stopping point so only the passengers can really enjoy this. This was once the passage of the railway line that brought equipment, workers and supplies into the dam area when it was being constructed in the early decades of the 20th century.

The Burrinjuck area is very attractive, even if the water capacity is low. The lake down near the dam wall is surrounded by steep mountains. The road travels around the long narrow arms of the lake and when there is no water, you can see the stony bed. Boats tethered to trees far above the waterline indicate how high the water can go. There is a village of houses built into the side of the mountains out here, including a conference centre set on the lake. There are no general services. The dam wall itself is closed but there is a turnaround circle at the gates, which you will need.

On the way to the dam wall, you will have passed the Burrinjuck Waters State Park caravan park, gloriously set in a large native forest. The park provides a wide range of accommodation from cottages and ensuite cabins to unpowered bush camping sites. You must BYO linen for all types of accommodation although some can be hired. In among the trees and off the maze of sealed tracks around the park are BBQs, parkland, kangaroos, a shop with fuel, a playground, boat hire and a launching ramp. What is particularly enticing about this park is that all of the accommodation is distributed in a way that gives you a sense of privacy in the bush setting. The park is operated by the NSW Department of Land and Water Conservation. The staff told us that school holidays are busy, but other than that it shouldn't be too difficult to get accommodation here. We highly recommend it for a night in a bush hideway (02 6227 8114).

Back on the Hume Highway, on the way to Gundagai, you will pass two small towns. Jugiong is 2 km off the Highway, Coolac is still on the highway. Jugiong, 65 km past Yass, identifies itself as a town on the Murrumbidgee River. The Jugiong River joins the Murrumbidgee to the south of the town. There is fuel and a motel here, an old two-storey hotel with a verandah, some old cottages, and several abandoned fuel stations. A lookout at the west end of town just before you rejoin the Hume Highway provides great views over the Murrumbidgee Valley and to the mountains to the east and south. Rejoining the Hume is not easy here. There is no feeder lane and there is a bend in the highway just before the junction. Also, the speed limit is 110km/hr along here.

Ben Hall and the hold-up at Jugiong

Ben Hall was another one of the 'wild colonial boys', the Australian-born bushrangers who used their knowledge of the countryside to their advantage. Hall was one of the smartest of the bushrangers; his men were well armed and well mounted, often on stolen racehorses. Hall himself was described as a tall, robust-looking man with a fine, frank-looking face. Despite his notoriety, it is believed that he didn't kill anyone during his career, although some of his henchmen did.

Hall was particularly active from 1863 until he was shot dead in 1865 at the age of 28. He and his gang robbed banks, hotels and stations, and held up travelers and mail coaches. When Henry Keightley, a station owner, killed Mick Burke, a 17-year-old gang member, Hall decided to spare Keightley's life on condition that his wife found a ransom of 500 pounds, the price on Burke's head. Mrs Keightley had 24 hours to get the money and returned with minutes to spare.

One of the Hall gang's more audacious highway robberies took place near Jugiong in 1864, on the road between Sydney and Melbourne. The gang of three held up sixty travelers, robbing them and herding them into the bushes where they were to wait together under guard. Then the target of the hold-up arrived, the mail coach. As they robbed the coach a fight broke out and some of the captive travelers came out of the bush to watch, although not one went to help the coach escort. One of the police officers escorting the mail coach was killed. The gang escaped with the loot.

Not long after this hold-up, the NSW Government passed a law that made harbouring an outlaw a crime in itself. It also legalised the shooting of known outlaws on sight. This was a response to increasing lawlessness in the bush. Between 1862 and 1867, twenty people were killed by bushrangers, 23 bushrangers were killed or hanged, and 20 policemen were wounded. Ben Hall was shot dead after being surrounded by police near Forbes on the Lachlan River.

Coolac is another small town. It is still on the Hume Highway and has a historic hotel and a general merchant shop.

Before you reach Gundagai, you will see the 'Dog on the Tuckerbox' statue and tourist lay-by, 8 km east of the town. Here you will find the 1932 tribute to early pioneers, along with monuments devoted to the Australian film and radio characters — Dad and Dave, Mum and Mabel. The Rudd family are fictional characters who featured in several early Australian books and films, and later in a very popular radio serial. The broadcast ended with the song, 'The Road to Gundagai', and consequently the town on the Murrumbidgee entered rural folklore. The tourist lay-by on the north side of the road contains these and several other Australian icons, such as an old tram, a wooden dray, wagon-wheels, and a flag with paw marks flying beside the Australian flag. The location of this collection of icons was selected because this was a favourite resting place for outback workers, drovers and dray transport drivers in the 19th and early 20th century. Nearby you will still see the ruins of the Five Mile Inn, a popular drinking place built in 1851. If you are travelling through in November, you may encounter the 'Dog on the Tuckerbox' festival featuring bush bands, bush poets, yarns, and line dancing.

Gundagai

The town of Gundagai is built on the river among treeless mountains, with Mt Parnassus on the east side of town providing panoramic views down into the Murrumbidgee floodplain and the hilly landscape beyond. The floodplain dominates the town. It is vast and green, with three exceptionally long bridges stretching over it: the old wooden Hume Highway, a railway bridge, and the modern Hume Highway. Large river red gums stand at intervals through the plain. The view from Mt Parnassus lookout is an exceptional opportunity to see this scene from a distance.

Down at river level, you can get close to the bridges. The old wooden bridge over the floodplain is the longest such bridge in Australia. It was built in 1867 to take over from the overworked punt that was part of the road between NSW and Victoria since about 1840. The Prince Albert Bridge carried the Hume Highway until the nearby Sheahan Bridge was opened in 1979. You can walk out over the old Prince Albert Bridge and get a sense of the floodplain. A cairn marks the place where the first

Hume and Hovell

Hamilton Hume and William Hovell were the first Europeans to travel overland to Port Phillip from the settled districts of NSW. Hume (1792–1873) was the Australian-born son of a convict superintendent. At the age of 22, he headed off on exploratory trips into the uncharted areas of NSW. Hovell (1786–1875) was born in England. He went to sea as a boy and rose to be master of a ship. He migrated to NSW in 1812 with the support of his father-in-law, who was one of the colony's early medical practitioners.

Hume, Hovell and their party of six men set out from the Lake George district in NSW in October 1824. They crossed several rivers including the Lachlan, the Murrumbidgee, the upper Murray and the Goulburn before ending up in what is now Corio, near Geelong in Victoria. Hovell charted the location and recorded positive descriptions of the land for future agricultural use. However, his calculations were out by a degree and his mapping coordinates referred to Western Port, country that was not immediately suitable for agricultural development. The error was discovered in 1826 when settlers attempted to establish themselves there. As a result of this miscalculation, Hume and Hovell are credited with delaying the colonisation of Victoria for a decade.

Their expedition wasn't a failure overall. They returned with valuable data about the geography of the rivers and tributaries of this region. What was particularly intriguing was the existence of the large Goulburn River flowing north or north-west — this suggested that there was a major river or outlet to the north of this region. This of course proved to be the Murray, and the information about the Goulburn contributed to the success of Charles Sturt's expedition along the Murrumbidgee and then down the Murray in 1829.

William Hovell joined the government party in the boat that sailed to Western Port in 1826. Hamilton Hume was a leading member of Sturt's expedition to the Darling in 1828. After those adventures, Hume settled on a station near Yass and Hovell settled near Goulburn, NSW.

The Hume and Hovell Walking Track was developed by the NSW Department of Lands as part of the 1988 Bicentennial celebrations. The track follows Hume and Hovell's overland route as closely as possible. Overall it is estimated that the walk would take 20 days, but guides identify much shorter trips suitable for the casual walker or families. The guides are available from visitor information centres at Yass and close to the route.

school house was located, which was washed away in the disastrous flood of 1852. In between these two bridges is the lengthy railway bridge that was built in 1901 and closed in 1986.

When you see the dry floodplain, it is difficult to imagine the river flowing through here so fast that it wiped out the original town of Gundagai in 1852, killing 83 of its 250 residents. Gundagai was first established nine years before, with its buildings erected near the water's edge. Now the three-storey flour mill on Sheridan Lane near the bridge is the only building in Gundagai that survived the flood. Nearby you will see a memorial to Yarri, one of numerous references to the Aboriginal man around Gundagai. During the flood and in the darkness of night, Yarri single-handedly rescued many of the townspeople in his bark canoe. Guided only by their voices, he battled the raging river, then 1.5 km wide, to bring them to safety.

The town itself is beautiful with many deciduous trees, old buildings, and several parklands. At the Visitor Information Centre you can pick up an excellent guide to the town, as well as purchase a walking guide that will take you around the old buildings and monuments. In the Information Centre itself there is an extraordinary marble replica of St Marie's Cathedral in Paris, constructed by local resident Frank Rusconi over a period of 28 years. He also sculpted the statue of the 'Dog on the Tuckerbox'. The historic walk will take you down the main street, past the 1928 Gundagai Theatre, the magnificant 1859 court house, several 19th century hotels with low verandahs and tiled walls, and around to the bridges and the flour mill. There are a couple of museums in town, including the Dr Gabriel Gallery on the first floor of Butcher Robert's Store in Sheridan Street. This displays a collection of interesting photographs of Gundagai taken in the early 20th century.

Gundagai is one of those places where you could easily spend a day exploring and still find things to do. There is plenty of accommodation here with at least six motels, four hotels including the 1858 Family Hotel (02 6944 1019), two caravan parks, and several B&Bs. The Visitor Information Centre can provide details of accommodation to suit your needs. It is open from 8 am to 5 pm, Monday to Friday; and 9 am to 5 pm, Saturday, Sunday and

The road from Hay to Maude (Photo: Catherine de Courcy)

Fishing on the Murray River (Photo: Bill Bachman)

Shearing shed at Poltalloch Station (PHOTO: CHRIS AND BETH COWAN)

public holidays. It is closed for lunch from 12 noon to 1 pm at weekends.

GUNDAGAI TO WAGGA WAGGA

The back route between the two towns is the first section of the Murrumbidgee that could almost be called a river drive. The Murrumbidgee flows through the pasture country with bare hills on the north and the river appearing periodically on the south. Occasionally there are old stone houses and farm buildings that give you an indication of how long this land has been settled. Now the land around the Murrumbidgee is beginning to flatten and, if you are on this road at sunset, you will get glorious scenes with the golden light of the setting sun disappearing behind the line of low ridges.

You will notice that the Murrumbidgee is acquiring a line of trees along its bank, although they are still not as big or as dense as those along the lower reaches of the river. This is a most picturesque drive with riverbank features such as fallen trees, rocks, and banks of stones or mud when the water level is low. There are some deciduous trees along here, which break the muted native green eucalyptus colour with bursts of gold in autumn. Most of the river access is on private property, so this is not a good place to plan some fishing.

To reach the back road between Gundagai and Wagga, follow the signposts that direct you to Junee. The back road is a narrow, winding road, 80 km long. At the tiny township of Nangus, 22 km past Gundagai, take the south fork to Wantabadgery and on to Wagga. Wantabadgery, another small settlement 39 km from Gundagai, was close to the scene of the shoot-out and capture of the bushranger Captain Moonlight in 1879.

Wagga Wagga

This is the first Murrumbidgee town that really feels like it is built on the river. The river flows through the largest provincial city in NSW (population 57,000) and there is plenty of interaction with it. What is particularly attractive about this city is that the river is

lined by great red river gums and a flourishing natural environment. So, just two minutes from the town centre, you can sit on
the sandy banks of the river in the shade of the trees, and fish for
yellow belly, trout and redfin.

The wide streets of Wagga Wagga have an eclectic variety of
architecture which makes the streetscape attractive. There are
several large 19th-century buildings with ornate mouldings,
columns and architraves. Mid to late 20th-century architecture is
also evident along Baylis Street, the main street through the
town. Wagga Wagga Town Planning Department has produced
three walking tour guides to the town with the assistance of the
National Trust. The tours take you off the main streets and provide basic information about the offices and houses that you are
passing. The emphasis is on the 19th-century structures, many of
which have been sympathetically restored.

Around town there are several places worth seeing. Chief
among these is the National Glass Art Collection. This is housed
in its own elongated gallery at the back of the Civic Centre, near
the Tourist Centre. The permanent glass collection is displayed in
the upper part of the gallery, and temporary exhibitions are displayed downstairs. Glass is a very accessible art and the colours,
textures, shapes and sizes are very impressive. The design of the
gallery, with a glass wall and natural timbers, promotes the beauty and light of the collection.

The spacious Regional Art Gallery is also inside the Civic
Centre and hosts temporary exhibitions, as well as an active education program for which regional galleries are well-known. It
also has a small permanent collection of paintings and a good collection of contemporary Australian prints, a selection of which is
often on display. Next door to the modern Civic Centre is the
original Town Hall with its elegant Council Chambers. This
building was built in 1881 and its corner position on the main
street highlights the majestic look of the building. Inside, the
arched wooden beams and dark wooden cathedral ceiling are
striking. The chambers are open to the public as a museum. The
spacious rooms in the building are used to display temporary
exhibitions. Inside the chambers there is a large painting of the
famous Tichborne Trials of 1873–4. Wagga Wagga's own historical museum is scheduled to open late in 2001.

Captain Moonlight

Andrew George Scott was one of the more unusual bushrangers who plagued the countryside in the 19th century. He was the son of an Irish clergyman who became a lay preacher himself in preparation for joining the ministry. In 1869, a bushranger calling himself Captain Moonlite [sic] held up a bank in Bacchus Marsh, Scott's local bank. The bank manager later identified the thief as Scott but no one believed him. He was charged with the robbery himself but was acquitted when the case collapsed. Some time later Scott sold a gold ingot that was identified as having been stolen in Bacchus Marsh and he was arrested and convicted. In gaol, Scott acted as a lay reader in the prison bible class. He was released early for good behaviour.

In 1879, Scott roamed the countryside with several friends, unsuccessfully looking for work at a time of high unemployment. Frustrated and hungry, they stormed Wantabadgery Homestead, a place where they had been refused work and even shelter from the rain. They gathered together 52 hostages, including all visitors and some guests from a local inn. After one of the hostages escaped, the police moved in. The gang escaped but the police caught up with them a few kilometres later. About 300 spectators gathered to watch the ensuing battle. Two gang members were killed, including a 15-year-old. A police officer was shot by Scott. At his trial, Scott asked that the lives of his three surviving colleagues be spared. Two were given life sentences, Scott and another were hanged.

Scott was tried in the Gundagai courthouse, in the presence of up to 2000 members of the public who reacted to the event and subsequent trial with behaviour bordering on hysteria. This was a time when bushrangers were the curse of the highways in the settled areas of country NSW and Victoria. Scott was sentenced to hang and he asked only that his body be buried with his friends. At his death, at age 37, Scott was relatively old for a bushranger. His body remained in an unmarked grave from 1880 until 1995, when his last wish was granted.

As well as promoting its buildings, Wagga Wagga also encourages visitors to become familiar with the river. They have laid out the Wiradjuri Walking Track, a 30 km walk that starts along the banks of the river. The walk takes you through the trees and undergrowth, and under the 19th-century Wiradjuri Bridge that is no longer used. The full walk heads south across the Sturt Highway and out of Wagga Wagga; a shorter walk of 10 km goes along the river and around Wollundry Lagoon. Of course you can join or leave the walk at any stage. A guide is available from the Visitor Information Centre and describes natural features and constructions along the way. Wagga Beach, just a 2 minute sign-posted walk from Fitzmaurice Street, is a beautiful place with sandy banks, green lawns, a playground, tables, toilets and a swimming section that is patrolled in the summer.

Tichborne Trials

The trials were held in London and were reputed to be the longest running in the world, lasting for 290 days. The focus of the trial was a young Wagga butcher known as Tom Castro. He claimed to be the missing heir to the Tichborne fortune in England. Roger Tichborne had gone missing on a trip around the world some time before this; his mother had never given up hope that he was alive and had con-tinued to search for him. Castro learnt of the story and claimed to be the sole Tichborne heir. Other members of the family challenged him and the court case dragged out for nearly a year. In the end Castro was found guilty of perjury and sentenced to jail. On his release, he went off to America, gave lectures and joined a wild west show. He died in 1898, claiming until the end that he was the Tichborne heir.

Later research suggests that he was an English man named Arthur Orton, born in 1834. The Wagga connection is now illustrated in the large painting hanging in the old chambers.

Outside town, 7 km to the north, is Charles Sturt University, a major feature of Wagga Wagga. The University teaches viticul-ture, among other subjects, and out of this has developed a win-ery with a cellar door. They have several good wines that are worth tasting. They also sell olive oil and recently they branched into making cheeses flavoured with bush ingredients such as lemon myrtle and wild berries. You can taste this interesting range of cheeses at the cellar door. Access to the winery is sign-posted through the grounds of the university. The cellar door is open from 11 am to 5 pm, Monday to Friday; and 11 am to 4 pm, Saturday and Sunday.

In May 2001, another significant feature was created at the university. On a hill overlooking the Murrumbidgee Valley and the town, the Wiradjuri people celebrated the opening of Indyamara, a place that means 'give honour, be respectful, be polite, be gentle, patient and honest with each other.' Indyamara is a simple place with a path leading to the top of the low, treeless hill; several large boulders mark the path. Informative interpretative signs have been placed at intervals along the path describing the natural history and geology of the Murrumbidgee Valley, as well as the Wiradjuri's relationship with the region and the arrival of the Europeans. Access to Indyamara is via the road to the left of the roundabout at the entrance. There is no parking on the narrow road, but there are university car parks in the area.

There is plenty of accommodation and places to eat in Wagga Wagga. The town boasts over 2000 beds in a variety of places, from the 7 caravan parks, 22 motels, 5 hotels, and several B&Bs. There is no bush camping in the immediate vicinity of the town, but 19 km downstream marks the beginning of some excellent opportunities to camp out. Several of the hotels and motels in town have nice restaurants attached to them where you can get good meals, including dinners. There are also cafés, including the colourful Hipomoto on Peter Street. The café (which is very hard to miss as it is painted in strong primary colours) serves good coffee and excellent cakes, such as quince or rhubarb cake. Hipomoto is also an art gallery that sells a variety of items, including pottery.

The Visitor Information Centre is on Tarcutta Street behind the Civic Centre. The signage leading you there from the west side of town is not great but you can't miss the Civic Centre on Baylis Street. The Information Centre staff can give you some good brochures about accommodation and facilities in Wagga Wagga. There is also a free map of the town available. It is one of the excellent series of Blue Guide Handy Maps, so we would recommend that you start at the Information Centre before exploring the town. The Information Centre is open from 9 am to 5 pm every day. The Centre does not operate an accommodation booking service, but the staff will be happy to assist you in identifying accommodation to suit your group.

Fishing information and advice is available from Rod's Custom Rods out at 110 Harmond Street. The staff are very helpful in providing up-to-date information and advising on what bait to use. Opposite the shop is a good children's play centre that kids up to the age of 12 would enjoy. It has all of the usual slides and bouncing places, as well as nooks and crannies to hide in.

WAGGA WAGGA TO NARRANDERA

Now at last is the first real opportunity to camp along the river without human intervention. About 19 km west of Wagga on the Sturt Highway you will see a sign indicating a truck rest stop. Just after this, and around a corner, you will spot a small street sign announcing Kohlhagen's Road and see a faded wooden sign by a gate saying 'Riverside Drive'. You will also see the trees along the Murrumbidgee not far north of the road. This is the entrance to a public reserve. Although the 2 km dirt track goes through sheep paddocks, it is a public road. This leads down to a beautiful place on the river with river red gums and the best bush camping along the Murrumbidgee so far. It is a popular place with the locals, but off-peak during the week you may have the area to yourself. The track is a dry-weather track only and would become impassable when wet.

From here on along the Sturt Highway, there is great bush camping by the Murrumbidgee at reasonable intervals. Also, the river red gums are now as large and majestic as those on other major inland rivers. Between Collingullie, 24 km west of Wagga, and Narrandera 74 km further on, there are several access points on the river. For example, 17 km west of Collingullie is Central Island Road, a sealed road through fields that leads to Bulgary Bridge and campsites with fireplaces and toilets. If you take Central Island Road and then continue along the graded track towards Narrandera, you will arrive at Weir Road 14 km later. This track follows the course of the river but the land along the riverbank is private and there is no access. The weir, however, 10 km down Weir Road and then Station Road, is another popular place to camp. This area is well signposted so river access is easy to find.

If you continue your journey to Narrandera along this back

Floods of Wagga

The origin of the name 'Wagga Wagga' comes from an Aboriginal language and means 'the place of crows'. It is also the place of many floods, as Sherry Morris documents in her book, *Wagga Wagga Floods*. The town is set on the alluvial floodplain of the Murrumbidgee, which was first charted by Charles Sturt in the 1820s. A station called Wagga Wagga was established near here in 1832 and four years later Thomas Mitchell made camp on the site of the town. From there on the settlement grew quickly as land-hungry colonists followed the explorers into the interior. It was proclaimed a town in 1849.

From the beginning of its settlement, Wagga Wagga was threatened by swollen river waters. The first flood to be recorded was in 1844, and depths of 150 centimetres were recorded in some station huts. However, it was the flood of 1852 that highlighted the danger to the townspeople as fast-flowing water rushed through the main streets of the town unexpectedly. This was the floodwater that had cost Gundagai so dearly. It didn't claim any lives in Wagga, but it caused such damage and hardship as it rose to over 180 centimetres, that many people found themselves stranded on the roof of their house for days, losing all their possessions. After the flood, further housing lots in North Wagga were eliminated and building along the northern banks of the river was restricted.

Since then floods in Wagga have become a way of life, with the degree of damage varying. In 1962 a levee bank was built on the south side of the river to protect the business district and most of the residential area. In 1974, when the river reached the same level as the flood of 1852, the small suburb in North Wagga suffered with up to 250 centimetres of water flowing through the houses. At Hampden Bridge, the river was recorded at a depth of nearly 11 metres. On this occasion, Burrinjuck Dam had filled to capacity due to extensive rainfall and winter snow; the water spilled over the dam wall and flowed on to cause havoc at the towns beyond it. The town levee was not breached. Since then levees have been built to protect the streets of North Wagga.

road, you will find several more signposted public tracks into the river. Some distance past the weir, the road is sealed. You will begin to notice that the countryside is becoming flatter with fewer features on the horizon. From here until you reach the junction of the Murrumbidgee with the Murray, flat, almost fea-tureless plains are characteristic of the landscape. The back road rejoins the Sturt Highway 35 km from Narrandera.

Narrandera

The small service town that sits on the northern banks of the Murrumbidgee was once the major town in the region and you can see evidence of this in the wide streets and old, elegant build-ings. Its role as an important river crossing place and a pastoral regional centre was usurped in the early 20th century with the development of the new towns of Griffith and Leeton as focal points for the Murrumbidgee Irrigation Area (MIA), but Narrandera has retained its charm and historical interest. It is still an important service centre situated on the Newell Highway between Queensland and Victoria, and also plays a role as pastoral centre. The Narrandera Visitors' Centre is on the Newell Highway and the very helpful staff are delighted to give you informed and detailed information on whatever you are interest-ed in. You can also have a look at the largest playable guitar in the world!

Besides the natural environment of the riverside in Narrandera, the distinctive features of the town are several spec-tacular buildings. Two of these are close to the railway line on the north side of town. The beautifully preserved Star Hotel was built in 1916. The federation building is situated on a street corner and has a verandah trimmed by ornate lacework. It was once a pub and still gives this impression from the outside. Today it is run as an elegant B&B with prices ranging from $88–110 for a double room, or $55 for a single. Because it is a listed heritage property, there are no ensuites to the rooms. Anyone can go to the Star Lodge for dinner by making a reservation in advance (02 6959 1768).

On the next corner is Hall's Hotel, also built in the 1880s as a pub. This is now open as a tea room and is worth taking a break in. The pressed-metal ceiling in the restaurant is notable, con-taining more detail than usual for such ceilings. The high ceilings, large windows and polished wooden floor are perfect backdrops for home-cooked food and cakes. There is a small local craft shop in another part of the building that sells a mixture of items from cloth dolls to fine wooden bowls. The original rooms of the pub are actually underneath the tea rooms and are inaccessible.

You can get a guide to the historic buildings in Narrandera from the Visitors' Centre. Many of the 19th-century buildings such as the police station, Hit & Miss Hotel, and St Thomas' Anglican Church on Larmer Street are not obvious on the streetscape, largely because they are set so far apart and are shaded by trees. The Tiger Moth plane displayed in Narrandera Park near the Visitors' Centre is a memorial to the thousands of pilots who trained here before going off to fight in World War II. If you want to spend a day exploring the history, we would recommend that you walk around using the guide and map for directions.

Star Hotel in Narrendera

Narrandera is on the Newell Highway that links Queensland and Victoria and, as you would expect, accommodation and places to eat are readily available. There are several licenced restaurants, five hotels, and numerous cafés, mostly in the centre of town. In terms of accommodation, there are at least nine motels, two caravan parks and five hotels with rooms starting at $20 for a single. The Visitors' Centre is open from 9 am to 5 pm, seven days a week.

NARRANDERA TO HAY

The Murrumbidgee bush camping continues along this part of the river and there is plenty of choice in the forests on the north side of the river close to Narrandera. The maze of tracks through the riverbank forest continues for many kilometres, so it will be up to you to choose your spot. Outside of the busiest times of year, you are likely to have as much isolation as you like. Here you can light a campfire between April and November inclusive, cast a fishing line into the river, and be woken by flocks of screeching corellas at dawn!

The hidden treasures of this area are not well signposted. To find the forest, take the Leeton Road out of Narrandera on the north side of the river. About 12 km from the town, you will see a street sign pointing into the forest towards the river saying 'Pistol range'. This is the only indication that you are entering a large, wild public area with masses of bush camping opportunities. After turning into the track, a grid and a notice welcome you to the MIA 1 Forest. From here the tracks could become confusing. You can pick up a mud-map to the forest tracks from the Narrandera Visitors' Centre and we shall also give you some broad descriptive information about how to find your way in and out. However, there are so many tracks leading to and from the main ones, you need to have a good sense of direction to feel comfortable in here. The advice we would give is keep the river trees in sight, and be aware of your location in relation to the river. The more dense the trees, and the taller they are, the closer you are likely to be to the river.

The effort is worth it if you want to camp down by the natural environment of the Murrumbidgee. The most direct route from Leeton Road to the river will take you to Platt Beach after 4 km. From here, the main track runs through the trees, roughly following the course of the river. If you meander along the track,

History of Narrandera

The history of this small town, with a population of around 5000 people, is far richer than most visitors would realise. The first European came through here in 1821, then Charles Sturt made camp here on his epic journey down the Murrumbidgee and the Murray rivers in 1829. As usual, pastoralists followed the explorers into this country and by the 1830s the NSW government had introduced squatting fees. The pasture lands of the region were rich and the area became known for its ability to produce fat cattle. Until the 1850s, the cattle were driven up-river to the markets in NSW. Then gold was found in Victoria and the role of Narrandera as a river crossing exploded.

During the gold rush, Victorians were desperate for meat and Riverina cattle prices soared. The crossing at Narrandera was reliable, the business district of the town remained flood-free, and enterprising land-owners pushed the development of facilities. Squatters bought store cattle from the north, fattened them on their runs in the Riverina, then drove them over the river at Narrandera and sold them for good profit in Victoria.

The railway reached Narrandera in 1881. At the same time, Narrandera was home to the largest concentration of Chinese people in NSW. The gold rushes had drained the region of labour and the Chinese were prepared to live here, do heavy scrub-clearing work, develop market gardens and feed the people of the settlement. A Chinese sector with 30–40 houses was developed on the north side of the river with a joss house, a hospital, stores, gambling and opium dens.

The role of Narrandera as an important regional centre was diminished by the development of the Murrumbidgee Irrigation Area. Experimentation with irrigation in the region began in 1899 when a local pastoralist, Samuel McCaughey, became frustrated that the creeks on his property at North Yanco would dry up for years at a time. He established a 320 km irrigation network involving artesian wells, trenches and canals, and dams to provide water to around 10,000 hectares of land. McCaughey's station was converted to an agricultural high school in 1922; later an agricultural college was established in Yanco. Already the value of irrigation in the area was being recognized by a newly established citrus industry, and a cannery operated by the state government was built in 1914. Shortly afterwards, rice-growing began in the region and wineries were later established.

you will see plenty of tracks off it that will take you to a camping place by the Murrumbidgee. The tracks to named beaches are marked from the main forest track. About 10 km from Leeton Road turn-off is the marker to Yanco Weir; the weir itself is 1.3 km down the track. It is a stunning location — both for fishing and for bush camping — but as with most bush camping, there are no amenities.

The forest drive continues along the Murrumbidgee for about 20 km. Exact distances are difficult to gauge because there are so many track options. As you reach Catfish Corner, Nandirong Bend, or Long Beach, you can turn back towards the main road and rejoin the highway 4 km from Yanco. Yanco is 24 km west of Narrandera by the highway. Beyond Yanco, you can turn back into the MIA forests and find many more camping opportunities by the river. These are all favourite camping and fishing places with local people, which may explain the maze of tracks that are not on the printed mud-maps. Rely on your instincts and use the river to navigate. Also, as in all remote areas with uncharted tracks, monitor your trip-meter closely. Be aware that these are dirt tracks in a floodplain; if there is any rain about or there is flooding from the river, you will become hopelessly bogged, so get out at the first sign of rain. When the tracks are bone dry, they should be accessible to all vehicles with good tyres and suspension; however, drive gently as the ruts and potholes could damage suspension, and the corrugations can shake your vehicle up.

The conventional route between Narrandera and Hay is via the Sturt Highway and the small 19th century river of Darlington Point. The turn-off to Darlington Point is 54 km from Narrandera on the Sturt Highway and the town itself is 3 km from the Highway. This is part of the road labelled as the Kidman Way, which leads north to Bourke. You can also drive into Darlington Point from the north side of the river; it is about 91 km from Narrandera via Leeton.

There is a caravan park set under the bridge on the river. Despite its location under a bridge that seems to have trucks going over it all night, it is a peaceful place where you have natural river access as well as the option of staying in overnight cabins or pitching a tent with amenities nearby (02 6968 4237). In 1905, a bascule bridge was built, replacing the punt that had operated on this bend in the river since the 1850s. The metal section of the bridge was replaced in 1979, but was later re-erected at the entrance to the caravan site by students from the Engineering Faculty of the University of NSW.

Other facilities in Darlington Point include a hotel, post office, several shops, and a club with a restaurant. There is also a river beach on the north side of the bridge near the entrance to the caravan park.

Back on the road to Hay, you are entering extraordinary country. The land is flat to the horizon, broken by rows of native trees. The Hay Plains, covering 4.4 million hectares, are among the flattest country in the world. The dense trees of the Murrumbidgee are visible to the north. Grass pasture stretches out to the horizon. This is the landscape for which Hay is famous.

There are numerous public access tracks to the Murrumbidgee along here, most with bush camping. Those where camping is prohibited are identified. The tracks are not prominently signposted and there are many private station tracks. So if you want to camp or simply visit the river, look closely at all signs and follow those that indicate public access to the river.

As the river moves towards the Murray, it is wide and lined with great river red gums. The bird life is active and varied with flocks of white corellas that talk loudly at sunrise and sunset, and hundreds of native green budgies that chirp in the trees. There are plenty of places where you can drop a line in and hopefully catch Murray cod and yellow belly, and perhaps redfin, bream and catfish. Bait is available in Balranald and Hay, although it is easy enough to gather worms or shrimp along here. Happily, there are fewer and fewer carp in this stretch of the Murrumbidgee thanks to the restocking policy of the NSW fisheries department. They have been restocking the waters with native Murray cod and, further upstream, trout cod. These fish are so aggressive that they will eat anything, including the young carp. Now people are once more reporting being able to catch 'fish you can really eat!' However, trout cod are still protected and there are restrictions on when you can catch Murray cod so check the details of open and closed seasons that are issued with your annual licence.

There is another riverside caravan park 11 km east of Hay — the Bidgee Camping Ground and Caravan Park. It offers powered and unpowered sites, wood BBQs, and plenty of space, particularly outside peak school-holiday periods. If you want to camp here during school holidays, phone ahead and make a booking (02 6993 4808).

Hay

This is a great town to visit with loads to explore. The Murrumbidgee here is wild, flowing through its natural course thickly lined with river red gums. The spacious town with its wide trees and colonial town streetscape stretches out to the north of the river. The Visitors' Centre is again the place to start and, just as in Narrandera, we received well-informed and friendly assistance with all of the features, services and facilities in town. Bush camping, river access and fishing are promoted along the Murrumbidgee around Hay so you can get good detailed information about areas that interest you. The centre is open from 9 am to 5 pm, Monday to Friday; 10 am to 12 pm on Saturdays; and 9 am to 12 pm on Sundays. The hot showers and toilets are open from 6 am to 8 pm, seven days a week.

Hay began as a river crossing in the 19th century and is roughly halfway between Sydney and Adelaide. It has a rich history, with a Cobb & Co. coach factory and the Dunera prisoner of war and internment camp. These are now the focus of the town's historical presentations.

Discarded remains of Cobb & Co. coaches are piled high in the old gaol on Church Street. The gaol was built in 1878 and was used for its original purpose until 1915. Since then, it has been used at various times as a hospital for the insane, a military prison during the war, and as a high security institute for girls. In 1974 it was handed over to the people of Hay and it has since been developed as a museum.

This is an unusual museum in that a massive number of items are on display, few are labelled and there are no staff on duty. You are asked to put a dollar in an honesty box at the entrance, and then you can explore. Cobb & Co. material is only one part of the museum's collection. A few coaches are still intact but, unlike other displays, these coaches have not been polished up. They simply stand there alongside other old forms of transport, including a mid-century motorbike, looking like they were used very recently.

The other items have been arranged in a clutter in each of the 15 cells behind metal grids. One cell retains all of its original bars. The bars are inside the standard metal cell door, so giving the prisoner an L-shaped space, presumably to allow some air flow for the inmate by leaving the heavy cell door open. Another cell has been set up as it originally was, with the bed at an angle to the wall. Typewriters, bottles, telephones, farming implements, domestic equipment and other items reminiscent of olden times fill the remaining cells. Little attempt has been made to make them look other than what they are — old, discarded items. They don't shine and there are few notices. This gives the gaol museum collection great charm and interest.

Hay and the Cobb & Co.

Hay's position on a low point of the Murrumbidgee made it a natural crossing place for drovers who needed to cross the river in the 1840s. The settlement was based in a vast pastureland, grazing fat sheep and cattle. As demand for fresh meat in Victoria increased enormously following the gold rushes in the 1850s, Hay boomed as a river crossing. The town was gazetted in 1859 and named after a local politican.

Cobb & Co. began a regular run to Hay in 1860. The successful coach company had started in Victoria in 1853 with American backing and had soon spread its network all over the settled areas. In 1862, Cobb & Co. arrived in Hay with a long cavalcade including coaches, horses, drivers and a brass band. They established a coach-building factory specialising in 6-seater and 24-seater coaches. They also set up a stud farm to maintain their horse supply. In the 1880s, this was the largest coach factory outside Sydney and continued to operate until close to the end of the century. 'Sunbeam', the restored and polished coach on display next to the Visitors' Centre, went into operation in 1886 on the Deniliquin–Wilcannia run, and continued running as a mail coach until 1901. Then it was converted into a passenger coach and used on special occasions.

Up the road on Murray Street, the 1882 former railway station houses the exhibition devoted to the Dunera POW and internment camp. Hay was selected as the location for a POW camp in 1940 because it was on flat land, far from the coast, and on soil that was difficult to tunnel through. There was also a small local population and plentiful supplies of water from the Murrumbidgee. The first prisoners who arrived here were German and Austrian, and there were many Jewish people among them who had escaped Nazi Germany. They were transported to Australia on the ship *Dunera*, and the name became associated with the camp. These first prisoners were later joined by Italian POWs and Japanese internees, some of whom had never been to Japan. The prisoners farmed, dug irrigation canals, and were encouraged to play music, organise theatrical performances and organise an educational program. The stories of Dunera Camp and the inmates who lived here are displayed on the walls of an old railway carriage. The railway building itself is now used as government offices.

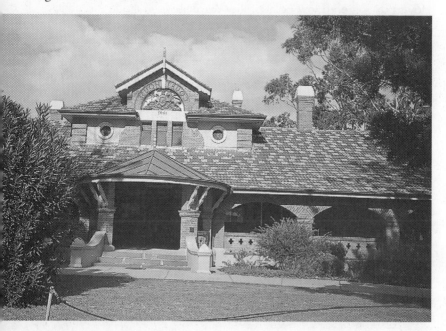

Courthouse in Hay

Back in town on Pine Street, behind the Information Centre, is the still functional redbrick courthouse. This redbrick building with its deep verandah was built in 1892. Inside it has wooden panelling, marble fireplaces and high, ornate ceilings. When there is a clerk of court in attendance, visitors are welcome to look through the building. This is usually during the office hours of 9 am – 5 pm, Monday to Friday. It is not open to tourists on the one day a month when the court is in session. It is probably best to check with the staff in the Information Centre to see if it is open.

Close to the river on the Sturt Highway are the remains of the 1904 sewerage works, the second rural sewerage works to be completed in NSW after Narrandera. The residents were concerned about the contamination of the river from the waste being poured into it. Their concerns were realised when there was a typhoid outbreak here in the late 1890s. The signs by the old brickworks describe how it operated and the scientific significance of the works.

Another feature of note in Hay is the Bishop's Lodge, 2 km along the Sturt Highway towards Narrendara. This is worth visiting even if it is closed. The Bishop's Lodge is a grand residence clad in corrugated iron, with a splendid rose garden that is still carefully tended. The gardens were planted in the late 19th and early decades of the 20th century. By 1988, 50 roses were still growing in the garden, and several roses are believed to be unique to the lodge. These are all now protected as heritage roses. The house itself was built in 1889 as the official residence for the Anglican bishop of the Riverina. The pale galvanized exterior walls have little holes in them so you can see the sawdust that was used as insulation. When you knock on the walls, the dull sound indicates how effective the insulation is. Many Riverina homesteads used this building method in the 19th century. Inside, the wood-panelled rooms with wooden floors, ceilings and elegant fireplaces are in grand proportions. The Bishop's Lodge is only open for a limited time, from 2 pm to 4 pm on Saturdays; however, you are welcome to wander around the garden at any time. If one of the committee who look after the place is there, they will give you a tour. The Lodge is used for functions to contribute to its upkeep.

The Hay Visitors' Centre has a couple of historic walking and driving guides, as well as leaflets on the buildings of historic interest around the town. There is plenty of accommodation in Hay, as it is on the Cobb Highway between Echuca and Wilcannia. There are seven motels, two hotels, three caravan parks and plenty of bush camping. The staff in the Visitors' Centre can give you information on accommodation that would suit your needs. You can also get a free hot shower here — always useful if you are bush camping.

There are plenty of places to eat, including one of the best cafés along the Murrumbidgee — Our Coffee Lounge. In this ordinary-looking country coffee shop, the coffee was excellent and the home-made cakes superb. They also sell a locally produced 'fruit leather' which we have never come across before. It is a sheet of pure fruit that has been pureed, then dehydrated and formed into sheets. It is slightly chewy and full of flavour. There are no preservatives or added sugar in it.

HAY TO BALRANALD

If you want to stay with the Murrumbidgee, turn onto Cadell Street and follow the strip of bitumen out to the tiny settlement of Maude, 48 km from Hay. At one stage, close to Hay, the road travels through fields of lettuce that are sent down to Melbourne and other coastal cities. Several times the river travels close to the road and you will see billabongs in the floodplains. About 14 km from Hay there is the turn-off to the Hay Weir where, 2 km down the track, you will find sandy banks, tables and opportunities for bush camping.

From Hay Weir, the river leaves the road and takes off through the flat, almost featureless paddocks until it reaches Maude. Semi-trailers use this road and although the bitumen is just wide enough for two cars, it is probably wise and courteous to give trucks the whole road. There are bitter, native paddymelons by the side of the road. As you drive towards the tiny settlement of Maude, you will see its communications aerial rising from the cover of the trees.

Maude, with a population of 60, is set by a weir that was built in 1940. You can't fish near the weir, but there is easy river access elsewhere around here, and you can get bait in the shop. There is a hotel and a shop, as well as more bush camping opportunities. You can also stay in a bunkhouse in the Maude Hotel, as well as get snacks and dinner here. Local information about camping, fishing and general river-based activity is readily available from the pub. Two enormous Murray crays have been mounted on the wall of the pub to show you what can be caught in the area.

The road from Maude back to the Sturt Highway is 58 km across a dirt track. This is a great dry-weather drive through floodplain, pasture, rain channels, black clay, picturesque bill-abongs, cotton fields and wild, flat scrub. There is no river access but in the northern section of the drive you will see the river trees to your north. If the road is wet, it will be slippery and probably impassable, so you will have to return to Hay in order to get to Balranald. But if it is dry, it is an adventurous road and quite beautiful. If you are building your experience to take off to a desert track, this sector will give you a good sense of what kind of road surface and remoteness you will experience out there.

Balranald

Top-class visitor information centres seem to be characteristic of this end of the Murrumbidgee because, yet again the assistance we received at Balranald Heritage Park and Visitor Centre was enthusiastic and informative. Balranald is a service town, set on the Murrumbidgee in country with red sandy soil and scrub ground cover. The streets are wide and the streetscape not especially noteworthy. But the town is very close to the river and the tourism staff are setting up signs that give you some historic information about what was once here.

Several of these signs have been placed along the banks of the river. One gives some information about Charles Sturt, the first European explorer to chart this country. Another describes the inland river transport industry that used to use one of two wharves here. The *Pevensey*, a riverboat that starred as the *Philadelphia* in the TV series 'All the Rivers Run', was made in Balranald. River transport continued to Balranald until the railroad arrived in 1926.

Aboriginal culture is not easily accessible in Balranald at the moment, (or for that matter in any town since Wagga Wagga). However, this may change in the near future. In the meantime, you may like to try to find the scrub-covered red dune on the north-western side of town (head to Endeavour Drive, on the outskirts of town, and follow the dirt track towards the river). This fenced-off dune is an Aboriginal sacred site. There actually isn't anything to see; however, we like to visit these places — if we are allowed — to get a sense of the ancient history of the region.

Balranald has five motels, three hotels, and the Balranald Shire Council Caravan Park (03 5020 1321). You can get dinner in one of the hotels or in the Shamrock Motel; there are also coffee shops in the town centre. Although the Murrumbidgee looks wild, there is no camping along here. The Balranald Tourist Information Centre is open from 8.30 am to 5 pm, Monday to Friday. At the time of printing, it was planning to open at weekends but hadn't announced its opening hours. The staff here can assist you with planning your accommodation in Balranald.

JUNCTION OF THE MURRUMBIDGEE AND THE MURRAY

The easiest access to the junction of the Murrumbidgee and the Murray is actually from the Murray Valley Highway near Boundary Bend on the southern side of the Murray. We have described this in the chapter on the Upper Murray. You can get access to the junction of the two rivers on the northern side of the Murray, although it is on private property and access is restricted. About 29 km past Balranald, there is a signpost leading you to Weimby, 34 km to the west. This takes you close to the junction of the Murrumbidgee and the Murray. However before you go out there, talk to Terry Cook at the Balranald RSL, a member of the Balranald Anglers' Club (03 5020 1205). If Terry is not there, staff at the RSL will direct you to someone else who can assist. There are camping facilities out there erected by the Anglers' Club, and to keep this going, as well as to assist with the restocking of the waterways, there is a $5 per person charge.

4 The Goulburn River
LAKE EILDON TO ECHUCA

A trip down the Goulburn is a journey of surprises as the river changes character with the countryside and the needs of the people who live in the catchment area. Victoria's largest river rises in the wild forest country of the Great Dividing Range near Woods Point. Its natural course is altered by the great dam system at Eildon and the weir at Nagambie. Sometimes the river is a rippling stony creek, sometimes it flows calmly through a town, and at Eildon and Nagambie, it feeds vast lakes. The diversity of the river flow gives this trip down Goulburn River its character. You can leave a busy town where the river sweeps by majestically, and soon find yourself a quiet stretch of water where you can cast a line and relax in the shade of the red river gums and eucalypts. Alternatively you can hire a boat and fish from the middle of one of the lakes.

Away from the water, the pleasures of the Goulburn include regional wine and food. There are several well-known wineries, some boutique wineries, a few good restaurants, and a variety of outlets for local produce. There are also plenty of interesting places to stay, a few excellent places to camp, art galleries, vintage trains and carriages, a little Aboriginal history, a bit of early European settlement history, and some of the best fishing in Victoria.

Once you leave the mountain tracks of the Great Dividing Range and the narrow, winding roads around Lake Eildon, much of the trip is on the Goulburn Valley Highway. Occasionally we recommend alternative routes that run close to the river to pro-

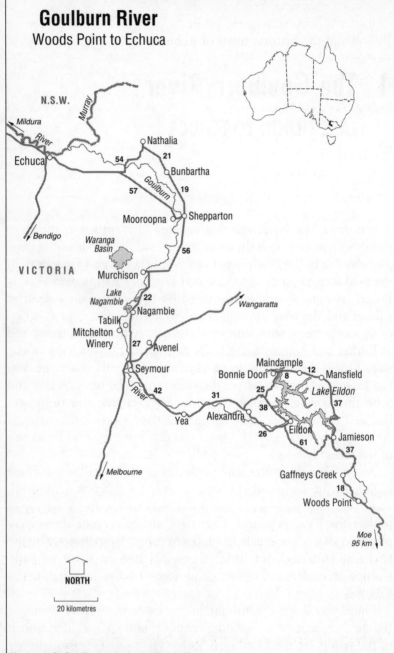

Goulburn River
Woods Point to Echuca

N.S.W.

Mildura

Murray

River

Echuca

Bendigo

VICTORIA

Nathalia

54 21

Bunbartha

57 Goulburn 19

Mooroopna Shepparton

Waranga
Basin

56

Murchison

Lake
Nagambie 22

Nagambie

Tabilk
Mitchelton
Winery

27 Avenel

Wangaratta

Seymour

River 42

31

Yea

Alexandra

Maindample
Bonnie Doon 8 12 Mansfield

25 Lake Eildon

38 37

26 Eildon
61 Jamieson

37

Melbourne

Gaffneys Creek

18

Woods Point

Moe
95 km

NORTH

20 kilometres

Map drawn by Flat Earth Mapping using data from Westprint Maps.
More detailed maps are available from Westprint Maps. Ph (03) 5391 1466.

vide some variation. Several of the highlights along the way are well-known features of the Goulburn, such as the lake system at Eildon and the historic town of Echuca. Other highlights for us were real surprises, for instance the wildness of Woods Point, the excellent collection of vintage train engines and carriages in the Seymour Railway Heritage Centre, and the large SPC canning factory outlet in Shepparton!

Main route

Woods Point — Jamieson — Eildon — Alexandra — Yea — Seymour — Nagambie — Shepparton — Echuca

Maps

Touring Atlas of Australia, Melbourne, Penguin, 2000
Jamieson–Licola Adventure Map: Covering from Aberfeldy to Wonnangatta, Buxton, Victoria, Rooftop Mapping Services, 2001
Lake Eildon, Vicmap Survey and Mapping Victoria, Government of Victoria, 1991
Lake Eildon including Goulburn River, Eildon Pondage, Fishing Map 5, Australian Fishing Network
Seymour and District Blue Guide Handy Map, 1999 (free)
Shepparton District Tourist Map, City of Shepparton, 1993 (free)
Echuca–Moama Blue Guide Handy Map, 2000 (free)

Passes and licences

A Victorian recreational fishery licence is required to fish the Goulburn, its tributaries and billabongs. A NSW Freshwater Recreational Fishing Licence is required to fish in the Murray around Echuca, even if you are fishing from the Victorian bank. The fruit fly zone starts at Nagambie; to protect the fruit industry it is forbidden to carry fruit north of Nagambie along the Goulburn.

Maximum distance between supplies

55 km from Woods Point to Jamieson.

Minimum number of days required in dry conditions

433 km from Woods Point to Echuca via Lake Garry. Three days if you only have time for a quick visit.

Best time of year to visit

The winter months from May to September can bring heavy snow to the headwaters of the Goulburn in the Great Dividing Range. In the summer months, October to April, the weather can vary from hot and dry to just perfect.

Warning

The unsealed roads to and from Woods Point, and around Lake Eildon, can be slippery and dangerous when wet. While the roads would be manageable in a 2WD, a 4WD would be more comfortable. Roads around Woods Point may be closed due to snow in winter; check the road conditions before travelling in winter.

Accommodation and camping

There is plenty of accommodation of all sorts and it should be easy to get outside of school holidays and peak holiday periods. The most comprehensive guide to accommodation along the Goulburn is in the *Goulburn Murray Waters, Victoria : Take to the Waters* booklet, which is published by the Goulburn Murray Waters Campaign Committee and is available free of charge from the tourist centres along the river.

The Visitor Information Centre in Mansfield operates an accommodation reservation service for 130 places in the region; this includes most of the holiday settlements around Eildon. The Echuca Information Centre also offers an accommodation reservation service for a variety of places.

The best bush camping is between Woods Point and Jamieson. There is also bush camping available around Lake Eildon in the National Park. Other than that, the only camping grounds are connected to caravan parks as most of the land along the riverbank is private or government property.

Local information and useful telephone numbers

Parks Victoria Information Centre	13 19 63
Mansfield Visitor Information Centre	toll-free 1800 039 049
Eildon Tourist Centre	03 5774 2909
Alexandra Visitor Information Centre	03 5772 1100
Seymour Regional Visitor Information Centre	03 5799 0233
Nagambie Lakes Visitor Information Centre	03 5794 2647
Shepparton Visitor Information Centre	03 5831 4400 or toll-free 1800 808 839
Echuca Information Centre	toll-free 1 800 804 446
Echuca–Moama Visitor Information Centre, Echuca (accommodation)	03 5480 7555 or toll-free 1800 677 679

THE ROUTE

Woods Point

The Goulburn rises close to Woods Point and this is the place where we begin our journey up the river. The roads leading to Woods Point from Moe or Warburton can be difficult, and suitable only for 4WD when wet. It is a beautiful drive that leads up into the mountains and through old-growth forest. It is 88 km to Woods Point from Moe and only the first 52 km is sealed. The unsealed road is narrow in places, has many potholes, and is stony. When it is wet, it is slippery. It is also steep in places. It is slow driving in any vehicle when it is dry, so a 4WD would be the most comfortable car for this section. But the rough ride is worth it.

The 55 km road south from Jamieson to Woods Point is a better road and we have described it in some detail in this chapter. City access to Jamieson, Mansfield and the other towns around Lake Eildon is via highways and minor sealed roads.

Woods Point is an extraordinary town. It looks and feels like a town straight out of the 19th century. It is a goldmining town, with a population of 39, nestled in the side of the mountains and surrounded by thick forest. The old, lopsided wooden buildings give the town its unique atmosphere in the modern world. In fact, most of the town was burnt out in the horrendous 'Black Friday' 1939 bush fires.

Fuel station in Woods Point

Woods Point is a very friendly and comfortable town to visit. We stayed overnight in the Woods Point Commercial Hotel and had a most enjoyable evening in the mid-20th-century hotel with its first-floor verandah, wooden panelling, high ceilings, wood heating, rustic metal implements hanging out of the rafters, and a great welcome from Don and Ann Woods. We had dinner, a chatty evening learning more of the long history of the town, then a large cooked breakfast that comes as part of the overnight deal, ($35 per head), and coffee in the morning sun on the verandah upstairs (03 5777 8224).

The Goulburn River rises to the north of the town close to the home of one of the local residents. Skinny's home is readily identifiable by the large wooden seats and highly polished red gum mushrooms outside. Skinny has developed the landscape around the river, using stones to channel it through the grassy bank. The river runs under a bridge and southwards before doing a U-turn in the mountains to the east and flowing north towards Lake Eildon. Up here, the bed of the river is stony. Because of this, the trout that you'll catch here are tastier than the trout from the country north of the lake. The flesh is whiter and doesn't have the slightly muddy taste that can sometimes characterise trout. There are plenty of places to fish; local information suggests that the best places are about 2 km south of the town.

The existence of Woods Point is based on goldmining, but the last remaining goldmine is out of bounds. The surrounding countryside is very beautiful with plenty of opportunities to walk and fish. There is a well-stocked shop with a large pot-bellied stove. Here you can get a good selection of maps and books, including the excellent *Rooftop Jamieson–Licola Adventure Map*. Across the road are the public toilets, identifiable with the only neon sign in town announcing their presence! There are two signposted camping grounds with tables, toilets and fireplaces, and both close to the Goulburn. A fee of about $2 is payable in the shop.

WOODS POINT TO JAMIESON

This is an adventure in its own right and the best opportunity for driving along the banks of the Goulburn. The road is winding and narrow in places, has potholes, and is steep. In the course of the drive you will drop up to 400 metres. It is an easy drive for a 4WD even when it is wet, but be aware that in winter, when there is snow, Woods Point may be cut off. The road is unsealed for 42 km north of Woods Point; from there the road is sealed.

Travelling north, the road first travels along by Raspberry Creek, then Gaffneys Creek. About 24 km north of Woods Point the Goulburn joins the road and from there until you get to Jamieson the river is never far away. Sometimes the road rises over a spur and the river is visible in the valley below. Most of the time, the wide, glistening river is within metres of the road, lined by acacias, gums and low ferns. Much of the land along here is private property, so restrict your picnicking and fishing to the generous, signposted reserves along the route.

There are nine designated bush picnic or camping areas with

toilets between Woods Point and Jamieson. In fact, we have never seen so many toilets per kilometre along a bush road before! The camping areas are all located on large grassy clearings by the banks of a creek or, as you get further north, on the banks of the Goulburn itself. There is a small fee for camping in the two campsites between Kevington and Jamieson. The rest are free. This is unquestionably the best camping available along the Goulburn.

History of Woods Point

When gold was found in the creeks around this area in 1861, hardy miners cut their way through the dense forest to try their luck. One of these was a storekeeper named Wood who set up a shop; the settlement became known as Woods Point and grew rapidly. By the end of the 1860s, roughly 2000 people lived here. There were 3 suburbs, 30 hotels, any number of shanty pubs, a brewery, a police station, banks, a post office, and other features of 19th-century Victorian mining towns, including a newspaper and dancing saloons.

The track from Jamieson was the main route into Woods Point. While there was gold to be found, the town prospered. When the gold ran out, there was little to keep many people in such a remote place. By 1927 only one mine was operating, and has continued to operate spasmodically since then.

In 1939 the 'Black Friday' fires killed one resident, and destroyed about 300 houses and buildings. Only seven buildings survived. The locals still have stories to tell about this catastrophic time. After the fire, many people left the area. The town has remained small ever since and, despite the destruction of 1939, still retains the character of a 19th-century mining settlement.

There are several tiny settlements between Woods Point and Jamieson, all with a goldmining background. A1 Settlement is 13 km north of Woods Point. There is very little here, the only real sign that you are in what was until recently a working goldmining settlement, is the 1 km strip of bitumen through the town.

About 4 km north of this is another 19th-century settlement called Gaffneys Creek, named after Red Gaffney, one of the early miners. It was once home to a large population of miners and there are many remnants of their cottages and mines in the hills around the town. There was a hotel here but it burnt down in 1993. The media at the time suggested that the fire had something to do with escaped criminals, Gibb and Butler, who had been assisted by a female prison warder. The trio tried to hide in this area; they spent the night in the hotel and were later arrested by the Goulburn River north of Knockwood Reserve. Local lore insists that the Gaffneys Creek fire was a coincidence of timing and had nothing to do with the prison escapees.

Kevington is another small settlement with its origins in the gold rushes of the 1860s. The Kevington Hotel was established in 1868 and is the last remaining hotel from that period in the region. Kevington is 44 km north of Woods Point and there is little here other than the hotel and a few houses.

About 4 km north of Kevington, the Goulburn crosses the road and there is a lovely picnic spot near the bridge. The forested country of the headwaters of the Goulburn is stunningly beautiful. As you draw closer to Jamieson and leave the Great Dividing Range behind you, the character of the countryside changes. Here, 19th-century settlers cleared the land for agricultural development; they also planted rows of European trees. Native eucalypt forests remain in the national park areas.

Jamieson

This is a small town with a population of about 60, but it doesn't have the small intimate atmosphere of Woods Point. It is fairly spread out and the trees are sparse. It is a service town for the region and, despite its lengthy history as a supply town to the goldmining settlements dating back to 1854, Jamieson doesn't have an old feel. Yet there are several historic buildings, including the 1864 courthouse. The courthouse was used for petty sessions right up until 1977; the long wooden bench is still there. Now the building houses a museum that is open at weekends during the busy summer months. It displays a collection of clothes, farm implements, and other domestic items from the region. The display is changed every year. There is also an emphasis on family history.

Other old buildings, including miners' cottages, have been

preserved. There is a map with a list of historic buildings and sites around Jamieson, giving a potted history of each.

The accommodation ranges from riverside camping to luxurious B&Bs. Jamieson itself has two standard motel/hotels, the Lakeside (03 5777 0515) and the Courthouse (03 5777 0503). You can get cold drinks and pub meals in both of these places. There is also a well stocked shop and service station.

The Goulburn River

This is the largest river in Victoria. It rises in the Dividing Range near Mt Singleton and Woods Point, and flows north for nearly 600 km to join the Murray close to Echuca. It drains a large area and now most of the Goulburn water is diverted for irrigation, firstly via the 1951 Eildon Dam, and further north via the 1891 Goulburn Weir at Nagambie that rises 15 metres above the river bed.

On their pioneering overland trek from NSW to Victoria, the early Australian explorers Hamilton Hume and William Hovell reached what is now called the Goulburn River near the current location of Alexandra. On the way back to the settled areas of NSW, they crossed back over the river again near Seymour and named it the Hovell. But by the time another explorer, Major Mitchell, arrived at the Hovell River in 1836, it had been officially renamed the Goulburn after the Colonial Secretary of NSW. Thomas Mitchell wasn't impressed, preferring Hovell since there was already a Goulburn River in NSW. He noted that the Aboriginal name of the river was Baunga, but that name wasn't used by the settlers either.

JAMIESON TO MANSFIELD

This 37 km journey takes you along a good, sealed road to Mansfield around the east side of Lake Eildon. The lake comprises a network of flooded valleys and is now characterised by a series of inlets with a river or creek flowing into it. At high water level the lake shoreline stretches almost 500 km! Several of the inlets have holiday settlements close to the water, or at least the lake bed. When water levels in Lake Eildon are low, many of the inlets around the jagged bank of the lake are dry, with only the river or creek flowing into it through a narrow channel. The woody weed ground cover only takes about six months to grow and makes the lake bed look as if it has never been covered by water.

The dry inlets continue around the eastern and northern shores of the lake when the water level is low. Even at Bonnie Doon where the Brankeet Inlet is wide, the water level becomes so low sometimes that it is difficult to believe that the town is situated on a lakeside. Nevertheless, there are still great expanses of the lake to be seen in places. The fishing also remains good, particularly if you hire a boat and head out on to the water.

About 25 km north of Jamieson is the turn-off to Goughs Bay, which is 8 km down that road. There is a mass of designated camping sites out along an inlet known as the Delatite Arm, many of them set in pine plantation forest. It is a spacious area, especially if the water level is low! The camping grounds are under the control of Parks Victoria and fees apply. There are toilets and rubbish bins at each of the designated camping areas; fires are not permitted during the summer. Despite the great number of campsites, it is essential to book in writing with Parks Victoria if you want to stay here around Christmas or Easter. This is a very busy camping area all year round and there are usually rangers on duty who will collect your fees.

About 32 km from Jamieson is the turn-off to Delatite Winery and the cellar door outlet. The grapes at Delatite were first planted in 1968 when high-altitude grape growing was not common in Australia. The Ritchie family produced its first vintage in 1982 and the label has been growing in popularity ever since. The cellar is well set up for tastings from its large range of wine, from unwooded chardonnays to late-picked reislings. However, unlike the big wineries around the Goulburn near Nagambie, Delatite celllar door is not an experience in itself. Nonetheless, keen wine drinkers will enjoy this cellar door, as Delatite have several good wines that are only available here.

MANSFIELD

This is a large town (population 3000) that looks after the tourist needs of visitors to the summer water activities on Eildon and the winter snowfields of Mt Buller. The busy Mansfield Visitor Information Centre, in the old railway station, runs an accommodation booking service for 130 registered hotels, motels, boathouses, B&Bs and cottages.

There are several nice places to eat in Mansfield, especially along High Street. Choose from Bon Appetit, the Callopy Street Café, or the Mansfield Hotel, which serves wood-fired pizzas that you can eat in the afternoon sun on the verandah.

There is a gift shop in High Street, beside the banks, where you can buy high-quality locally produced pottery and wooden objects. Pickatooth Pottery, which used to sell its work in the Meat Market in Melbourne, uses this shop as an outlet, with the great advantage that the prices are much lower than Melbourne prices.

There are plenty of river fishing opportunities in the area and fly-fishing for trout is particularly popular. The European pest, carp, have made their way into some of the rivers and creeks, notably the Howqua. Some rivers have managed to stay clear of carp. The Delatite, for example, has several natural and constructed barriers to stop the pest fish making their way upstream. A cold winter will push them all back into the lake, but in the warmer months, be aware that if you go bait fishing, you may catch a carp.

If you are keen to go fly-fishing and don't know what to do, you might consider taking lessons or joining a guided tour. There are several fishing services available here that will provide tuition in the elegant and highly technical skill of fly-fishing, as well as guide you to the best fishing places in the creeks. Tours and tuition tend to be expensive, but you can expect value for money. Out at Merrijig, 21 km east of Mansfield, John and Teresa Pincombe provide lessons on their privately stocked lakes. They also provide guided tours into good fishing places in the river system, with or without tuition. They supply all of the gear, including tackle, lures, meals and transport. Two hour lessons or guided tours are $90 for one person, all day will cost you about $275. Prices vary for groups and different lengths of time (03 5777 5697). For information about other fishing tour operators, contact the Mansfield Visitor Information Centre.

MANSFIELD TO EILDON, VIA THE LAKE EILDON NATIONAL PARK

Leaving Mansfield for Eildon, you can take the back roads through Lake Eildon National Park. This is a beautiful drive, but 16 km of the 58 km journey is along unsealed, windy, narrow and occasionally steep tracks. It is accessible to any vehicle when it is dry, but regardless of what vehicle you are driving, it is a slow drive and too dangerous to try in a hurry.

Before you come to the high road turn-off you will pass one of the highlights of the region, the Bridge Inn Hotel in Maindample. It is 12 km west of Mansfield and was once the centre of a large settlement with a population of 1300 and about 20 shanty pubs. Now Maindample is noticeable by a red boat hanging out of a tree and a large sign saying 'Oh bugger'! The Bridge Inn Hotel has recently been taken over by the Moores, a family that ran the William Creek pub on the Oodnadatta Track in

Sign outside the Bridge Inn Hotel, Maindample

South Australia for many years. They have brought in some of that unique atmosphere that seems to characterise outback South Australian roadhouses — intimidating from the outside, full of warmth and a family environment on the inside. There are sofas around the fireplaces and a kids' play corner. You can also get excellent caffe lattes and cappuccinos, as well as large slices of delicious cakes. On Thursdays, the Moores fly down to Phillip Island to get fresh fish. Their fish platters are renowned, so if you want to eat there on a Thursday or Friday, it would be wise to book (03 5778 7281). The seemingly extreme nature of this flying shopping mission falls into perspective when you realise that this was once a family that could park its plane outside its door in the outback!

About 7 km west of Maindample is the signposted turn-off to Eildon via Lake Eildon National Park. The Eildon National Park covers a vast region and was once made up of two parks, Fraser National Park and Eildon State Park. It contains many bush walks, track drives suitable only for 4WD, excellent camping opportunities with or without facilities, loads of places to fish, and heavenly places to sit and read, or sleep under the stars.

The northern section of this high road is known as Maintongoon Road, the southern section as Skyline Road. The scenery along here is stunning as the road (most unsealed) first travels high above the eastern bank of the Brankeet Inlet, then up into the eucalypt forests of the national park. In sections, there is old-growth forest to the east and grazing country to the west. There are only a few designated lookout points along here, one of which is just before you reach the bitumen.

The high road meets the northern road between Alexandra and Eildon 35 km after Maindample. A side road at this junction leads to the Fraser Camping Area, one of the popular designated camping sites in the national park. From the junction, it is an easy 11 km into Eildon following the south side of Lake Eildon National Park.

If this route through the National Park is too wet to travel safely, you can of course take the long route from Mansfield to Eildon. The 93 km journey travels along the highway via Alexandra.

JAMIESON TO EILDON (ALTERNATIVE ROUTE VIA BIG RIVER)

This narrow, windy and mostly sealed 61 km road travels between the Lake Eildon National Park to the north and the Rubicon State Forest to the south. It is another very attractive drive through the forest that it is possible for all vehicles, although careful driving is required.

Besides the sheer beauty of driving through eucalypt forest, the only major feature is Big River. It flows along by the road for about 3 km before joining Lake Eildon at the Big River Inlet. Darlingford, the town completely submerged by the development of the lake, was at the northern end of the inlet. This was the junction of Big River and the Goulburn River.

Darlingford and Lake Eildon

Darlingford began as a settlement in the 1850s to supply local gold prospectors, particularly along the Big River. As Jamieson and other supply towns closer to the mining action grew, the people of Darlingford turned to agriculture on the lush river flats. At its height, Darlingford had a hotel, a post office, a store, and a shearing shed that doubled as a dance hall.

Darlingford was first flooded when the small irrigation dam, the Sugarloaf, was built between 1914 and 1927. Sugarloaf was designed to harness the water flowing into the valleys from the numerous rivers and creeks that drain the area. Then in the 1950s, the great dam and weir of Eildon was created and a network of valleys was flooded to become Lake Eildon. Darlingford was completely submerged. On occasions of very low water, the ruins of the town can be seen.

Eildon

Eildon is a functional town that looks after the immediate needs of the many holidaymakers, particularly families, who come here regularly. The small town, which was built in the 1950s for the dam construction workers, is about half a kilometre off the Goulburn Highway. Disappointingly, there is no great sense of 1950s nostalgia about the small U-shaped town centre. Holiday towns are problematic for passing visitors; out of season they look a bit scruffy and tired, in season they are much too crowded for comfort. But the spin-off for visitors on a driving holiday down the Goulburn River is that it is easy to do things here, like hire a boat or buy bait and other fishing-related equipment.

There are numerous take-aways and cafés; the Sugarloaf Restaurant in the centre of town has a pleasant atmosphere. There is also plenty of accommodation from six budget-priced caravan parks, five motels, self-contained units, houseboats, camping grounds, and a few very luxurious and expensive B&Bs. The caravan parks are large; the 30-acre Eildon Caravan Park is at the west end of town, while the 25-acre Blue Gum Caravan Park is on the Goulburn River. Both are set close to the water and are hidden by trees. They provide self-contained cabins, as well as the usual variety of accommodation that you get in caravan parks. The Eildon Tourist Centre can provide you with a list of the 18 or so places of accommodation, but can't give you prices.

If you want to camp there is a popular camping area in the National Park at Jerusalem Creek, 10 km from Eildon township. Jerusalem Creek has bush camp sites with fireplaces, toilet blocks, tables, shelters and water. Fees are payable at the honesty box at the entrance to the campsite (it costs $8.30 per vehicle for up to four people). Other designated campsites, similar to caravan park sites, have a set fee of $14 per site. For bookings during busy times call (03 5772 1293).

Other services in Eildon include a service station, police station, a playground and picnic tables. On Christmas Eve, there is a large street party, the shops open late and alcohol is well controlled to ensure it is a family day (there is only one pub in town, so that helps). At Easter Eildon hosts a well-known 'trash and treasure' market that attracts a lot of people. During this time it is difficult to move in Eildon and impossible to find parking.

The Eildon Tourist Centre is open from 10 am to 2 pm, seven days a week. It is staffed by volunteers and during peak periods they open for longer hours. The Alexandra Visitor Information Centre also has information about Eildon.

LAKE EILDON

The Lake Eildon dam, about 1 km from the town, is the focus of the lake system. The Goulburn Highway leads to the dam wall and a lookout between the spillway and the lake. From here there are photogenic views out over the lake, the spillway, and the pondage to the west, and the huge metal gate to the Goulburn River beyond. The lake is spectacular, surrounded by steep inaccessible mountainous slopes covered by trees.

The mechanics of the dam and the irrigation and hydro-electric systems are explained on charts at the car park. The anonymous, dull-looking buildings that always seem to be associated with electricity generation are nestled into the hillside below, but they don't detract from the views. High on the ridge over the carpark lookout you will find a shelter marking Pinniger Lookout. From below it looks dramatically high, but it is only a 20-minute drive from the spillway along a mostly sealed road. There is a small shelter and a BBQ up here.

EILDON BOAT HARBOUR

For a change of pace and a little activity, go down to the Eildon Boat Harbour. When you leave the dam, turn right and follow the signs. When the water level is low, the slipways and steps that normally provide direct access to the water are suspended halfway down the side of the grassy slopes. But whether the water is high or low, you will still be able to launch a boat here.

There are toilets, a shop, and other basic facilities. You can hire a wide range of boats from Lake Eildon Holiday Boats at the Boat Harbour. Choose from luxurious holiday boats to small aluminium six-seater powerboats ($30 per hour). The Boat Harbour also sells tackle and bait. The staff in the Boat Harbour centre are happy to chat about fishing on the lake and give you advice. As well as supplying fishing and general Eildon information, the Boat Harbour sells fishing licences and general supplies.

FISHING AT EILDON

One of the main reasons so many people take holidays at Eildon all year round is for the fishing. There are plenty of opportunities to fish around Eildon. Firstly there is the lake itself, then there is the pondage that stretches out to the west of the dam, and of course there are the creeks and rivers that feed the lake.

European settlement in the Goulburn region

In 1837 squatters were permitted to take up as large a run as they could stock on Crown land for a small fee. This coincided with the settlement of Melbourne and a wider push for land outside the settled areas. Peter Snodgrass was the first European squatter to arrive at the Goulburn, settling near Yea in 1837. He was quickly followed by other young men and their stock, sheep and cattle.

The early squatters were often middle-class men of independent means who had migrated from Britain; many who came to the Goulburn were of Scottish origin. In preparation for heading out into barely charted country, the squatters gathered sufficient funds to buy a large herd of cattle or a flock of sheep. They bought supplies for a year, hired staff, including shepherds to look after their flocks in fenceless lands, and headed overland from NSW with a team of bullocks and a dray.

Once out here in the bush, the men lived in very rugged conditions for a few years. They had no tenure over the land in the early days so there was little point in building an elaborate house. A well-set-up home was a sod hut with an earthen floor, a stone or mud chimney, a bark roof, basic furniture made from local timber, and perhaps a bookshelf. Windows were unglazed, but might have had shutters that could be closed in bad weather.

By 1839 most of the Goulburn River country had been taken up by squatters. It was a tough life, made worse by the recession in the 1840s. The squatters' assets were in their stock, and if anything happened to that they could be ruined. Quarantine methods to control the spread of disease were not effective in the 1840s and 1850s. In fact, the Upper Goulburn was one of the last areas in Victoria to eliminate scab, a skin condition that caused sheep to lose condition. Dingos and native cats threatened their stock numbers, as did the cattle duffers and bushrangers.

Communication was also difficult, as the tracks into the heavily timbered area and between holdings were hard going, often muddy and wet, or overgrown. River fords were unpredictable — sometimes passable, sometimes a raging torrent. As sheep and cattle prices fell dramatically, the pastoralists could no longer afford to keep their shepherds. In a desperate response a tallow and skin industry was established. This proved moderately successful, and allowed some pastoralists to survive. The down side of this was the stinking smells of burning mutton at the tallow works along the valley. Then, as families moved in the late 1840s and laws were changed to improve tenure, the pastoralists built houses and farm buildings, and a community life developed.

The next threat to the squatters came with another change in law and the arrival of the selectors. When the population of Victoria increased dramatically, following the goldrushes of the 1850s, the demand for land from smaller farmers was huge. With male suffrage, the government had to listen to these calls to 'unlock the land'. The size of the squatters' licenced areas was reduced when selector farmers moved in on their water frontage in smaller lots. Rentals for the land also increased so much that squatters could no longer afford to maintain large station runs, and by the mid-1870s the squatters along the upper Goulburn had all but vanished. The selectors who bought up the land were often family men who had tried their luck on the goldfields with mixed success. They were drawn to the Alexandra area by the potential for a gold find, and then remained, managing to buy a small block of land with income from mining work.

For total beginners, the Eildon Trout Farm is a good place to start. A catch is virtually guaranteed, so beginners can experience the feeling of a fish wriggling at the end of the line, control the flapping about on the ground, and experience the joys of gutting and cleaning a fish. In fish farms your catch is weighed, and you usually pay by the weight. Some people maintain that farm trout don't have the same flavour as wild trout, but it is good for beginners to learn what to do if they actually land a big one in the bush. All of the necessary equipment including lines and baits, and cleaning and gutting facilities are available at the Trout Farm. Trout paté, smoked trout and fresh fish are also available for purchase.

Eildon provides for all-year-round boat and bank fishing. There is no closed season on the dam or in the pondage. You will need a licence to fish in any of these places, which you can get at the Eildon Garage, at Eildon Industries in the shopping centre, or at the Eildon Boat Harbour. You can hire a boat at the Boat Harbour, or take a charter with Ivor Bumbers of Eildon Industries. Ivor's charter boat accommodates up to five people and costs $75 per hour with a minimum of two hours. The advantage of this is that you will get inside information and advice from

Ivor — always useful if you are not a confident angler. You can also hire tackle, as well as buy tackle and bait from him (03 5774 2712).

Lake Eildon holds rainbow and brown trout, redfin, yellow belly and Murray cod. Redfin can be caught by spinning from the bank or out of a boat, or by using yabbies as live bait on a hook. Trout can be caught by trolling, fly-fishing in the upper reaches, or by using bait. Seek local advice from the bait and tackle shop, they should be able to tell you where the fish are being caught and what bait is the one to use. Don't be put off if you are told to use maggots, as they attract trout and other fish. Used in conjunction with a ground-bait cage they can be dynamite bait.

The pondage is home to some very big trout, thanks to periodic releases of stock from Snobs Creek Hatchery when their role as brood fish has ceased. The dates are deliberately not announced as the trout are so disorientated when they are released into the water that you could catch them by hand. So to give the fish a chance to acclimatise, the release dates are closely guarded secrets. When releases do take place, and the word gets out, the banks are lined with anglers trying their luck. Here again, the choice of fishing styles is up to the angler. Fly-fishing can be successful in some areas of the pondage, whereas bait fishing using a variety of baits can be effective in other areas. Lure fishing can be successful too and, once again, local advice will point you to the direction of the popular lures.

EILDON TO ALEXANDRA VIA THORNTON

There are two roads between Eildon and Thornton — the Goulburn Highway and the back road. Both are pleasant drives of around 26 km through agricultural land punctuated by rows of poplars, elms, oak and other European trees. In autumn, the colours on the landscape are glorious. Both roads are well sign-posted. The Goulburn Highway runs along the south side of the pondage, the Back Road is on the north side. About 200 metres from the town on the back road you will see the fishing platform designed for wheelchair access. At the end of the pondage is the massive weir gate leading to the Goulburn River.

The roads meet near the distinctive blue hotel in Thornton

Woven baskets at Camp Coorong Ngarrindjeri Aboriginal Cultural Centre
(PHOTO: BILL BACHMAN)

Trout fishing on the Delatite River (PHOTO: BILL BACHMAN)

The pondage at Lake Eildon (PHOTO: GARRY TICKNER)

where there are spillover tourist facilities for the Eildon region. The Acheron River runs through the township and you will find some good trout fishing; almost all river fishing styles will catch fish here.

Thornton is also home to Snobs Creek Hatchery. The hatchery was once open to the general public and the entire process of breeding trout was on display. Now, in order to maintain high levels of hygiene, visitors are only permitted to go into the discovery centre. It is open Friday to Monday, 11 am to 4 pm; the entrance fee is $5.50 for adults, children $2.75. We would suggest that its main value now is for groups of school kids on an excursion.

Alexandra

Alexandra is a pretty town that sees its role as providing a range of services to the region, including Eildon. It isn't promoted as having features that encourage visitors to travel out of their way to see it. However, the town itself is charming, with several attractive 19th-century buildings and an excellent parkland. Following the brown tourist signs, we also found a good pottery and an old railway museum. The Visitor Information Centre, staffed by friendly and knowledgeable volunteers, is on Grant Street, near the historic shire hall. Across the road from the Visitor Centre is parkland with several clean BBQs, tables, toilets, and a fenced playground.

The activity of the town is focused on the busy shopping centre in Grant Street where there are several inviting coffee shops and other stores including one that combines a large vegetable shop with an antique outlet. There are several old pubs along this street. The Shamrock Hotel, in the centre of the shopping strip, is renowned for its meals. The quality of the food, with menu items such as whole baby snapper, is well above average for a pub meal (03 5772 1015). You can also get accommodation here in single and double rooms, none with ensuite (roughly $25 per head).

Around the corner from the Shamrock Hotel, in a converted church on Downey Street, is the Alexandra Pottery. Katelyne and Wytze Kylstra make pottery from local clay and have some of the natural substance in the shop. They can tell you about the process of converting the raw clay into pottery. They produce a range of items — large bowls and plates, mugs, jugs, cheese dishes and vases — many painted in bold colours and in several different styles. Their shop is heated by an ingenious construction involving a 44 gallon drum with a brick lining.

Alexandra Timber Tramway and Museum

The Alexandra Timber Tramway and Museum is hidden away in the old railway station on Station Street, off Vickery Street, about 1.2 km from the Information Centre. The rail line to Alexandra was built in 1909 after years of lobbying by the local community. The trains ran for over 40 years but often with very few passengers. On one occasion in 1930, there were nine passengers and six crew! The timber industry brought some business but the Alexandra rail line incurred losses most of the time. The line closed to regular traffic in the 1950s, finally beaten by the motor car. Today there are lots of bits and pieces gathered at the museum associated with the railroad and Alexandra's agricultural past. These include steam engines and tractor wagons that used timber wheels with solid steel threads, farming implements, the narrow-gauge iron, bits of engines and carriages, and lots of well-used metal equipment. The highlight of the collection is the 1909 Fowler Locomotive; the brightly painted engine now looks a bit like a toy train.

Outside, Ernie Le Brun, a local man with many years of milling experience in the region, has built some large-scale models of typical buildings found at sawmill settlements. They are boxy, wooden buildings with corrugated fireplaces lined with stone. These cottages would have provided the most rudimentary of accommodation for timber workers. The Museum is open on the second Sunday in the month, when you can also get a ride on the restored 1909 steam train. You could also get a trip on the 1939 diesel locomotive, the first to be built in Victoria. Even if the museum itself isn't officially open, you can still see the old railway station, historic train engines and carriages, the model buildings and other relics of pioneering history, all of which are accessible.

FISHING

Now for the fishing — and the Goulburn River at Alexandra is pretty good. The river crosses the Maroondah Highway 2.5 km to the west of Alexandra. There is a small carpark on the west side of the bridge. The river is beautiful here, particularly in autumn when the colours of native and deciduous trees are reflected in the rippling water.

Fishing access is better out by the Breakaway Caravan Park, south of Alexandra. The long way around to the caravan park is to drive 10 km west of Alexandra on the Maroondah Highway, then turn east and follow the signposts to the caravan park about 2 km down the road. The short way is to drive south along Grant Street in the town itself and keep going for 6 km. This will take you to an old attractive wooden bridge over the Goulburn. It may or may not be there when you visit because it is in poor condition and, as we write this, the shire is deciding whether to preserve it or let it go.

There is some fine trout fishing at the Breakaway. People have been known to catch trout of up to 3.5 kg around there, but the average trout would be about 30 centimetres long, or about 0.5–1 kg. The Breakaway was formed around 1914–6, when farming activity and levee building forced the river to alter course. The bridge was built at about the same time. The Breakaway is close to the confluence of the Acheron River and the Goulburn, another indicator for good fishing. The wide banks are ideal for fly-fishing.

The Breakaway Twin Caravan Park has a variety of accommodation, including self-contained cabins, powered and unpowered sites, as well as the usual facilities of a caravan park. Prices range from $15 for unpowered sites in off-peak periods, to $75 for the air-conditioned apartment in peak periods (03 5772 1735).

History of Alexandra

In the 1850s and 1860s, small farmers moved into the Upper Goulburn area. They had few resources and life was hard. Besides dealing with the hazards of the land and the destruction of crops by dingos, kangaroos, possums and rabbits, they had rates and selection fees to pay. The markets for the produce were inaccessible and many of the farmers failed. However, the discovery of gold in the district brought change, bringing the markets closer. The town of Alexandra grew in this environment. The first settlement was near a gate in the track between two properties; this gave the town its first name of Red Gate. The town prospered for a while. Community life was lively with dances, debating, church functions, annual agricultural shows and other activities.

During the goldmining boom, the town had a shanty look to it with most buildings being slab huts or lean-to shanties. There were 24 hotels at one stage. Sly grog was readily available. Indeed, the first shanty was erected by an enterprising man who realised that there was money to be made from thirsty goldminers. His first dray load of beer was tapped while still on the dray! The publican was so successful that he built a large hotel with a ballroom and offices. Chinese market gardeners supplied the growing population with fresh vegetables, and an Irishman opened a bakery.

The town was still pretty much a shanty town surrounded by partly cleared scrub with unsealed roads when it was declared a shire and named Alexandra after the Princess of Wales in 1869. The shire hall was built in 1882. After the number of miners in the area dwindled in the 1880s and 90s, the town survived as a service centre to the local agricultural industry.

The caravan park staff will give you advice on where the fish are biting and what bait to use. They gather information from the keen fisherfolk who will tell them whether the fish are going for worms or maggots or flies, but won't necessarily tell them where exactly they caught the fish. A very large trout named 'Harry Humungous' lives under the bridge. It is believed that it must be about 50 centimetres long. Visitors pop into the small shop at the caravan site and tell the staff that they have just seen a whopper but not to tell anyone! Harry Humungous has been around for a long time; he seems to have learnt to stay close to the bridge to avoid being caught.

ALEXANDRA TO YEA

The Goulburn Highway south of Yea travels through pasture land, sometimes with a five metre strip of native trees. The Strathbogie Ranges are to the north of this 31 km stretch of road and the Great Dividing Range is to the south.

About 3 km south-west of Molesworth, there is a large bill-abong called Sheepwash Lagoon close to the main road that has good fishing potential. There is a pleasant parking and picnic area under the trees beside the lagoon. If you are lucky, you may catch tench, carp, roach, redfin, blackfish and — if there has been flood

Sheepwash lagoon

The billabong got its name during the early pioneering days when John Cotton washed his sheep here prior to shearing. This was not unusual in itself, clean wool could increase the value of the clip in the marketplace by up to 50%. The traditional method was to wash each sheep individually in a dam with about six men rubbing and squeezing the wool. However, Cotton developed a more efficient method of washing the sheep by setting up a spray system in this lagoon. The sheep were soaked in a dam for about half an hour, then held under a spout of water for ten minutes. This reduced the number of men required to assist and they could do a more thorough job. The sheep were then left to dry in a clean paddock for several days before they were shorn and the wool was baled. Cotton was fortunate in having a large lagoon as most pastoralists didn't have the natural resources suitable for such a process. Hence the name of the lagoon.

connection between the billabong and the river — you might get trout. They don't breed here, they just get fat on the smaller fish.

At Molesworth, contact with the river is brief. The highway travels over it, a modern bridge running alongside an old railway bridge. Then we lose the river again as it vanishes off into the distance.

Yea

The spacious town of Yea is another service town in the region with a wide range of facilities for travellers. It is set on a tributary to the Goulburn, the Yea River. At first glance there doesn't seem to be much to excite the traveller, but again, there are a few surprises.

One of the first surprises we came across was in the large, ordinary looking supermarket in the centre of town. This was once called The Empire Store and was established in 1882. It was never an elegant or glamorous place. However, inside, near the bottle shop section that displays cask and flagon wine, is a new wooden staircase leading to a cellar. A sign invites you down to the original 19th-century cellar. This is a joy. The cellar is cool and musty-smelling with a constant temperature of 12–14°c. The well-worn wooden shelves look original, and overhead metal railway lines have been used to support the floor above. In one corner of the cellar is a mechanical loading mechanism leading to a trap door. On sale here is a range of good Victorian wines such as Plunkett, Traeger, Passing Clouds and Tahbilk. A series of photos tells you about the original owner who ran the store at the turn of the 20th century.

Down the road, Marmalade's Café sells the best cakes along the river. The simple-looking homemade cakes are moist and full of interesting flavours. The genteel wooden café is situated in the renovated 1887 Commercial Store and has retained the heavy wooden features of a country grocery store. On Friday and Saturday nights you can get dinner here also. It has been receiving awards and recognition from Australian food experts, including being the winner of the 'Top Victorian Place to Visit' in *Mietta's Guide to Eating and Drinking 2001*. Two self-contained units attached to it are used for B&B at prices ranging from $130 to $150 (03 5797 2999).

Next door, the Country Club Hotel will give you an unintentional surprise if you stop there for dinner. The servings of home-cooked food are huge. We are not sure quite what the market is but someone must want to eat that much food in a single sitting! The menu is reasonably extensive and a bit more interesting than the average hotel. With main courses at about $15, it is pretty standard for rural hotels. John had an excellent roasted local trout that had a well-textured flavour.

About 2 km east of Yea on Killingworth road is Yea River Gallery, a recent addition to the town's secrets. Access to the gallery is clearly signposted; the turn-off to Killingworth road is 800 metres from the Mobil petrol station on the east side of town, and the track out to the gallery is 1.8 km along the road. The Yea Gallery is in a restored wool building. It is owned by Jim Walduck, who used to run a gallery at Red Hill, on the Mornington Peninsula. He has gathered a wondrous collection of art, including local paintings and drawings, 19th-century prints, Chinese basket-wear and pottery from all over Australia. The gallery is open from Thursday to Sunday, 10 am to 5 pm.

Killingworth Road runs along the Yea River Wetland Walk, a peaceful bush path that has been laid out in the wetlands around the Yea River. It is close to town and within walking distance from the motels and town centre. A walking guide from the tourist centre will tell you what to look out for, including black swans, coots, swamp hens, cormorants, kingfishers and moorhens. It also points out the regrowth of the natural vegetation of the region, such as the tea tree and the swamp gum, following the removal of imported willows, ivy and honeysuckle.

Accommodation in Yea is available in one of the two motels, or in the caravan park. Yea Motel is off the main road on Millers Street and is about $60 per night for two (03 5797 2660). The Tartan motel is situated in the town centre (03 5797 2202). The Yea Family Caravan Park is situated on the banks of the Yea River on Millers Street and attracts keen birdwatchers and enthusiastic fishing people (03 5797 2972). The Country Club Hotel is one of several in the town that provides accommodation; its rooms are

Taungurong people

The traditional lands of the Taungurong Aboriginal people were around the Goulburn catchment area near Eildon, Alexandra and Yea. They are part of the Kulin nation, sharing similar languages and intermarrying with people of the country as far south as Melbourne. In the 1840s, they lost access to their land when the European squatters moved in. When Peter Snodgrass, the first squatter, arrived he estimated that there were 500–600 people living in the region. But smallpox, flu, tuberculosis and other European diseases may already have taken their toll because they indicated to Snodgrass that they had once been more numerous. The Aboriginal people got on well with some of the settlers, working with them and for them. Squatters who treated them badly soon found themselves without local labour.

According to the squatter John Cotton, the Taungurong lived in temporary shelters with bark and thickly leaved branches supporting beams to a height of about 1.4 metres. They lit a fire in here for cooking and heating. They had bags, spears, tomahawks and shields as part of their basic equipment. They wore their hair in ringlets. Cotton described a corroboree that he attended: the women and children sat in a circle and beat time on their possum skins, making a sound a bit like a muffled drum. A male singer beat time with a stick. The dancers then came out of the darkness and danced and clapped sticks around the blazing fire. There was continuous music and dancing for two hours.

Like the other Kulin people, the Taungurong were prepared to work with the colonists and establish a new lifestyle for themselves. They needed land to be able to farm like the white settlers, and access to rations, equipment and other supplies. In 1841 a reserve was established at Murchison by the Board for the Protection of Aborigines. However, William Le Souef, the Protector, was a harsh man who was dismissed on grounds of cruelty and misappropriation of government supplies in 1843. Then rations to the reserve stopped, and over the following years, neighbouring squatters took over the Aboriginal reserve land. The Protectorate was finally disbanded in 1849.

William Thomas, an official with the Protectorate in Melbourne, worked hard to try to secure land and a reasonable deal for the Aboriginal people. He worked closely with clan leaders and came up with various workable solutions. One of these was to establish a station in Acheron, south of Alexandra in 1859. The land was selected by the Aboriginal people, it was marked out, and crops were planted, including five acres of wheat and ten acres of potatoes. It was also intended to run 1500 sheep. It had the potential to be a reasonable solution, the elderly and sick had a place to stay, the younger people could farm the land and, when rations were scarce, go out and find work. It seemed secure. Peter Snodgrass, the squatter and by then a member of parliament, was appointed as the local Protector. But by this stage, land politics in Victoria were volatile and destabilising the Government. The squatters were a powerful force trying desperately to retain their lands. The land interests of the Aborigines were at the bottom of the priority list.

At Yea, Hugh Glass, a well-connected local squatter, coveted the land of neighbouring Aborigines at Acheron. Snodgrass, an associate of Glass, appeared to act in the squatter's interest rather than the people he had been appointed to protect. After nearly two years on the Acheron property, the Taungurong were forced by Snodgrass to move off the land they had cultivated and onto a much poorer station to the south of it. The Aborigines knew that it was poor land, it was cold and would be bad for their ill and old folk. But Snodgrass insisted, ordering the European superintendent to move them. Later when the superintendent went back to the Acheron property to check on the crops, he found that the fences had been deliberately broken and the crops destroyed by cattle.

In 1863, 117 surviving members of the Kulin, including the Taunguroug, were listed by officials. A year later, 67 were settled in Coranderrk, now near Healesville.

above the bar and bistro with single rooms at about $25, double rooms at $35. Family rooms are also available. They all have shared bathroom facilities.

YEA TO SEYMOUR

The Yea River meets the Goulburn River 7 km by road northwest of the town on the Ghin Ghin Road. This is one of the recommended fishing locations near Yea. Ghin Ghin Road turn-off is 3 km from Yea and 35 km from Seymour. It is signposted from either direction. The road drops down into the river valley to the north of the main Goulburn Valley Highway. Several old wooden bridges take the road over the creeks to the junction of the Yea and Goulburn Rivers. You can fish here, ideally on the south side of the bank because the inflow water is dirty and the trout and redfin tend to be in the cleaner water picking up the food from the dirty water. No camping or fires permitted. It is a pretty place, and a popular fishing location with a launching ramp for boats. It has been spoiled a bit by careless visitors who leave rubbish and ignore the fire bans. But there is enough space to find a clean spot. To get back to the Goulburn Highway, return the way you came.

Yea

Yea began as a shanty settlement on the river and was originallly named Muddy Creek by Hume and Hovell. In 1855 the Surveyor General, Andrew Clarke, sent one of his surveying staff, out to the settlement to lay out a town formally. As a result of that visit, the settlement was renamed Yea after a Crimean war hero, Colonel Lacy Yea. Colonel Yea had been Clarke's commanding officer in England about 15 years earlier and had been particularly popular with his fusiliers. He led them from the front, taking his turn in the trenches in Crimea. He organised hospital huts for his wounded, and took a keen interest in their welfare. Five months before the surveyor arrived at Muddy Creek, Yea was killed in battle. Reports in the paper contributed to his heroic status, and emphasised the great affection his men had for him. His name was pronounced 'Yaw', but calling the small settlement 'Yaw' was considered an affectation and it vanished from use to be replaced by 'Yay'. Nearby Molesworth was also named after a war hero who fell in the same battle.

The drive between Yea and Seymour is through pasture country, with the Strathbogie Ranges in the distance to the north. Several tracks lead north from the main road towards the river but it is private property and you can't go fishing there unless you have permission from the owners. For visitors passing through, it is possibly best to stick to the standard fishing areas. In terms of actually catching fish or indeed the number of fish you catch, it makes little difference.

The Trawool Valley Resort will jump out at you along this stretch of road. This was once a great soldiers' pub, a pokey place where the elderly owner would serve the young soldiers large steaks. Now there is a multistorey modern building with its own lake, lawns, trees, a car park, tennis court, gazebo and panoramic views over the valley. The dining rooms are spacious and comfortable with wide windows. There is a big log fire in one corner, and a glass garden restaurant for residents. The cost for rooms is $95 and upwards for two, with a luxury suite at $260 per night.

Just down the road on the western side are the Rosehill Guest Cottages. The gardens of this cottage were planted in the 1880s by Ferdinand von Mueller, the government botanist and influential director of the Botanic Gardens in Melbourne. The coffee shop serves Devonshire teas. You can sit and relax on a verandah overlooking the garden, with the valley and mountains beyond.

John as a young soldier fishing in the region

John came out to Australia from England by himself at the age of 16. He joined the regular army, did his recruit training and was then posted to the 1st Armoured Regiment. As a young soldier based in Puckapunyal (near Seymour) in Victoria in the 1960s, he used to go fishing near Trawool and catch coarse fish like tench, carp and roach. He threw those ones back, it was fun just to catch them, and there were no rules at the time about not returning carp to the water. Any redfin caught were kept for the pot. Access to the billabongs was through private property but John, knowing that permission was rarely given to young soldiers, would sneak through the fields and scrub to fish in one of the many billabongs along this stretch of the river.

This was such good fishing country that he used every opportunity to fish. When he was on sentry duty at one of the entrances to the tank-firing range, he would take a handline and a few worms in the hope that he would be close to one of the many creeks that ran through the Puckapunyal range. A narrow and mostly shallow creek under Mt Puckapunyal regularly produced redfin up to 2 kg, with garden worms as the prime bait. A dozen or so redfin broke the monotony of sentry duty. Other creeks such as Sugarloaf Creek, near the old Hume Highway, were the source of brown trout, and he would usually go after tench and carp in the billabongs.

In the very early days, John brought the cleaned and gutted fish to the army cooks who were happy to cook them for him. The excess fish went to mates in the camp's married quarters.

Seymour

Seymour is a large town that used to thrive on the nearby army base at Puckapunyal, although the young soldiers were not particularly welcome in the past! As you travel in from the east you will see the former army married quarters, neat box-like buildings that line the street on the Goulburn Valley Highway from the east.

It is now a service town, but has an interesting centre based on its mid-19th-century role as the crossing place of the Goulburn on the main route between Sydney and Melbourne. The Goulburn snakes around the town with a large bend by the Goulburn River Caravan Park on the south of the town, and comes close to the historic area on the north of the town.

Old Seymour is close to the Seymour Regional Visitor Information Centre and this is a good place to start your visit, as it is easy to find using signposts. The staff here will give you a guide to historic Seymour, most of which is within walking distance of the Centre. The Information Centre itself is in the old courthouse on Emily Street, which was once the Hume Highway. The maze of rooms that made up the magistrate's court are open to the public. All of the features of the courtroom are there including the dock, the clerk's desk and the bench. The courtroom now displays Australian art. The Information Centre is in an adjacent room, and is thoroughly stocked with material on the region.

Opposite the Information Centre is the Old Post Office Gallery, which was the first post office building but is now an art gallery and restaurant. The surroundings are elegant and ideal for time out at lunchtime, or a luxurious dinner with an interesting international menu. It is also a gallery that displays a wide range of award winning Australian artists with an emphasis on pottery and painting.

Down the road from the Old Post Office Gallery is the Royal Hotel, made famous by Drysdale's painting, *The Cricketers*, painted in 1910 when the pub was known as Moody's. The Royal Hotel was built in three stages, the first stage was in 1848, the second in 1852 and the front of the hotel in the 1890s. Sadly, by some legal necessity, the old two-storey verandah was removed in the 1970s. Inside, the hotel looks like any other rural pub, with a long bar and a bistro to one side and few notable features. It serves good pub food.

To the west of the Royal Hotel, there is a small concrete stall that is the source of Stella Salakowski's famous hamburgers that have been made to a secret recipe since the 1950s. Now the hamburgers are so well known that travellers 'in the know' still take a diversion off the Seymour bypass simply to buy one. The burgers are made on a hot plate inside a window; all transactions with the public are through a string-covered hatch retaining the atmosphere of the original caravan stall. Give the burgers a go — they are fabulous!

Stella Salakowski's famous hamburger stall, Seymour

There are other old buildings along Emily Street, most with 20th-century additions. The single sheet historic guide of the town will give you good information about these. The banks of the Goulburn are around the back of the Royal Hotel where there is a carpark and good fishing access.

Then when you have finished exploring the old part of town, one further joy awaits you on the other side of town — the

Seymour Railway Heritage Centre. Give yourself lots of time there, this is one of the highlights of the Goulburn Valley.

The Railway Heritage Centre is situated in the old railway yards on the southern side of the railway line off Watson Street. Access is not well-signposted; if the street map lets you down, use the railway line to guide you here. The large yard is crowded with railway engines and carriages. For the rail enthusiast, this is heaven because the fleet is so large and so much of it is operational. The place is run by volunteers, many of whom once worked on the railroads. The Centre began in 1983 when a steam locomotive was transferred to Seymour from the Newport rail yards in Melbourne for restoration. The job took four-and-a-half years to complete, and the locomotive is now used for special trips along the tracks.

The jewel in the Heritage Centre's fleet is the Yarra Parlour Car, an elegant old-fashioned carriage with lead-lighting in the windows, ornate ceiling, panelled walls, heavy lights, tasselled curtains, upholstered bench seats along either side, the original brass fan, and open rear platform that is decorated with metal lacework. It was designed to provide elegant comfort to 1st class travellers who travelled between Sydney and Albury in the early decades of the 20th century. Originally passengers would have been sitting in armchairs but these proved too difficult for the modern restorers to maintain so bench seating was installed. You can see similar armchairs in the smoking section at the other end of this carriage. This is a smaller section but no less elegant. In between is a kiosk and other crew facilities to cater for passenger comfort.

Another gem is known as State Car No. 4, which was used in the 1980s when Prince Charles and Princess Diana visited Seymour. The carriage and small private rooms were made available to the royal couple and their immediate staff. The standard washbasins in this carriage look like round shiny metal shields against the dark wooden panels. They are clipped onto the wall and fold out in a simple mechanism. During the time of the royal visit, this was not Victoria's primary state carriage but it was used because the open platform at the rear of the carriage made it easier for people to see the royal couple, especially the popular princess.

At the other end of the scale, but no less intriguing, are the carriages that routinely carried 1st and 2nd class passengers on the four-hour trip between Sydney and Albury. These carriages have compartments that appear to fit about eight people; each has a door opening into it. In the cheaper seats, passengers sat on plain wooden benches with no padding at all. You can see how the seats and floors have been worn down with wear. The 1st class passengers had padding on the seats but no other luxuries.

These are just a few of the notable carriages at the museum. The great steam engines and the old diesel engines are all there and are shunted around as required. To give you an idea of the size of this place, in all they have three steam engines, and at least ten diesel engines of various types. On top of that they have about 20 carriages. The volunteers have bucket-loads of enthusiasm and knowledge. The Centre isn't officially open as it is a working depot and still needs to upgrade its visitor services but when volunteers are there, they are happy to show visitors through some of their prized carriages. They don't charge a fee but rely on donations from the public. Tours can be arranged by phoning (03 5799 0515). It is definitely worth a visit, and definitely worth ringing someone in advance to see if they can show you around.

As a major stopping point along the Hume, there are plenty of places where you can stay in Seymour. There are five motels and three caravan parks, including the Goulburn River Caravan Park, which is situated on a bend in the river near the Goulburn Park. It is set in a natural environment on seven acres. Besides a number of powered sites, it has several cabins with ensuites (03 5792 1530).

SEYMOUR TO NAGAMBIE

The 27 km road from Seymour to Nagambie is mostly single lane, each way, with occasional overtaking lanes. There are some excellent diversions not far from the river along the way. The link to the Hume Highway is 5 km north of Seymour.

Along this stretch of road there are several turn-offs to the historic town of Avenel. This was once the home of Ned Kelly; his father, Red, is buried here. Plunkett's Winery and Café is also in Avenel and is open from 11 am to 5 pm everyday. Another feature

History of Seymour

Seymour grew up around a crossing place over the Goulburn. It was on the main route between Sydney, Melbourne and Adelaide. In 1838, a man called John Clarke, who had worked at a crossing on the Murrumbidgee River, set up a slab-hut hotel with a store and stables on the Goulburn. A year later, he moved it upstream to a better crossing that is now Seymour. The river punt was set up just behind what is now the Royal Hotel.

Other services followed — a blacksmith, a store, another pub, and an official name. The small township was named after Lord Seymour, the son of the 11th Duke of Somerset, who had no apparent ties to anything around here!

By 1850 Seymour had a school, a police station, part of what is now the Royal Hotel, as well as a range of services required by travellers and local station staff. But it remained small until the gold rushes. First gold was found in NSW and hopeful diggers flocked east through Seymour to reach those fields. Not long afterwards, a richer source of gold was found in Victoria and they all flocked back again through Seymour. Then gold was found in the Ovens area and other areas nearby, and Seymour boomed, despite not having any gold in its own immediate vicinity.

The railway arrived in 1872, making the town a centre for commerce. River boats began coming down from Echuca in 1878 carrying wheat, flour and other agricultural produce to the rail head, but the construction of the Goulburn Weir at Nagambie put an end to Seymour's brief history as an inland port. The influence of the railway continued and Seymour became a railway town including an administration centre and workshops. As rail workers and their families moved in, the population increased. A railway institute, designed to provide an educational and recreational club for the workers, was opened and the connection with trains became a way of life for Seymour.

In 1910 Lord Kitchener visited Seymour as part of his inspection of Australia's military position. Seymour was already host to a regiment, and Kitchener noted that the area was suitable for field exercises and training. A year after the outbreak of World War I, a military camp was established here. At the outbreak of World War II, the military base at Puckapunyal was set up east of Seymour. The American defence forces came there for a short time and set up a hospital for its wounded soldiers. On being discharged from the hospital, American defence force personnel had to march to Melbourne to prove they were fit to return to duty!

of Avenel is the historic 1860 Harvest Home Country House
Hotel; it operates as a B&B, and its restaurant is renowned for its
homemade and home-grown food. Although this is to the east of
the Highway, and therefore further from the Goulburn River, it
is worth taking a side trip to the historic town.

Further north and right on the river are two of Victoria's well-
known wineries, Mitchelton Wines and Tahbilk. These are two of
the highlights of the Goulburn River track, whether you are a
wine-drinker or not. Mitchelton Wines is modern with large
spaces and an airy atmosphere; in contrast, Tahbilk is old with
cobwebs hanging off the arched brick room of its cellar. You could
even visit them in succession on a wine cruise on the Major
Mitchell, a small cruiser that carries 50 people and serves morning and afternoon tea, and hosts moonlight cruises and BBQ parties. Details of the cruises are available from Goulburn River
Cruises, (03 5794 2877). Prices vary, for example a cruise with
lunch is about $30 per adult.

MITCHELTON WINES

Access to Mitchelton Wines is well-signposted along the
Goulburn Highway, 20 km north of Seymour. The winery itself
is 4 km west of the highway; its distinctive tower makes it an easy
place to find. The road to the winery passes through swampy paddocks in all but the drier months, and you may see some elegant
white egrets, spoonbills and ibis alongside the road. Just before
the entrance to the winery there is a narrow bridge over the
Goulburn River.

The facilities at the Mitchelton Wines are superb, and could
keep you there for a whole day, even if you have no interest in
wine. Inside there is historic wine-making equipment. Outside
there is a display of different grape varieties. You can also see
some great views over the Goulburn Valley from the top of the
observation tour.

Across the lawns around the cellar door, the renowned
Mitchelton wine bar and restaurant serves lunch from midday.
The restaurant has been awarded *The Age's* 'Chef's Hat' for four
years in a row. This is a place for a planned lunch rather than
something quick to eat. For example, the winter menu served by

the large open fire includes duck and several river fish dishes, with main courses priced around $20. Another option is to bring a picnic and take a table down by the riverside under the trees, where there are coin-operated BBQs. Mitchelton has laid out 5 km of paths down by the riverbank. This is an attractive place and visitors are made to feel very welcome. The winery is open from 10 am to 5 pm, seven days a week and the grounds close at 6 pm. The wine bar and restaurant is open for lunch every day, while the Preece Lounge in the observation tower is open for lunch from October to May.

TAHBILK

The Tahbilk winery, until recently known as Chateau Tahbilk, is on the east bank of the Goulburn and is a great contrast to Mitchelton. There are two routes to Nagambie from Tahbilk. One is via the Goulburn Valley Highway; the turn-off is 20 km from Seymour, and the short route is well-signposted along straight roads. The other is a 9 km picturesque drive along a tree-lined anabranch of the Goulburn River between Nagambie and the cellar door.

From the south or north, the tracks to the vineyard run down by the waterside. The old trees and ancient-looking bridge near the cellar set the scene for a visit to a vineyard that was founded in 1860 and is still family owned. On the way you will pass a sign identifying some large, gnarled vines that were planted in 1860 and claimed to be the oldest shiraz grape vines in the world!

The Tahbilk cellar door is situated in the long white stone building with timber shutters, an iron door and a distinctive tower at one end. The ground floor of this building is the cellar-door outlet, a long dark hall with worn wooden floorboards and a wooden counter that takes up about one third of the room. A small hatch in the middle of the room leads down to the old cellar. The 92-metre cellar is chilly and has a strong smell of fermented wine; enormous barrels line the narrow corridor down the centre. It was originally dug out by hand over an eight-week period and then lined with bricks. The bulky timbers on the ceiling beams clearly show the age of the place, and the cobwebs add atmosphere.

Tahbilk is open from 9 am to 5 pm, Monday to Saturday, and from 11 am on Sundays. The vineyard has provided a self-guided tour that lists the function and date of the buildings around Tahbilk. By the way, if you join the Tahbilk wine club, you can get a 10% discount at Scullers, in Killara Gardens B&B, and several other places around Nagambie. Contact the winery (03 5794 2555) to arrange this or join when you are visiting.

Tahbilk

Tahbilk is the Aboriginal name for the land by the Goulburn, shortened from tabilk-tabilk (the place of many waterholes). The vineyard is on rich river flats with 11 km of river frontage. It was founded in 1860 by a group of partners, including the English poet, RH Horne, and a businessman of Scottish origin, John Pinney Bear. They developed the vineyard from scratch.

A community grew around the vineyard and it prospered over the next 25 years. Following Bear's death in 1889, the winery passed into the hands of his family. The annual yield dropped, and natural hazards such as floods and frosts took their toll.

Reginald Purbrick purchased Chateau Tahbilk in 1925, with only modest reports about the future of the winery, and in 1931 his 28-year-old barrister son, Eric Purbrick, took over the management. Purbrick gradually re-established the sense of the Tahbilk community, built a new homestead and began to develop markets for the wine.

Tahbilk chablis was served at an official lunch organised by the Commonwealth for Queen Elizabeth in London in 1953. It became an in-flight wine for TAA airlines in the late 1950s and is now one of Australia's better-known wines.

Tahbilk recently dropped the Chateau from the title it had carried from 1860 to 2000. As part of an agreement between Australia and the European Community, Australia has agreed to drop traditional European expressions from its wine labelling. Words such as 'champagne', 'burgundy', 'sauterne', 'port' and 'sherry' are to be phased out by about 2010.

Nagambie

The location of Nagambie by the lake is very attractive. The Nagambie Lakes Visitor Information Centre on the Goulburn Highway to the south of the town has all the brochures you will require and the staff can help you with advice on where to stay, places to eat, and what to see. There is also an unusual nut shop in the Visitor Information Centre where you can either buy edible nuts or look at decorated nuts!

Lake Nagambie, created by the Goulburn Weir at the end of the 19th century, dominates the town. There is little on the western side of the road to impede your view of the lake; the most striking building is a small redbrick church by the water's edge. The redbrick buildings on the eastern side of the highway remain from the town's earlier years, and include the Royal Mail Hotel, the post office, a doll shop and museum, and another church.

Much of the activity associated with Nagambie that interests us lies outside the town, primarily Mitchelton Wines and Tahbilk, and the weir. But before you leave, schedule dinner at Scullers. This is a stylish à la carte restaurant in the centre of town that has a good reputation throughout the area. The night we were there a large party of journalists and others, who were following the Olympic Torch's slow journey through Victoria, had travelled some distance to eat here. The food is elegant and tasty, and quite a contrast to pub counter food. Scullers is open for dinner Wednesday to Sunday from 6 pm, and lunch on Friday to Sunday from 11 am. Prices are similar to medium city prices with main courses around $20 each (03 5794 1828).

For accommodation, there are four motels in Nagambie, several caravan parks, including the Nagambie Lakes Country Resort (03 5794 7221) by the lake which has self-contained rooms (that will take up to six people for about $70 a night for the room), and some B&Bs. The breakfast at Killara Gardens (03 5794 2421) is superb with freshly stewed local fruit, and Daisy Lodge (03 5794 7271) near the Goulburn Weir has self-contained cabins for $100 a night close to the water's edge. The Visitor Information Centre can send you information about all of the accommodation in the area.

NAGAMBIE TO SHEPPARTON

The Goulburn Highway continues north and is the direct route between the two towns. The major feature along this 56 km route is the splendid Goulburn Weir, 9 km north of Nagambie. The small town of Murchison is also worth looking at along here.

By the way, be aware that if you are going north from Nagambie, you will enter the fruit fly zone. You cannot take fruit into the fruit-growing country of the Murray River. So if you are carrying fruit, you must eat it or dump it before you travel.

GOULBURN WEIR

The Goulburn Weir turn-off is 9 km north of Nagambie and is clearly signposted. It is then 3 km out of the weir on a sealed road. The lakes of Nagambie spread out before you with scores of blackened treetops and jagged limbs sticking out above the water. The road passes over a small canal system before winding back around the lake.

The weir was first built in 1891 but was replaced in 1987 as part of a major maintenance program. A two-gate replica of the original weir has been built on the western side of the river. The Goulburn Weir needs to be looked at from all sides. The most thrilling angle is from the top of the metal bridge where you can look through the mesh at the water cascading below you.

The quality of the fishing in Lake Nagambie depends on the volume of water entering into the lake from the Goulburn, and that in turn depends on how much is released from Lake Eildon. The usual collection of fish will be here, particularly redfin and trout. There are restrictions as to how close you can get to the weir; the limit is identified by buoys. On the downstream side of the weir the water is oxygenated but it is usually discoloured, having picked up sediment from the bed of Lake Nagambie. However, this shouldn't affect the fishing. From this point on, there won't be any trout in the river, but you will catch redfin, yellow belly and the inevitable carp. There are also trout cod and silver perch but both are protected and must be thrown back alive. On the north side of the weir the river follows its natural meandering course, flowing gently over the large stones of the riverbed.

Goulburn Weir

The concept of irrigation and building a weir was initiated by Hugh McColl, a bookseller and printer from England, who emigrated to Australia in 1852 with his family.

At first McColl worked as a commercial traveller around Victoria. During his travels he became convinced that the colony would benefit enormously from irrigation. He became a printer and newspaper proprietor in Bendigo, and later a member of parliament. He continued to promote irrigation in the hinterland despite government indifference. Eventually a royal commission was set up to look into the project, and there was progress. McColl died in 1885. Two years later, work on the Goulburn Weir began at Nagambie.

Goulburn Weir featured on Australia's first ten shilling note in 1913. The dramatic drawing on the back of the note has all of the gates open and the weir in full flight. It had 21 wrought-iron river floodgates supported by cast-iron piers. The weir was the first major work in irrigation development in Victoria and contributes to the water supply for agriculture in a huge area from Shepparton to as far west as Ouyen.

MURCHISON

Murchison is a small town over the Goulburn, 23 km north of Nagambie and 33 km south of Shepparton. It is about 1 km off the main Goulburn Highway, and has a few attractive redbrick buildings, and the Ossario in the cemetery. The town had its origins as an Aboriginal protectorate in 1841. This had failed by 1849, but the town survived because it remained a river crossing-place. Now there is a narrow, twisting bridge over the river and huge gum trees along the river banks. In one of its redbrick buildings, you will find a classic country Devonshire tea room.

Just to the east of Murchison is the cemetery with the Ossario Italian war memorial. Access south by the river towards the cemetery is signposted. There was a prisoner-of-war camp near Murchison in the 1940s. It was one of several POW camps and was designated to house about 4000 German and Italian POWs captured in North Africa and the Middle East. The camp was finally closed in 1947, the delay caused by the shortage of ships to repatriate prisoners to Europe.

During the war a number of prisoners in the Murchison camp died and were buried nearby. In 1956 a flood damaged their graves. Gathering donations from the Australian Italian community, the regional Italian community built the Ossario in Italian white marble. The remains of Italian POWs and internees whose graves had been disturbed were buried here. In addition, permission was sought from families and officials to have the remains of all Italian POWs and internees who died in other Australian camps to be interred here. As a result, 130 men were buried here and their names recorded on plaques on the wall. The Ossario was dedicated in 1961, and a ceremony is held here every year in November. The Garden of Remembrance was planted, surrounding the area in a great sense of peace.

King Billy, or King Charles Tatrambo of the Molka Tribe of the Ngooraialum people, is also buried in the Murchison cemetery. Tatrambo was the leader of the Molka group of the river area when the Aboriginal protectorate moved in here in 1840. Before Tatrambo died in 1866, he requested that he be buried like a white man in a box in the ground. His grave is at the north-east end of the graveyard; beside him is the grave of his wife and son, who both died some years later. A small metal breast-plate and boomerang have been fixed to the metal surround of Tatrambo's grave.

Shepparton

Shepparton is a city of food — fresh, canned, dried, pickled and preserved fruit and vegetables, and, if you are lucky enough, some fresh fish also. It is the home of two major Victorian canneries, Ardmona and SPC, as well as smaller producers. This large regional city, with a population of 50,000, once had some fine public buildings, including a post office and several banks. These gave the town centre that interesting elegance that we still see in substantial rural towns such as Broken Hill, Bourke and Ballarat. Unfortunately these buildings were demolished in the 1970s to be replaced by dull, low buildings that sadly now contribute to Shepparton's town centre having a dull, low feel to it.

Shepparton is very spread out and you will need a map to get around it. It has the usual range of family leisure activities with golf, swimming, cinemas and fishing anywhere along the river-bank. The Visitors Information Centre is situated on the Goulburn Highway by Victoria Lake. There are plenty of brochures, maps and lists of accommodation and restaurants available here. The free maps are particularly useful because, unless you are just driving through, you will probably need them to get around.

Travelling from the south, our first food experience was at the Belstack Tourism Complex and Strawberry Farm at Kialla West, 10 km south of Shepparton. The farm itself is about 1 km down a straight road from the Goulburn Highway, and is signposted. It is set in a beautiful location on the banks of the Goulburn River. The farm has a large bistro-style restaurant with home-cooked food. Peter and Margaret Tacey created this oasis along the high-way. The Tacey family moved into this region as pastoralists in the 1860s and Peter has a wealth of anecdotes about five genera-tions of family life in rural Victoria. The Taceys make a wide range of interesting preserves, including sugar-free jams made from pure fruit, and spicy sauces that merge chilli and strawber-ries in a flavoursome mixture. They are also moving towards organic produce, and haven't used sprays for six years now. Visitors can pick their own strawberries, boysenberries, blackber-ries, nashi pears, and other fruits in season. This is a great place to have a Devonshire tea, a long lunch or even dinner and go for a walk along the peaceful Goulburn (03 5823 1324).

Back in town, Shepparton's two large canning factory outlets — SPC and Ardmona — are a highlight of the trip down the Goulburn River! We have not had a lot of experience with facto-ry outlets, but in the interests of research, we included these in our travels. And it was fun. Exploring the huge warehouses full of cans of fruit, vegetables, beans and other produce is like explor-ing a fresh vegetable market. There is so much to choose from, including cans of foods we were not familiar with. Generally cans are sold in a carton with maybe a dozen in each. Sometimes the cans are damaged, sometimes there are no paper labels on the cans, mostly they are as you would find them in the shops, only cheaper and in bulk. Ardmona is 5 km from Shepparton on the way to Mooroopna, and SPC is about 2 km north-east of the main shopping centre on the Old Dookie Road just past the railway line. Ardmona is open from 9 am to 5 pm; SPC opens from 8.30 am to 5.30 pm, Monday to Friday, and from 9 am to 5 pm, Saturday and Sunday.

About 2 km east of SPC on the Old Dookie Road is Redbryne Pottery, and this is another Goulburn delight. It has a large stock of items for sale, including bowls, mugs, plates, vases and, if you wish, an entire dinner service. This pottery was established in 1975, and displays the works of several potters. Redbryne Pottery is open every day from 9 am to 5 pm.

On New Dookie Road, closer to the centre of town, you will find the famous Furphy foundry. This was opened by John Hare Furphy, a blacksmith and Methodist lay preacher who arrived in town in 1873. Furphy's water tanks served the immediate needs of agriculturalists in the region, but they later became famous during the World War I when they were used by the Australian soldiers on the battlefields. As the water carters carried gossip and stories, the name 'Furphy' became synonymous with tall stories. Enthusiasts of large metal objects will probably find the small museum of interest. It is situated around the side of the foundry, and is open Monday to Friday from 10 am to 4 pm.

Over the river near the Ardmona factory outlet is a popular place for children called Kidstown. It was built and developed by the Mooroopna and Shepparton community. There are loads of activities for children, in a safe environment, including enormous slides, a huge sand pit, a fruit-bin pyramid, monkey-bars, swings and other joyful things. It is open every day from dawn to dusk, and entry is a gold coin donation.

Deep in the northern suburbs is an Aboriginal display centre. The Aboriginal Keeping Place is an interpretative centre with large-scale exhibits on the Bunerong culture that stretches down as far as Murchison, east to Albury and north to Barmah. The cultural officer, Kevin Atkinson, and the staff there are happy to talk to you about the artefacts and culture of their people. The Keeping Place is situated in Parkside Gardens, a garden area that was once an international village. Now it is a bit of wasteland with several lakes and the home of the local radio station, 98.5 FM. It is easiest to get to the Keeping Place via Numurkah Road, then turn into Parkside Drive rather than take the scenic route around by the Goulburn. The Keeping Place is open from 9 am to 4 pm

Monday to Friday, and at weekends by appointment (03 5831 1020).

There are many places to have lunch or dinner in Shepparton. If you ask the staff at the tourist centre, they will give you six pages of restaurants with brief descriptions and a map. We particularly enjoyed lunch at the Lemon Tree Café in the central shopping area on Fryers Street. The polished wooden floorboards, fresh lasagne, homemade cakes and good coffee all make it a very comfortable place to relax. Restaurants that people recommend for elegant dinners are Cellar 47 on High Street and Sebastian's Restaurant on Wyndham Street, both near the town centre. There are more than a dozen motels in Shepparton, many obvious from the main road, and at least five caravan parks. During the week, the Shepparton Visitors Information Centre provides an accommodation service but this is not available at weekends. Shepparton is busy during the school holidays so we suggest you make accommodation arrangements in advance if you plan to travel during these times.

FISHING

The Goulburn sweeps through Shepparton to the west of the Goulburn Highway and the town centre. The lake beside the Visitors' Information Centre provides reasonable fishing but the reeds can get in the way and you would need to be selective with your casting. The Goulburn is to the west of the lake and there is good access there. Generally people catch redfin and yellow belly. You can also get Murray cod and trout cod. Early in 2001 the Rex Hunt Foundation released one million Murray cod fingerlings into the Goulburn with the promise of great fishing in the future.

The Goulburn River at the northern part of town also provides easy fishing access. The riverbanks near the cemetery and the golf course are particularly good because they are on the outskirts of town and are less likely to be crowded.

If you want local fishing information, go to the Shepparton Outdoor Sports Centre at the corner at Rowe and Corio streets. The staff in the Centre are enthusiasts and will be able to tell you which fish are biting and what the best bait might be. They sell bait and tackle, but don't hire out equipment.

History of Shepparton

Like other Goulburn River towns, Shepparton began as a punt across the river in the early 1850s. The effects of the gold rush and station life seemed to pass it by. By the late 1860s there were still only three buildings, some shepherd and squatter huts, and about 30 people living in the settlement. It is believed that the name Shepparton came from an event known as 'The Siege of Tallygaroopna' in which an Irish squatter called Sherbourne Sheppard reclaimed land that had been sold on his behalf. In the 1840s, Sheppard had returned from a trip to Europe and found that the property on which he had been squatting for a number of years had been sold in his absence to pay his debts. He refused to accept that anyone had the right to do that and moved back on the land. The case was eventually resolved in his favour in the Supreme Court. The publicity associated with this case gave the river crossing the name 'Sheppard's town'. Then, as Shepparton historian Ron Michael says, 'The lazy Australian accent did the rest!'

SHEPPARTON TO ECHUCA VIA LOCH GARRY

The quickest way between the two towns is 70 km via Mooroopna. However, if you want to see the Goulburn River at Loch Garry near Bunbartha, take the Barmah–Shepparton Road that runs north towards Nathalia and then, just before Nathalia, turns south towards McCoy's Bridge over the Goulburn. This route is clearly signposted and is about 97 km. It travels through pasture, vineyards and orchards, often in fairly straight lines. It is a very pleasant drive and it is not a very busy road. The trees in the distance to the south-west indicate the course of the Goulburn, which is now meandering into the Murray River.

Loch Garry at Bunbartha is surrounded by gum trees and soft forest floor. The fishing isn't great because if the water levels are low, the lake is more like a series of swampy lagoons. However it is a pleasant place to camp and enjoy the bush atmosphere. It is a popular duck hunting location so it is probably best to avoid it at the beginning of the season.

Then, 59 km from Shepparton, you pass over the Goulburn. There is a reserve and picnic place under the trees with a fireplace beside the river so you could have a tea break or a hot lunch. The road along here has many bends, a sure sign of the proximity of the river.

Echuca

The Goulburn joins the Murray just east of the town — one of the best tourist towns on any of the rivers. The activity around the Port of Echuca combines history with excitement and excellent tourist facilities. We have described the town in detail in the Upper Murray chapter (see pages 58–63). The Echuca–Moama Visitor Information Centre, in Echuca, is situated in the 1877 railway engine-house on the river bank. It runs an accommodation service and provides information on all of the tourist activity around town.

5 The Darling River
BOURKE TO WENTWORTH (NSW)

The Darling River trip is an easy outback adventure that travels through remote semi-arid desert country on good, gravel roads. It is an ideal trip for travelers who want to experience the Australian outback for the first time. The roads are well-defined and maintained, and suitable for any vehicle in good condition. There is also enough passing traffic so that you could call for assistance if you get into trouble. Yet it is beautiful and remote country with the magnificent river running close to the roads. Between Bourke and Wilcannia, there are gravel roads on either side of the Darling, both roughly following the course of the river. You can cross the river at Louth and Tilpa and take the other road for a while. Both roads are suitable for conventional vehicles when it is dry, but will be impassable after rain; also the quality of the road surface will depend on recent rain and when it was last graded.

There are interesting towns along the way and some easy access to the river, particularly on station riverfront camping sites. In the northern reaches of the river, stations have designated bush campsites on their property; this gives you the opportunity to meet the station owners and learn about the real outback. The fishing tends to be better than in the Murray because it is not so heavily fished and it doesn't have the same problems with salt and pollution. In the river towns, the history of the European settlement is evident, with historic bridges and large inland wharves. The extent of the inland river-transport network will probably surprise most visitors.

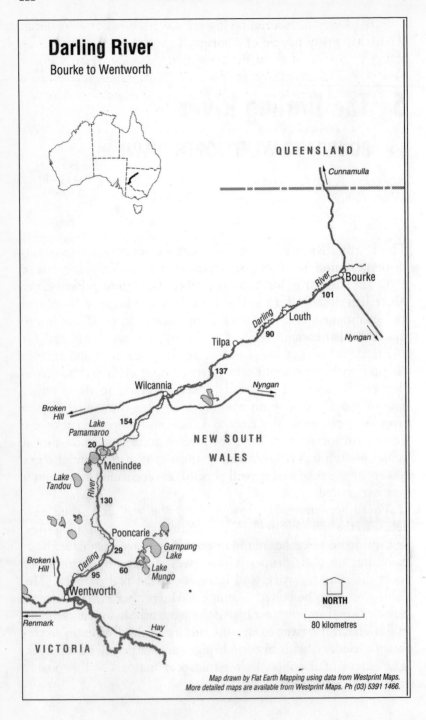

Darling River
Bourke to Wentworth

QUEENSLAND

Cunnamulla

Bourke
101

Darling River
Louth
90
Nyngan
Tilpa

137

Wilcannia
Nyngan

Broken Hill
Lake Pamamaroo
154
20
Menindee

NEW SOUTH
WALES

Lake Tandou

River

130

Pooncarie
29
Garnpung Lake

Broken Hill
Darling
60
Lake Mungo
95
Wentworth

Renmark
Hay

NORTH

80 kilometres

VICTORIA

Map drawn by Flat Earth Mapping using data from Westprint Maps.
More detailed maps are available from Westprint Maps. Ph (03) 5391 1466.

The history of Aboriginal life on the river is not so obvious. There are many people of Aboriginal origin in the towns along the track, many of them Barkindji people of the Darling River area. But although there are few related things to see, there is information available about Aboriginal culture before white settlement, so we can get some sense of their river culture.

Main route

Bourke — Louth — Tilpa — Wilcannia — Menindee — Wentworth

Maps

Touring Atlas of Australia, Melbourne, Penguin, 2000
A Touring Map of the Outback Area in New South Wales, NSW Government 1989

Passes

A NSW freshwater recreational fishing licence is required.

Distance from starting point

733 km from Bourke to Wentworth on the east side of the Darling River. The trip will take a minimum number of three days in dry conditions, if you don't look at anything!

Maximum distance between supplies

158 km from Wilcannia to Menindee.

Best time of year to visit

April to October — during this period daytime temperatures range from about 15 to 30°c. During the summer, temperatures soar to over 40°c.

Accommodation

Hotel, motel and caravan park accommodation on the Darling is available in the towns along the routes. As the extent of the accommodation in each town is limited, it is possibly wise to book ahead as you go along, particularly if you want to stay in motels or cabins with ensuites in the caravan parks.

There is plenty of bush camping by the river, but most of it is on private property. We have identified stations where the owners are happy to give permission to camp on the waterfront on their properties. This usually involves a camping fee. We have also identified places where there is bush camping is permitted.

Local information and useful telephone numbers

Tourist Centre, Bourke	02 6872 1222
Trilby Station, river camping	02 6874 7420
Wilcannia Shire Visitor Information Centre	08 8091 5909
Menindee Information Centre	08 8091 4274
National Parks and Wildlife Service, Mungo National Park	1300 361 967
Wentworth Visitor Information	03 5027 3624

PREPARATION

Fuel and supplies

Although there are towns at intervals of less than 158 km along the Darling, this is an unsealed road so you should carry some emergency provisions. Unless you plan to travel far off the road, there is no need to carry spare fuel because it is available in each of the townships along the way. However, some emergency rations and extra water should be carried just in case of a breakdown or if rain closes the road. Emergency rations can be as simple as extra lunch or snack food, but make sure to keep the salt and sugar levels down, and drink water.

Water is available along the route, however, extra water should be carried just in case of a breakdown or being bogged. Carry 5

Wooden bridge over the Darling track, south of Louth (PHOTO: GARRY TICKNER)

PS Canberra *approaching the Port of Echuca* (PHOTO: BILL BACHMAN)

Morning mist over the Central Murray Riverina
(PHOTO: BILL BACHMAN)

litres of water per person per day and extra in the summer when the dry heat can zap your energy levels if you don't maintain your liquid intake.

Fruit fly exclusion zone

Note that you cross the fruit fly exclusion zone 40 km south of Wilcannia.

THE ROUTE

Bourke

Bourke has the exotic and rugged ring of an outback Australian town. It is a substantial and busy town of about 3000 people, with a strong Aboriginal presence. Many are descended from groups who once lived around here or who were moved here from other parts of Australia. Bourke's recent history is associated with agriculture and transport, the river and rail lines. The town began life in the 1860s as a tough settlement that catered for the squatters who took up runs on the banks of the Darling River in the wake of the NSW exploration parties. It grew as the armies of seasonal workers (jackeroos, shearers and rouseabouts) were employed on the large cattle and sheep stations. In 1859 the first paddle-steamer arrived. Three years later the settlement became officially known as Bourke (after NSW Governor, Sir Richard Bourke). Police and other government officials were appointed and, of course, hotel licences granted.

The historic buildings in and near the centre of Bourke date from a 20-year period of activity beginning in the 1870s. The Telegraph Hotel (now the Riverside Hotel) and the Church of St Ignatius at the western end of town are the earliest buildings. Many of the substantial buildings in the centre of town, the post office, the police station, the Old London Bank, the courthouse and the Post Office Hotel date from the 1880s. By 1892, when writer Henry Lawson was in town, Bourke had 200 businesses, 5 doctors and 22 hotels!

While fine colonial architecture was giving the town style, the true industry of the town continued. At any one time during this period, there could have been up to 1000 working bullocks in the town! They were essential for getting the supplies to stations and transporting wool bales and other produce to the markets. The wharf thrived since river transport was the most efficient form of transport until 1885 when the railway arrived. As long as the stations produced, the town prospered.

Today the historic aspect of Bourke is one of the highlights of visiting this region. The staff in the Tourist Centre, in the old railway station, are knowledgeable and helpful; they have information about tours, facilities and accommodation available in Bourke. They also have a top-class free mud-map of things to see and do in the area; we found this a most valuable guide to exploring Bourke and the area around it. We also bought a standard street map of the town — the *Map Guide of Bourke* — which is easy to follow and identifies points of interest. The Tourist Centre is open from 9 am to 5 pm, seven days a week from April to October, and closed on Sundays from November to March.

We began by following the Maritime Trail on the far side of the river. Access to the trail is through station country along the north side of the Darling and is well signposted. To get there, drive along Mitchell Street and out to the North Bourke Bridge. Half a kilometre after the bridge on the Hungerford Road, past the Riverview Hotel, you will see a signpost directing you left down a dirt road towards the Maritime Trail. About 3.5 km along this track, you will see a signpost directing you through a gate. Please leave the gate as you find it (if it is closed, leave it closed, and vice versa). The 3.5 km Maritime Trail is well signposted. There is a fork in the track just inside the gate, both paths are part of the same loop. The right fork leads directly to the view of the replica wharf on the opposite bank.

The modern Maritime Trail consists primarily of a series of illustrated information boards that describe what used to happen along the opposite bank of the river around the wharf during its heyday. The first sign describes the reconstructed wharf directly across the river, built in 1994, slightly downstream from the original 1898 one. It follows the plans of the original, with three landing bays at different levels, depending on the amount of water in the river at the time; grass was added to the top deck in 2000 to provide a pleasant picnic spot. We haven't seen the river in flood so we find it hard to imagine water lapping the top deck! With the help of historic photos incorporated into the information boards, it is easy to imagine the bustle of people and produce when the wharf was at its busiest.

Early Bourke

Bourke's association with maritime history began in 1859 when William Randell's *Gemini* navigated the Darling. It was a risky trip, as no one knew the depth of the river or the location of the sandbars and snags. When the *Gemini* arrived in Bourke, there was great celebration. The settlers had been living on a limited diet of beef, native cabbage and spinach for some months because the overland team carrying the usual supplies of flour, rice, tobacco, alcohol and other staples had been stuck in floods for eight months to the east of the settlement. Worse still, there had been no alcohol available in the town for four months. The party celebrating the arrival of the boat lasted for three days! Incidentally, one of the passengers on Randell's second trip down the Darling was the notorious bushranger, Frank Gardiner, disguised as a Presbyterian minister. According to a contemporary report, the phoney padre delivered sermons on board the *Gemini* before it reached Adelaide. He later swapped his clothes for a stockman's outfit, stole a horse and vanished!

In between the levels, the great wooden beams are exposed and feel solid, but the steps are fairly steep. In 2000 a replica of the *Jandra* paddle-steamer began taking two-hour scheduled cruises several times a week from the wharf. They are on Tuesday and Thursday at 10.30 am, and Saturday at 10 am. However, these are subject to change, so check with the Tourist Centre in advance if you plan to go on one of these. It is a beautiful way to see the river and the only scheduled opportunity we are aware of of getting out on the Darling on a paddle-steamer today.

On the way back to town, the North Bourke Bridge is worth a close look. The mechanical bridge was built in England and brought up the Darling in sections. It was opened in May 1883 and is now the oldest surviving lift-span bridge in NSW. The bridge has tar macadam laid over it so, without close examination, it is difficult to identify exactly which part of the bridge was raised. However, it is possible to work out the mechanics: there are huge chains at the western end, enormous weights at both ends, and slots in the upright sections. These raised and lowered the bridge as if it were an open platform lift.

Just around the corner from the wharf is the Telegraph Hotel, now known as the Riverside Hotel, which is a most striking building. It was built in 1876 and has undergone an extensive renovation. The large rooms are beautifully proportioned and elegantly furnished. The building has plenty of 19th-century character with high, red cedar ceilings, cyprus pine floorboards, an original fireplace in the communal area and a verandah. The diningroom has lofty church ceilings which are part of the original hotel. The renovation of the old building is an ongoing process; John and Sitha Hickson even plan to renovate the cellars. Heritage rooms with king-size beds have been fully renovated and are moderately priced from $60 upwards per room (02 6872 2539). The Riverside is a splendid alternative to the standard Australian red or beige brick motel.

Back in Bourke, you will need a map to follow the trail of historic buildings along the wide, neat streets of the town. But there are so many buildings of note that, if you are walking, you may not want to try it all in one day. The Bourke mud-map or the *Map Guide of Bourke* provides directions to the historic buildings, and give some information about each one.

Other buildings that are impressively historical are also occupied. Some, like the courthouse and post office, still serve their original function. The Lands Department Building, close to the Riverside Hotel, was built in 1898 and still serves its original function. Visitors are encouraged to go in and look at the corrugated-iron walls and high corrugated-iron ceilings with their cross-shaped airy layout, designed to allow the maximum airflow through the building. You can also stroll around the magnificent wide verandah, look out over the well-kept gardens, and imagine trying to work in this place at the height of summer with no air-conditioning!

The courthouse on Oxley St, built in 1900, is an attractive structure with an open courtyard. Visitors are welcome if the court is not sitting. Before it was built, the post office next door, built in 1880, served as the courthouse.

The Aboriginal population

About a quarter of the population of Bourke is now of Aboriginal descent. Some of the Aboriginal people in Bourke descend from the group of about 80–100 people who came from Tibooburra and the Corner Country, 436 km west of Bourke. In 1935 the group was suddenly told to move from their comfortable settlement in Tibooburra to Brewarrina, north-east of Bourke; they were given two hours to pack their possessions into one of two trucks. The government officials threatened to take their children if they didn't go. Many of the older people died as a result of the dislocation; the others decided to walk back to Tibooburra. However, floodwaters stopped them at Wanarring, and they returned to Bourke and stayed there. Other Aboriginal people were drawn to Bourke as work became available. An Aboriginal reserve was declared and, in 1948, the official Aboriginal population in Bourke was recorded at 55 people.

In terms of accommodation, Bourke has four air-conditioned motels, two caravan parks, and lots of alternative accommodation, mainly out of town. The Royal Hotel on Mitchell Street also has rooms. It sounds a lot but on one occasion when we arrived in Bourke mid-week, quite late in the day and exhausted from a long day's driving, all four motels were fully booked. There was nothing specifically on in town; we were told by motel people that mid-week in Bourke can become quite busy. We asked a taxi driver if he had any suggestions. He led us to a delightful turn-of-the-century house called 'Tom's House', which had recently been renovated by the owners, Rob and Vicki Gransden (02 6872 2837). The three-bedroomed house sleeps seven, and has a well-appointed kitchen and a sitting-room with comfortable and tasteful furnishings. Truly a home away from home, and the cost of less than two average motel rooms. Families often book the cottage for a week and use it as a base to enjoy the facilities in the region, but, by happy chance, it was free that night. There is a list of accommodation on the mud-map, and the Bourke Tourist Information Centre can assist you in finding accommodation. The staff will also give you names and phone numbers of farm-stay accommodation in the area.

FISHING AROUND BOURKE

Fishing is a most popular and rewarding activity around Bourke. The banks of the river are accessible on either side of the town. You can fish at the wharf and you might catch a yellow belly, but the better fishing is down at the weir, 4.5 km from the Information Centre. The weir was opened in 1897, and is now a beautiful spot with a picnic area shaded by river red gums. You may catch Murray cod, which can grow to 30 kg — John has caught 17 kg cod here — but the best eating is up to about 7 kg. After that you will spend too much time cutting the fat off the fish to make them worthwhile. So if you do land a very big one, use it as a photo opportunity then throw it back.

After the big rain in 2000, Josh, in Loxley's Store on Mertin Street, told us that he was catching 2–3 kg yellow belly at the weir that were 8 centimetres thick — that is a huge fish! Perch and catfish were once common here, but, while you may land one, it is not as likely as in the past. The major baits are yabbies, shrimps and worms, but you may no longer use live fish like small carp for bait.

As usual, the best time to fish is after a flood when the water has had a time to settle. But any quiet stretch of the river will have fish that you can catch with patience and skills. The river red gums provide ample shade to protect you from the sun as you relax by the waterside. Bait (worms) and fishing gear are available from Brown's Service Station on Warraweena Street.

BOURKE TO WILCANNIA

The 328 km of unsealed roads between Bourke and Wilcannia on both sides of the Darling follow the course of the river, and both provide similar opportunities to get close to the water. Like all dirt tracks, they are good solid roads when dry and recently graded; when wet they are impassable. Of course, if the roads haven't been graded for a while, they will be rough. Generally, the road on the west side of the river between Tilpa and Wilcannia is considered the better road, sometimes having the quality of a highway! But overall, the roads on both sides of the river will give you a similar ride.

Although the map may suggest that this is a fine riverside drive, unfortunately this is not the case. The vistas to the left and right of the road are flat plains of muted green scrub with red sandy ground and bushy mulga and acacias breaking the horizon. In the distance towards the river, the thick line of tall trees indicates the course of the Darling. But there are few glimpses of the river itself — which is a pity because when the river does appear, it is a sensational view with steep banks and great gum trees. However, there are several stations, such as Rose Isle and Trilby, where you can camp by the river. We highly recommend that you stay overnight in at least one of these, but contact the neighbours for permission first. The Upper Darling roads are clearly defined and you should experience no confusion between identifying the main road and side station tracks.

The roads travel through station country, with a lot of station activity along the way including, sheep, cows, fences and grids. You may also see feral goats; there are so many of them that they are rounded up and slaughtered in the Bourke abattoirs for export. The roads are often fenced on either side. Occasionally you will see a track leading tantalisingly towards the river but with an unambiguous sign saying 'No trespassing', so you are restricted as to how far off the road you can wander. As usual, be careful when approaching grids, the ground might be washed away which could jolt your suspension if you approach it too quickly!

Besides the towns there are a few diversions such as the large shearers' quarters near the road, 203 km south of Bourke. There is a beautiful view of the river, 37 km south of Louth, that may even provide fishing opportunities. You will also see some fine examples of old wooden bridges in the southern stretch of the road, such as the one over Talyawalka Creek. This bridge is laid on enormous river red gum tree trunks. Three long trunks on either side of the bridge are supported by several thick trunks. The amount of modern traffic it still carries is a resounding testament to its sturdiness.

BOURKE CEMETERY

The cemetery is 1 km south of Bourke on the road to Cobar and Louth. Access is well-signposted. Like so many outback cemeteries,

Aboriginal people of the Darling River

The abundant resources of the Darling River once supported thousands of Aboriginal people. Collectively they are generally referred to as the Barkindji but in fact there are several distinct groups. The Gunu lived in the northern part of the river near Bourke, the Barundji lived near the river between Wilcannia and Louth, and the Barkindji lived in the lower part of the river between Wilcannia and Wentworth. They shared a similar language and seemed to have some similar customs, although much of this information was recorded by non-indigenous anthropologists and the local people didn't give much information away. Simpson Newland, writing in 1889 about the people he referred to as the Parkengees of the Darling, stated that the country belonging to different groups was clearly defined and, within that, further defined with names for every bend in the river and creek.

Overall, the people of the Darling enjoyed a rich lifestyle. They were skilled at fishing, using nets, man-made weirs, spears and other techniques to harvest from the water. They caught fish, ducks, tortoises, kangaroos, wallabies and other wildlife; they also gathered shellfish, local vegetables and berries. Land management ensured the maintenance of food and water during times of drought. In the northern section of their country, they built wells and covered them with bark to reduce evaporation. Some people of the Darling were known to bury grain for future use. They got pituri (a local shrub with narcotic properties) by trading possum skins and other local items with people from the Birdsville region, so it was important to maintain good relations with neighbouring groups in order to move through their country.

The Barkindji used possum or kangaroo skin as cloaks for warmth, and wore personal ornaments made from feathers, bones or wood. Fish grease or mud protected their skin from mosquitoes and other insects. When they required protection from the bitter cold of night, they built shelters with vegetation, sticks and branches. The people lived around the river during the summer months when the water was high, and moved out into the hinterland during the drier winter months. Groups of 10–30 people might form one camp, although during good seasons along the river the group might have been larger. Charles Sturt, the first European explorer to record life along the river banks in 1828–9, reported seeing large groups of dwellings resembling villages — one which had 70 huts.

Besides rich natural resources, the Darling people appeared to have a rich cultural and social life. Incised, oval shaped stones have been found in the region. One initiation ceremony included removing a front tooth of the young men; they also formed raised scars on their bodies and arms. They painted themselves and used feathers for adornment during celebrations. At the death of a member, the group all moved at once after burying the person with great care. They had rain ceremonies that were conducted in great secrecy by a select group of men — neither women nor enthusiastic visitors, like the 19th century anthropologist Simpson Newland, were permitted to attend. When rain fell, they believed that either their own ceremony or that of another group was successful.

Sadly, the information about real life along the Darling before the Europeans arrived is limited. Little information was passed on to the settlers, who quickly shattered the traditional lives in the river basin.

its tells a powerful story of the life of pioneering families in these remote areas. Premature death through accident, illness and crime are all evident on the headstones in the old section of the graveyard. Most poignant for us are the young mothers and children who perished out here in this isolated country in the 19th and early 20th centuries. Several police officers who died in the course of duty are also buried here. One was Sergeant John McCabe who was shot by the infamous bushranger, Captain Starlight. Another was killed when a barman in the Royal Hotel went berserk during a heatwave. A local character known only as Barefoot Harry was buried here in 1931. Barefoot Harry believed that his wife had drowned because he couldn't get his boots off in time to save her; after that he went barefoot around Bourke in preparation for saving another from the same sad fate.

A recent grave is that of the famous ophthalmologist Fred Hollows. He had worked on controlling trachoma among Aborigines in Australia as well as people in Eritrea, Vietnam and Nepal. He died of cancer in 1993 and was buried in Bourke. He loved that part of the country because, he said, 'It is a free country, no fences on the side of the road; you just drive off and light a fire.' The people of the Enngonia settlement outside Bourke, whom Hollows had visited for more than 20 years, screen-printed the cloth that was draped over his coffin. The wake was held at a claypan 60 km north-west of Bourke. Signposts on the road as well as in the graveyard will direct you to the pioneer eye surgeon's resting place. You can pick up a guide to the old parts of Bourke Cemetery from the Tourist Centre.

Lawson in Bourke

Australia's famous poet and short-story writer, Henry Lawson, spent six months in Bourke in 1892. He was sent there at the expense of the Bulletin magazine in Sydney to file stories from the outback. The wealth of experiences that he picked up on his adventure became a major source of inspiration for him.

Lawson arrived at a time of great unrest in Bourke. The shearers' conflict with the pastoralists had been going on for some time. Lawson was quickly drawn into the union circles, spending time in the Shakespeare Hotel, now the Welcome Mart on Mitchell Street. This was where the shearers' union was formed in 1887. Lawson wrote a wonderfully lively collection of poems and prose, recording life in the region at the time, all from a pro-union stance. He worked incognito, only his friends in union circles knew who he was.

Writing didn't support Lawson completely, so he had to find some work locally. He was employed as a housepainter, but left that to follow the work trail out into the bush. He worked as a rouseabout in a shearing shed in Toorale in November. At that stage, the shearing season should have been drawing to a close but because of the delay caused by unrest among shearers, shearing was still in full swing.

Lawson's travels and writings from this period have been collected in a remarkably gripping book called *A Stranger on the Darling*. Written by the late Alan Barton, a Bourke historian, and his daughter, author Robyn Burrows, it interweaves the history of Bourke with a large collection of Lawson's writings. This is lively reading for anyone interested in the area, and great campfire reading.

FORT BOURKE

About 11 km south of Bourke on the Wilcannia road, on the eastern side of the river, is the turn-off to Fort Bourke (also named after Sir Richard Bourke). This wooden construction marks the place where the explorer Major Thomas Mitchell and his party built a stockade to protect themselves and their equipment from potentially unfriendly Aboriginal people. The signposting to the fort is subtle. Drive down the track for 1.3 km, and turn left through a ramp. The 3 km track from there is comfortable when dry, but impassable when wet. At one point where it runs along the levee, the raised track winds through high trees with views of the river. It is a delightful drive, except for one thing — it is a single-lane levee with very few opportunities to pass another vehicle. So pray you don't meet another car because, if you do, one of you is going to have to reverse for a distance! If the other vehicle is towing a caravan or trailer, the unencumbered vehicle will have to do the reversing. We wouldn't like to be around if two cars pulling caravans met!

Fort Bourke stockade (PHOTO: GARRY TICKNER)

Despite the tourist promotion of the replica stockade in Bourke, it is not easy to spot. The only instructions we can give you is to turn right at the pile of stones about 100 metres before the wildlife refuge. If you find yourself at the gate of the wildlife refuge, you have gone too far. Go back along the water's edge and you will see the two-metre wooden stockade known as Fort

Bourke (again named after Sir Richard Bourke). This modern structure can only be considered a marker of the original that gave the town of Bourke its name. The stockade that Mitchell's men built in 1835 included a blockhouse for the men, and room to shelter the animals and carts. Mitchell returned to it on another expedition in 1839. Today there isn't much to do except climb in and out of the stockade, and take photos. But it is a peaceful spot beside a vast expanse of water with submerged trees stretching to the horizon and diverse bird life close to the shore.

ROSE ISLE STATION

This sheep station provides more permissible access to the Darling and some glorious riverbank camping. Rose Isle is 71 km from Bourke on the eastern side of the river to Wilcannia. There is no signpost welcoming visitors, however a white mail box with its name indicates you have arrived — and you are very welcome. Gary and Samantha Mooring of Rose Isle provide genuine, simple riverside camping with no facilities at a standard fee per vehicle ($12). There is one powered site that costs a bit more ($20). You may light a fire, although there aren't any officially designated fireplaces. There is also a shearing shed where, for $25 per person, you have access to full facilities including a kitchen, hot water, beds, showers, and so on; just bring your own bedding and food. If you plan to camp there, and are travelling from Bourke or even Louth, it is preferable to ring and say you are on the way (02 6874 7371). Otherwise, just call by the house which is between the road and the river, and the Moorings will give you good advice on where to camp, and valuable up-to-date local information on fishing.

FISHING ON THE DARLING

The quality of fishing on the Darling River has a lot to do with the flow of water from its catchment area to the north and east. When the water is flowing and the river is swollen, opportunities to catch Murray cod and silver perch increase. You may be very lucky and catch a catfish — a fish with a slimy eel-like skin that

Early exploration on the Darling

The river was first mapped in 1829 by Captain Charles Sturt, who was investigating the possibility of an inland sea. His party included the experienced explorer, Hamilton Hume. It also included two soldiers and eight convicts. When they arrived at what Sturt referred to as a 'noble river' early in 1829, it was the height of summer and the group was exhausted. There was great jubilation when they caught sight of the water. But their excitement was shortlived — the water was much too salty to drink! Sturt named the major inland river the Darling, in honour of Ralph Darling, the Governor of NSW at the time.

Sturt was determined to establish and maintain good relations with the local Aboriginal people during his expedition. For the river people, this visit seems to have been non-threatening. However, their encounters with the next European explorer, Major Thomas Mitchell, were not so pleasant. In 1835 Mitchell followed the Darling for 500 km from around Bourke to Menindee Lake. Initially he communicated well with the people around the Fort Bourke area, giving them gifts for access to their water and land. But soon he began to get annoyed at their demands, believing them excessive. Then his men killed an emu that was effectively the property of the Aborigines and didn't pay any compensation. There was also a suggestion that, unknown to Mitchell, when his men went to collect water by the river in the evenings, they took advantage of local women.

The trouble between locals and visitors came to a head at Laidley's Ponds (now Menindee). By this stage word of Mitchell and his party had preceded them — the white men were called 'Boree', meaning devil. There were many Aboriginal people at Menindee Lakes at the time, and Mitchell's party wasn't welcome. Nevertheless, he persevered, and set up camp. In the evening he heard shots from the riverbank where two of his men were collecting water. Some Aborigines, camped nearby for a major gathering, wanted the kettle. In the row that broke out, one of Mitchell's men was knocked down by a waddy (a heavy wooden club); Mitchell's men opened fire and shot the aggressor. More shots were fired and an Aboriginal woman was killed while fleeing across the river. Whatever the reason behind the initial attack, relations between the Darling tribes and the Europeans had gone sour. Mitchell's group retreated back up-river quickly.

As squatters, pastoralists and itinerant labour followed the explorers into this country, the life of the Darling people became much more difficult. They had a reputation for defending their country fiercely, and they had good weapons — spears and boomerangs made of mulga, and shields made of leopard wood. It is said that some people on the Murray put rotting flesh on the end of their spears to inject poison into a wound. After a fight with Europeans or neighbours, they would bury their own dead to ensure that the bodies were not robbed for mystical purposes — kidney fat rubbed on the body of a living person was believed to have special power. But ultimately it was an uneven battle and by the end of the century, European expansion had fundamentally changed Aboriginal society.

makes a great meal — but these are rare nowadays, as are black bream.

The murky waters of the Darling also dictate the type of bait you should use. Worms, maggots, yabbies and other standard bait are the most effective. When the river is low and the water is clear, you can use lures.

Good river fishing techniques are important for success on the Darling because so much of it is straight, murky river and stocks are not as rich as they once were. So aim for the outside curve of bends where the depressions are deepest and fish may stop to feed. The Darling has many snags, once the bane of boat captains' lives, now a good place to drop in a line. Large fish use the shade of fallen tree branches to rest and feed.

You will need a NSW Freshwater Recreational Fishing Licence to fish in the Darling. This is available from the hotel in Louth. You can also buy one in Bourke or any of the fishing outlets in NSW.

LOUTH

As a tourist diversion along the Darling, Louth is a little disappointing. It is a rugged male town that serves the local community, and tourist facilities are incidental and not advertised. It is strangely evocative of a 19th-century shanty town positioned to provide timely grog to weary and desperate outback travellers. Henry Lawson, who worked as a rouseabout on a station nearby, described Louth in 1893 as a small, crude town with a few wooden humpies, some decrepit boats, a rotten pub, and men standing or sitting languidly in the shade playing pitch-and-toss and spitting! In fact, Lawson never visited Louth but used a combination of impressions of the outback built up over a number of months, and his imagination. Today the Louth pub has rudimentary supplies, the usual cold beer and cordial, and flat, processed toasted sandwiches. Also, there is a caravan park with public toilets and showers.

However, that said, Louth is situated on the Darling and there is easy access to the river. Fishing and camping near the bridge is permitted, and the location is most attractive. In the 1890s Louth was a small but flourishing inland port. It was a stopover for Cobb & Co. coaches, the electric telegraph went through there, a ferry carried sheep across the Darling, and the buildings included a post office, a school, a police station, and of course a pub. Wool from nearby sheep stations and copper ingots from Cobar were assembled here for trans-

Entrance to Louth (PHOTO: GARRY TICKNER)

port to Bourke, or to Morgan in South Australia via the Murray. There is no sign of the wharf or any of that side of its history now, just the atmosphere.

For Catherine, Louth's Irish connection was initially appealing. The town was founded by Thomas Matthews from County Louth, just north of Dublin, and the relationship is proudly declared by the so-called 'Celtic cross'. Matthews was a success-

Pastoralists along the Darling

In the 1840s, adventurous pastoralists moved up the Darling River with whatever stocks they could afford and wagons loaded with shovels, axes, swags, food and other supplies. Land around the Darling did not provide the same good pastoral conditions as around the Murray or the Murrumbidgee, but that didn't stop them. The first licence fee was paid in 1841, with the first official squatter recorded in 1846. It is likely that there were Europeans grazing the land even before that. Pastoral runs were identified by landmarks, and the settlers built rough huts with bark and mud, and thatched them with the light lignum branches from the riverside. As they became more established, they built timber homes and stockyards. Stock was cared for by shepherds living in small huts along the run. By the end of the 1840s there was a lot of activity along the Darling.

But in the 1850s many of the pastoralists went broke. The gold rush in Victoria in the 1850s reduced the supply of European labour in the transport business, and access to supplies and markets was difficult. Then, following the arrival of river transport, the pastoral scene changed. Station owners began to shift from cattle to sheep. Cattle were a good option if the only transport to the markets was overland. But now that wool could be brought to market by river transport, it made sheep a more viable option. Forfeited runs were taken up again, shanty pubs and hotels were reopened. Other pastoralists, who had hung on but weren't doing well, now took the opportunity to sell.

When station owners began to erect fences in the 1860s, the role of the shepherd became redundant. Life was hard, with drought and flooding affecting the land and interrupting access to supplies and markets. Changes of ownership were frequent. A commentator in 1887 called the land along the Darling 'one of the greatest gambling tables in the world'. This was because one wealthy station owner could lose everything he owned and abandon the run with nothing to his name, while the next could start with nothing and leave with a fortune.

The 1884 Land Act in NSW caused havoc in stations in the region. The Land Act reduced the size of the squatters' titles. Huge stations, several exceeding 1 million acres, were broken up to increase the number of pastoral holdings. Pastoralists lost the improvements they had made to properties and found themselves having to run their stock on smaller properties. The years around the turn of the century were disastrous: the rabbit had become a pest, the land had been overused for sheep grazing, wool prices were low, and there was a national economic depression.

ful businessman with several hotels, stores and pastoral holdings in the region. He also provided a transport service to the copper ore mines in Cobar. He erected the cross in the memory of his wife, Mary, who died at the age of 42 in this harsh land. The construction of the cross is designed to reflect the light of the sun at sunset into the township; the experience lasts for about three minutes. Over a year the reflection travels a distance of a kilometre, depending on the position of the sunset on the horizon. On the anniversary of Mary's death in August, the light reflects on 'The Retreat', which was her home.

The Celtic cross is in the fields to the east of the town and is visible from the township. Various tracks through the scrub lead to it. But if you expect to see a traditional Celtic cross, you will be disappointed. It is difficult to see a Celtic influence on the style or design of the Louth cross, which rises to about 5 metres. If you wish to stay around Louth at sunset to witness this phenomenon, ask one of the local people where to stand for the best place for that time of year.

TRILBY STATION

The best option for bush camping along here is out on Trilby Station, 25 km south of Louth. Access to Trilby Station homestead is off the road on the western side of the river. Trilby Station was once part of the historic Dunlop Station, and Garry and Liz Murray have opened it up to tourists who want to find out what it is really like to live in this part of the world. Campers are welcome to join them for dinner and hear about what life is like running a sheep station in the outback. Garry and Liz will also tell you about the history of the area, then give you a mud-map that allows you to drive safely around their property. They have numbered the gates so that you can't get lost, a very practical and sensible way of providing directions! The station runs from the black soil floodplains to the higher ridges, and the vegetation changes on the way. You can watch sheep shearing and other activities in season — they run 15,000 sheep, as well as cattle. Old farming equipment that stood abandoned in a shed has now been labelled and captioned.

You can stay here, either camping somewhere along their 25 km of river frontage in one of the powered sites, or in cottage or modern bunkhouse accommodation. There is an overnight charge per vehicle for camping ($12 for camping, $15 for a powered site). For campers there is access to a kitchen, a BBQ and other caravan-park style facilities. This is a marvellous opportunity to camp by the Darling, either in isolation or near people. The station is accessible to conventional vehicles. Trilby is signposted from the road about 23 km south of Louth, and directions to the house are clear (02 6874 7420).

Fishing enthusiasts who are fed up with the poor quality of the fishing on the Murray are attracted to the available campsites of the Darling, including Trilby. You can catch cod, yellow belly, perch and, in season, yabbies. If you wish, Garry and Liz Murray can provide you with a flat-bottomed boat, yabby nets and some fishing gear. The river is a placid and safe place on which to take a small boat.

TILPA

Tilpa, 90 km from Louth, has recently developed into a good visitor stopover, similar in style and quality to the tiny townships that provide services to travellers in outback South Australia. It's famous pub is over 100 years old, and is made of corrugated iron and timber. It is one of the few true bush pubs in Australia.

Today you can visit the Tilpa Pub, have a cold drink, a meal and sign your name on the bar in exchange for a donation to the Royal Flying Doctor Service — one of the unique and highly popular features of this place. The shop next to it is in what was once the Weirwater Pub, then the puntkeeper's residence, and later the post office, during which time it was badly damaged by floodwaters before the levee was created. Graziers Carol and Bernie Williams acquired the by-now decrepit building and have recently opened it as a shop. Although the building is still in poor condition and it would be easier to demolish it, Carol is aware of

Shearers' strikes

As a major outback centre in a large sheep region, Bourke and the surrounding stations were centres of union activity during the shearers' battles with pastoralists in the late 19th century. The trouble began when a group of western NSW pastoralists posted a notice in *The Australian* in April 1886, announcing new conditions under which shearers would be employed in their stations. They dropped the standard rate of £2 per hundred sheep by 2 shillings and 6 pence. They also said they would drop the rate further if any work was unsatisfactory or if a shearer caused trouble. One poorly shorn sheep in a hundred could cause the shearer to lose a further 2 shillings and 6 pence per hundred. Bringing alcohol onto the property or even whistling when working could be construed by the foreman as misconduct and attract a penalty. On top of that, shearers were obliged to buy personal provisions from the stations at inflated rates because they were not allowed to bring their own supplies onto the station.

This prompted nearly a decade of unrest between the shearers and the pastoralists. A shearers' union was formed two months later. Its first branch was in Ballarat in Victoria; its second in Bourke in NSW. Over time it became a national political force. As the conflict escalated, there was trouble along the Darling. Several full-scale strikes occurred in the region, notably in 1886, 1891 and 1894. Neither pastoralists nor unionists were going to give in without a fight. Pastoralists used the paddle-boats to bring in non-union labour. Unionists retaliated by attacking the boats with missiles, including rocks and blazing sticks, graffiti, heckling, and even setting fire to a boat. Captains carrying non-union workers put up nets to protect their boats. Some non-union labour stuck it out and went to work, others joined the union and the fight. Other unions around Australia, notably the carriers' unions and the wharfies, banned the handling of 'black' wool as it was called.

The fight waxed and waned, but gradually the pastoralists' organisation and the union reached agreements. However, the truce was uneasy and in 1902 trouble threatened again. Relations eventually settled down in 1907 when there was a formal court conciliation, and the first shearers' award was made to establish rates of pay. It also dealt with issues like hut accommodation, cost of stores, and other details that had been the source of conflict in the past. Successive awards have continued to include such details in settlements.

its historical significance and is working out ways of preserving it. Carol and Bernie stock the usual outback stores: milk, bread, camera film, phone cards, some fishing gear, fishing advice and lots of great stories about life around Tilpa. It is open from about 7 am to 9 pm, although if a light is on and it is a genuine emergency, they are prepared to be disturbed after that.

Tilpa has great access to the river with a reserve and a weir. You may camp nearby, but there are no facilities and it is a bit public. There is a playground in Tilpa. There is also a rubbish dump — a useful service for anyone who has been travelling through the outback for a while! Two heritage signs in the town will direct you around the historical features. There are plans to create a caravan park in Tilpa now that the town is blooming as a tourist centre.

In the meantime you can find accommodation at Kallara Station Farmstay, 12 km north of Tilpa by the western side of the river. Kallara provides powered caravan sites, or the opportunity to stay in a brand new lodge, called Coolibah, overlooking the river. The original Coolibah Lodge, part of an ex-irrigation hut, burnt down in 2000. The new lodge has three rooms with ensuites overlooking the river. There is no riverside camping, but the caravan park has loads of space and there is no sense of crowding (02 6837 3964).

Wilcannia

Wilcannia, 137 km from Tilpa, is a well-placed tourist town with a stated population of 1000, a historic centre, and a reputation! In the town, 80% of the people are Aboriginal, mostly Barkindji people of the Darling. In the past there were incidents, not necessarily involving tourists, but enough to give the place a reputation of being rough. Yet on all of the many occasions we have visited Wilcannia, the place has been peaceful and quiet, the strong Aboriginal presence and the striking 19th-century sandstone buildings, all giving the town its own character. No doubt the sounds of late-night carousing might be threatening to some, the bars on the windows and hoardings on some abandoned buildings may also look a bit intimidating, but none of this impinges on our enjoyment of a stroll through the historic inland port or the pleasure of an overnight stop by the Darling near Wilcannia.

The demise of the Aboriginal traditional lifestyle

The influx of settlers and itinerant workers associated with the stations and river trade changed Aboriginal lives irrevocably. From the 1840s onwards, their access to the land was quickly reduced as pastoral runs were given to new settlers for their cattle, and later their sheep. The water was fouled, the land was grazed, and access to some areas forbidden, particularly as the fences were erected and station runs were pegged.

The river people began to work for the stations, the women as domestics, the men as station hands. They were given rations and supplies, and lived in camps near the towns. Their social order began to collapse, and the river and the land were no longer so abundant. From 1859, when the paddle-steamers began to use the river, their permanent stone fisheries were destroyed by the boat captains because they were hazards, or their weirs fell into disrepair as they were no longer used. The stock animals ate out their vegetables, berries and other land resources. Their skills in finding food on the land gradually began to fade. Initiation and other ceremonies were difficult to organise in the camps. People who worked for a station had two masters, the station manager and the tribal elder, so making it difficult to adhere to the traditional ways and customs. The Aboriginal population went into decline as the older people died, and fewer children were born.

Re-establishing a social order around this new colonial society may have been manageable, particularly on some of the better managed stations had it not been for the widespread availability of alcohol. The Darling was a rugged place, a place where even river boats and stations had licences to sell alcohol. Spirits of varying qualities — some viciously strong homemade stuff — were freely available. By law, it was forbidden to sell alcohol to Aboriginal people. But mixed-race Aboriginal people were excluded from this until 1906, and anyone could buy alcohol for medical purposes. Consequently, many hotel owners used the loopholes to continue selling grog, and the police did nothing about it.

This exacerbated the deteriorating situation for the Aboriginal people. Already treated poorly by many of the itinerant workers and others who lived out here, they had little tolerance for the rough settlers' brews, and found themselves the focus of taunts and brawls. Worse, the Europeans, many of whom were ex-convicts or tough misfits from the cities, brought alcohol into the camps to exchange it for the favours of the women. Disease followed as the traditional lives of the Barkindji, Barundji and others were destroyed. There were even stories about poisoning, shootings and ill-treatment against the people, but few incidents were investigated and there is little hard information about these stories.

Some of the people who moved into the district were concerned about the Europeans' intrusion on the lives of the Aboriginal people, and attempted to do something about protecting them. Religious missionaries and the NSW Government's Aboriginal Protection authorities were the two major groups who wished to provide a gentler transition from the old ways to the new world. They had mixed success, and, as with similar well-intentioned work in other parts of rural Australia, the solution of bringing people from different groups into reserves with minimal resources did not help to even the balance.

In 1910 the NSW Aborigines' Welfare Board placed regulations on the movement of Aboriginal people in the area. After World War I, many of the full-blood Aborigines in the region succumbed to the flu that had been carried back by ex-servicemen who moved to the area. Some Barkindji were moved by the Aboriginal Board to reserves, including to Murrin Bridge on the Lachlan River in 1948, but the major centre for the Barkindji is now Wilcannia.

Wilcannia is situated on the main route of the Barrier Highway between Broken Hill and Cobar, and therefore supports a lot of tourist and commercial traffic. It has no industries as such, but is a service town for the local pastoral industry and government work. The Liberty roadhouse is the hub of activity for travellers and has a comprehensive range of facilities. You can get fuel, eat-in or take-away typical roadhouse food, have a shower for a few dollars, buy bits and pieces of tourist paraphernalia including books, and chat with other travellers. Across the road from the roadhouse is a well-stocked IGI supermarket. Don't let the bars and shutters outside the store put you off. It is quite a substantial supermarket.

The European history in the town has been made readily accessible with the Wilcannia Heritage Trail. The guide to the Heritage Trail is produced by Tourism NSW and includes a clear map of the town, identifying places of historic interest. It is available from the tourist centre in the Shire offices on Reid Street, or in the shops and fuel stations in Wilcannia. Each place on the map represents a historic information board, usually with a photo. Many of the points of interest are centred either near the bridge over the Darling River or around the police station where there are several attractive government buildings.

The bridge over the Darling on the Barrier Highway is a fine example of a vertical or centre-lift bridge. Although the boards have been covered in tarmac, it is easy to see where the split was, and you can envisage the bridge being lifted in a vertical position by the pulley and wheels at either end of the bridge.

Information boards near the bridge direct your attention to past European activities, such as the Wilcannia Boat Club. This club was based in a floating boathouse that was moored nearby around the turn of the century. When Wilcannia was a centre of pastoral social life, the owners or managers were called silver-tails, while the station hands were called toe-rags! Part of the old wooden wharf is still visible, gently disintegrating with time. An old steam engine parked on the grass provides evidence of the other form of transport in the region.

A block away on Reid Street you will find a cluster of old sand-stone buildings in a row, with a courthouse, a police station and gaol. The middle building was built as a maximum-security prison in 1881, and is now used as a police station. Across the road from the police station are several large waterfront warehouses. Here, at the height of Wilcannia's prosperity in the late 19th century, wharf workers processed huge quantities of products such as wool, flour, wire and timber. The goods were loaded directly from the boats into the yards. The buildings are now closed up but they will give you a sense of how busy this inland port must have been in its heyday.

Some distance away are three more buildings dating from the late 19th century. The Catholic Church on Woore Street included a Catholic convent in the 1890s — a group of dedicated nuns opened a school in 1890 and built the convent in 1894. It was closed in the 1920s with the economic downturn of the town and a new convent was built in Parkes (over 600 km to the east). The Athenaeum Club and Library, two blocks away on Reid Street, held the municipal offices for a while; it also hosted a Pioneer Museum of old equipment. Now the shire is developing the Pioneer Museum as a computer centre for the local kids. The plan is also to have an Aboriginal art gallery to display local culture to tourists. The shire offices are now located in the old London Bank dating from 1890.

Sandstone building, Wilcannia

On or shortly after pension day, there are usually many people, mostly of Aboriginal background, congregating around the Club Hotel. While this may look a bit intimidating, it is actually a lot friendlier and more easy-going for a day time drink than some of the other outback pubs we have been into! Aboriginal culture is largely hidden from tourists like ourselves. There are some colourful murals on the walls, providing the only hint of how exciting the river culture is. A drink in the pub may provide more insight into life on the Darling. (Note that the pub doesn't serve meals.)

In terms of accommodation, there are two motels and a caravan park. Victory Park is on the banks of the Darling on the south-east side of town — turn right before the bridge. Victory Park has powered and unpowered sites — $14 and $9 respectively

— with access to tables, wood BBQs, toilets, showers, and a laundry. It is set in a large, grassed area by the river. The caretakers live there, and, despite the reputation of Wilcannia, this is a pleasant, peaceful place to camp. On occasion, local kids will try to sell you yellow belly or other fish they have caught; while you may feel a bit hassled by this, you can virtually guarantee the fish will be fresh! The caravan park is never very busy, so it is probably not necessary to book (08 8091 5874).

Wilcannia to Menindee

This track between Wilcannia and Menindee a 154 km dirt road that roughly follows the course of the Darling on the west side of the river. Like the other roads along the river, you won't see much water along the drive. If it has been raining, the road may be difficult or even closed! The terrain is a mixture of pale river sand or red sand, scrub, saltbush, and gumtrees, varying in size depending on proximity to the river. The land that the road travels through is either station country or wildlife reserve and you have little access to the river. However, there are plenty of lovely picnic spots in the scrubland under the trees. The bigger trees join the track along creek-lines, but these are likely to be dry.

There is one particularly attractive picnic spot by a beautiful lake 114 km south of Wilcannia, by some classic sandy red dunes. The unnamed lake is about 200 metres east of the road, and is ideally suited for lunch with birdlife, low trees and scrub. It is a sanctuary, so camping and shooting are prohibited. The lakes provide a peaceful break from the acacia scrubland along here.

A little earlier, about 102 km south of Wilcannia, is another lake called Balaka. You may see this marked on a map with a fish indicating that it is a place to throw in a line. However, it isn't! Balaka Lake is on private property, so you will have to wait until you get to the great fisheries of Menindee to drop a line in the water.

Further on, 130 km south of Wilcannia, the presence of the vast water system around Menindee is clearly evident. The region around Menindee has become a highly productive agricultural region with grapes and other fruit, cotton and cereal production, thanks to irrigation from the water system. Travelling this way from the north, it can be a bit startling after so much dry scrub and red sand.

Wilcannia

Wilcannia began to develop as a river stopover after the navigation of the Darling opened up the transport route. A woolshed and huts were built by the river to service Mt Murchison station and a settlement grew around this. By 1866 the settlement was proclaimed, with a population of 200. Following the discovery of copper, silver, opals and gold in the nearby Barrier Ranges in the 1870s and 1880s, the centre developed rapidly as a focus of commercial activity. The first school was built in 1868, and the first church in 1875. Travelling doctors of varying quality and degrees of sobriety provided medical attention until the first hospital was erected in 1879. One of the leading citizens in Wilcannia was Edward Dickens, son of the English novelist Charles Dickens. Known as Ted to his neighbours, he lived in the region for 25 years, working as a station manager, a justice of the peace, a municipal councillor, a member of the licensing court, a member of parliament in NSW, and a horsetrader.

In the early 1880s, steamers passed up and down the Darling by Wilcannia at the rate of about a dozen a week. Goods were stacked on the bank, the wharves not having been built yet. The air of prosperity and permanence was established with the construction of municipal and government buildings in the 1880s. The courthouse, the gaol, hotels, a warehouse and a library were among the buildings made with local sandstone. Ted Dickens was active in collecting funds to support the library.

There was a meet at the racecourse three or four times a year. Local services included up to a dozen local stores, two banks, a solicitor, two breweries, a cordial manufacturer, an optician and a jeweller. The local newspaper, the *Wilcannia Times*, was published three times a week. It folded in 1888 as the fortunes of the town began to shift.

Like so many other river towns, Wilcannia went into decline at the end of the 19th century. Unpredictable river flow and the railway line made river transportation less appealing. The pastoralists also suffered drought and plagues of rabbits, further reducing the economic life of the town.

Besides agriculture in this lush region north of Menindee, the lakes support a thriving water-based leisure industry. Signposts to the recreational centres and clubs, boat ramps, boat hire, caravan parks and so on, appear at frequent intervals to the north of Menindee. The lakes area is particularly popular with people living in the wider region, hence the number of water-based recreational clubs.

Continuing on, 135 km south of Wilcannia is a lookout over the lakes. This is a magnificent sight. The vast lake, which is 16 km long, disappears into the horizon. We were there once on a windy day; the rough water gave us the impression of being on the shore of an inland sea. Waves crashed up against the banks of the lake and birds hovered around the tops of partially submerged trees. The local literature boasts that the lakes are seven times the area of Sydney harbour and four times the capacity but, we don't need statistics to persuade us that this is one enormous lake system!

The lookout here provides access to just one part of the Menindee lakes system, which was developed in the 1950s. You could spend a week here following the complex system, starting with the dam on the Darling north-east of the town. If this interests you, the mud-map in Mary Wilson's book, *Menindee: First Town on the Darling*, or other maps available in the Information Centre, will give you the directions you need to follow the network of weirs, regulators, dams, canals, levees and lakes.

At the lookout, there is a railway line between the carpark and the lookout point that runs between Broken Hill and Wilcannia. The *Indian Pacific* passes here several times a week, the *Ghan* also travels through here, and freight trains may come through several times a day. At the lookout, there are litter facilities, but little else to make it an attractive camping place. There are plenty of places to stay around Menindee so we wouldn't recommend the lookout as a place to camp.

Menindee

Menindee is a pleasant town with lots of tourist-related activity and prosperous-looking businesses. It is a small place with a population of less than 1000, but numbers swell significantly during the holiday seasons. There are several different styles of accommodation available as well as plenty of great bushcamping locations. The clearly signposted Information Centre, in the old 1940s railway station on the hill in Maiden Street, is a good source of information. The staff are very helpful and will give you plenty of advice about tours and other facilities available for long or short holidays in the area. The centre is open from 9 am to 5 pm, Monday to Friday, and from 10 am to 1 pm on Saturdays and Sundays.

Although most of the interesting features of Menindee are in the country around the lakes, the town will give you a sense of a place that began life as a typical river settlement. Menindee grew up around Thomas Paine's hotel. He built the historic Maiden Menindee Hotel here in 1852, at a time when settlers were moving into the country along the river. At the time there were no permanent businesses or dwellings along this stretch of the river, despite the amount of stock movement in the region. Paine, an English convict who was transported for stealing a pair of boots, moved up the Darling with his Irish wife Bridget, and her parents. Determine to establish a solid settlement, they built a house using handmade sundried clay bricks, with timber roofing thatched with lignum branches. Relationships with the local Aboriginal people were cordial, and this encouraged more settlers to move in and develop the township. Bridget had nine children, and died at 33 years of age. Paine later moved to Queensland, where he died in 1882.

The outside of the Maiden Menindee Hotel is most inviting, with a well-preserved and attractive frontage. Inside, however, the central part of the hotel, including the bar, was destroyed by fire in April 1999. Before that, visitors could see the original hotel lounges and could eat in the diningroom with its wooden tables, white tablecloths and silver cutlery. The room where Burke and Wills slept in October 1860 had been altered and a wall removed before the fire, but even these have now gone. When we were there in 1999, it was business as usual with drinks being served in one of the rooms off the courtyard and tables set up outside in the gutted centre. The new diningroom and lounges have since been opened, and memorabilia has been put up in one of the lounges. There is still a historical atmosphere in the facade and the bedrooms in the front of the building.

Ah Chung's Bakery, 100 metres from the Maiden Menindee

Hotel, is also worth a visit. The bakery was built around 1880. Like so many outback bakeries, the cooking took place underground to conserve heat during the cooking process and to provide a more comfortable environment for the bakers. During World War II, this bakery produced 200 loaves at a time. The bakery has since been opened as an art gallery to display the works of local and Broken Hill artists. Howard Seddon has kept much of the original machinery, working benches and layout intact to provide visitors with the opportunity to see what an outback bakery once looked like — he even has the old bread tins there! The underground bakery is quite bright and didn't give us the sense of walking down into an underground environment, but we appreciated the opportunity to see a good example of an outback underground bakery. It is open from 2 pm to 5.30 pm, all days except Wednesday and Sunday (08 8091 4322).

Menindee Lakes

The lake area that became known as Menindee was first mapped and named Laidley's Ponds by Thomas Mitchell in 1835. Its popular name, Menindee, is a corruption of the Aboriginal name for the place, Minandichee. The existing lakes provided a good source of water for the area, but were subject to the extremes of drought and flooding that are characteristic of waterways in this region of Australia. This made them an unreliable source of water for European needs. In 1949, work on turning them into a water storage facility for the area began. Dams, weirs, levees and regulators were built. The work linked four major lakes, and was completed in 1960. Now floodwaters are harnessed for distribution as far as Broken Hill to the north and in Wentworth to the south.

The water-storage scheme virtually guaranteed a continuous flow in the Darling for irrigation, stock and general water supplies. In addition, water is sometimes released into the Anabranch to replenish water there. It is even used on occasion to increase water supplies down in the Murray River.

The remains of the Menindee wharf aren't marked on the map but they are visible on the river-front on the east side of town. The Information Centre will give you directions, no doubt local residents will also direct you on request. The wharf is located on the outskirts of town. Drive down Henley Street, past the junction of Chisolm street until you reach a maze of dirt tracks through tufts of grass. You will see the large trees by the Darling, and it is fairly easy to locate the wharf from there.

If you are interested in following the history of European settlement and the development of the town, you can pick up a copy of the Heritage Trail Guide at the Information Centre. It is another of Tourism NSW's easy-to-follow maps of the main historical features in the town. The guide is also useful as a map of the town if you are staying there for a few days.

As a major regional tourist centre, Menindee has a good range of facilities for visitors, including a variety of accommodation. It has full fuel services and some mechanical services. There is a post office with some basic banking facilities, a police station, a nursing service and access to Royal Flying Doctor support.

For accommodation, there is the Burke and Wills Motel, and two hotels, including Maiden's Hotel. There are three caravan parks, including the Copi Hollow Caravan Park on Lake Pamamaroo. This caravan park has several on-site cabins, as well as on-site vans. The turn-off to the Copi Hollow Caravan Park is signposted close to the lookout over Menindee Lake, 17 km north of Menindee (08 8091 4880).

Menindee has many excellent camping places and these will take you into the river and lake environment around the town. The best free camping is out by Lake Pamamaroo, 20 km to the north-east of Menindee. Take the Broken Hill–Wilcannia road out of Menindee for 11 km, and follow the signposts to the main weir. There is the large campsite here where Burke and Wills set up their expedition camp in 1860. The tree they blazed with their marker and the date has been protected, but other than that, the area is open and you may camp anywhere. There are toilets and BBQs, and a lot of space, but it can become quite crowded at busy times, so this is for people who don't mind the proximity of other campers. But around the lake and along the Darling there is 20 km of river camping. The track is marked out by other campers and is a bit rough. Small tracks lead into unmarked cleared spaces. Here you can have an isolated camp, light a small fire, fish all day surrounded by great river gums, and enjoy the peaceful bird life.

The other main camping area is in Kinchega National Park (see below).

The Information Centre can arrange fishing trips, birdwatching trips, visits to the sites associated with the Burke and Wills expedition, trips around the lake system and, of course, glorious river trips. If you plan to bring your own motorboat or jet skis, chat to tourist staff or local people about access and restrictions. The Kinchega National Park map available at the Information Centre gives clear directions on where you can use power boats and where this activity is restricted.

FISHING AROUND MENINDEE

The Menindee Lakes system is a popular fishing location with regular water flows. The yellow belly swim upstream when the lake system inlets and outlets are opened. Shrimp is the preferred bait in the summer; yabbies or worms work best in the winter. Lures are not a good idea because the water isn't clear enough. During peak periods, Lake Pamamaroo becomes very busy, particularly when the regulator has just been opened and the water is flowing. This means excellent fishing for yellow belly, Murray cod, silver perch, yabbies in season, and the inevitable carp. A media release is posted on the Information Centre door to inform everyone when the regulator has been opened. So, if fishing doesn't interest you, avoid Lake Pamamaroo at those times; if you do like fishing, this is the time to go. State fishing licences apply, and signs will point out the restricted fishing areas close to the regulator north of the town and east of Menindee Lake.

If you want direct assistance with fishing or want to head off in a boat to a fishing spot chosen with local knowledge, join one of the fishing tours available in Menindee. Geoff Looney is a keen and knowledgeable birdwatching and fishing guide operating around Menindee. He maintains a list of birds he has spotted in the area and has recorded 166 species. He said that this is an ongoing job as he spots more and more. This local knowledge, together with his cheery, chatty manner, make his fishing trips particularly popular. He provides gear, tackle, bait and morning tea on a trip through the wetlands area where there is great scenery and old homesteads. He brings visitors out in a boat for fishing and/or birdwatching at $80 for four hours for two people (08 8091 4437).

BIRDWATCHING AROUND MENINDEE

The Menindee Lakes system is a joyful place for bird watchers. This semi-arid oasis with permanent water, floodplain, river and lakes attracts a wide variety of birds, including grebe, cormorants, pelicans, egrets, ibis, ducks, kites and many more. Menindee Lakes are a stop-off point for birds on their migratory routes south from Indonesia and even northern Europe. In nearby Kinchega National Park, over 200 species of birds have been recorded. Rare species that you may see here include the pink cockatoo, the white-winged wren, the freckled duck or crimson chats. Tourism NSW and the National Parks and Wildlife Service NSW have produced information for keen birdwatchers. An informative brochure, *Outback Birding*, is available at the tourist centres in the region. This contains information such as the best place to see white-winged wrens (southern end of the lake drive in Kinchega). For visitors like us who just like the presence of lots of birds, simply head for areas with water and vegetation and you won't be disappointed.

KINCHEGA NATIONAL PARK

Much of the country to the south and west of Menindee town is now part of the Kinchega National Park. Kinchega National Park was a sheep station in the 19th century. When Burke and Wills set up an expedition camp here, the station was fully operational, and William Wright had just left his job as station manager. From 1870 Kinchega Station was part of a huge lease held by the Hughes family. At one stage the area covered 800,000 hectares. The park is now 44,000 hectares. In 1967 Kinchega became a national park and the last sheep was sheared in the wool shed, reportedly the six millionth sheep!

The National Parks and Wildlife Service of NSW have established several drives to help visitors explore the area. The total circuit along the river and west into the lakes is about 25–30 km. This provides visitors with an opportunity to drive close to the

Gunbower Creek, Gunbower State Forest near Koondrook (PHOTO: BILL BACHMAN)

The road between Noccundra and the Dig Tree (Photo: Garry Tickner)

Fishing in the Murray-Kulkyne National Park (Photo: Garry Tickner)

The Burke and Wills expedition at Menindee

Several of the dramas involving the tragic Burke and Wills expedition in 1860–1, were played out at Menindee. The tiny township of about 15 residents was the last outpost of colonial settlement in 1860. Here the explorers could get provisions, hire staff, send and receive messages, and make final preparations before heading into uncharted and inhospitable regions to the north.

By the time the group reached Menindee after their trek up from Melbourne en route to Cooper Creek, they were in disarray. Although the river transport pioneer, Francis Cadell, had offered to carry the group's supplies up-river in his paddle-steamer to Menindee, Burke would have nothing to do with Cadell because Cadell had opposed his appointment. So Burke and the expedition made slow progress from Melbourne via Swan Hill, leading heavily-laden camels, horses and drays. The drive to maintain some pace in difficult circumstances exhausted the group and the animals, so by the time they arrived in Menindee on the outreaches of settlement in the colony, they were already weary.

More seriously, Burke and his deputy, George Landells, were quarrelling frequently, primarily over the use and handling of the camels. Although there was a brief truce, it was broken by reports of Landells criticising Burke and his leadership behind his back. The squabbles in the party reached the newspapers, with most preferring to support Burke, despite evidence to suggest that his management of the expedition was suspect.

In Menindee, the locals were enjoying the diversion of the dysfunctional expedition. The characters who hung around Maiden's Pub were used to the comings and goings of men out into the bush. Menindee was the last outpost of any size before the promises of rich land up the Darling. The people had seen it all by the time the much-hyped expedition arrived in town. They listened to the squabbles, and speculated on the group's chances of success.

In October 1860 Burke and Wills set up camp by Pamamaroo Creek, although Burke and Wills stayed in the hotel in town. During that time Burke split the party, leaving a small group behind with some of the weaker animals and a large portion of the stores and provisions. He went on northwards towards Cooper Creek with some of his men, guided by a local man he had employed in Menindee, William Wright. Wright guided Burke's party as far as Torowotto, halfway to the Cooper before returning to Menindee.

Burke's instructions to Wright were to return to Menindee and bring back camels and other supplies. However Wright needed funding to prepare fresh dried meat supplies and to purchase better quality animals. He also wanted confirmation of his position with the Exploration Committee in Melbourne.

But communication with the Exploration Committee was disorganised, and the Menindee rear-party did not receive authorisation to continue preparations. Cheques bounced, important letters were carried by the slow, regular mail to and from Melbourne, and several almost-fatal forays were made to the north to follow Burke. Meanwhile, Burke, Wills and the rest of the advance group had arrived at Cooper Creek and were preparing to travel north, leaving William Brahe in charge of base camp at the Creek.

Then in desperation, one of the Menindee party, William Hodgkinson, set out in late December and rode for nine solid days to get to Melbourne to communicate directly with the Exploration Committee. They confirmed Wright's appointment and guaranteed funds to support the additional requirements of the party. At the end of January Wright eventually set out from Menindee with a party to provide back-up to Burke.

For a variety of reasons, Wright's trek towards the Cooper was a disaster. There had been little seasonal rain, so there was very little water at the hottest time of the year. They set up camps by Kooliatto Creek, and then at Bulloo, in places that greatly upset the local Aboriginal people. They also suffered from the rat plague that was infesting this part of the country at the time and several members of the group became ill. Wright's handling of all these disasters was questionable — his overriding goal was to make it to the Cooper to support Burke and he didn't want to spend resources and time on looking after sick members of the group. The artist Ludwig Becker, the experienced bushman Charles Stone, and a third member of the group, William Purcell, were near death at the Bulloo camp by April. Over the next eight days, all three died.

In April, Wright met up with Brahe and his party, who had left the Cooper after Burke and Wills had missed their return deadline by a month. When Wright met them on their return journey, they were all suffering from scurvy. Brahe and Wright left their combined party and returned together to the Cooper just in case Burke and Wills had returned just after Brahe left. Famously Brahe and Wright only spent 15 minutes at the Cooper base camp and noticed none of the small changes that Burke, Wills and John King had left there. They then collected their group at Bulloo, and returned to Menindee.

William Patten, one of Brahe's party, died on the way. They finally reached Menindee on 18 June. Wright chose to travel on to his family in Adelaide rather than organise a fresh party or even report to the Melbourne Exploration Committee. He left that to Brahe.

Burke and Wills died at Cooper Creek. In September 1861, King was rescued by a search party led by Alfred Howitt.

Darling through the river red gums. This is the only section of the Darling that is protected by a national park. The drive passes the historic woolshed and Visitor Information Centre on the homestead loop. The signposted ruins of the large homestead are on this loop.

The drive continues into the heart of the park to Cawndilla Lake and on to Menindee Lake. The whole circuit is fairly well-signposted, although there are plans for improvements. The drive is in three sections, the riverside drive, the homestead loop and the lakeside drive. Sections of the lakeside drive can become quite soft and sandy in the summer months so it is probably wise not to include this section if you are driving a normal sedan at that time of year. The tracks to the bush campsites are generally accessible for all vehicles in dry weather.

The entrance to the park is 1 km west of Menindee down Nora Street; access is well-signposted. The 35 bush camping spots by the river banks are clearly identified along the 20 km river drive. There is a small charge ($5 for two per night, and an additional fee for extra people), payable at an honesty box at the round hut near the entrance. You will find a map there. The marked and numbered campsites are situated on the Darling. There are toilet facilities at intervals along the drive, and campers are requested to use these. There is one minor problem with the campsites, however. Although they are close to the river, they are also close to the road and, depending on the time of year, there may be a lot of passing traffic. There may also be dust, particularly during the summer months. This makes the campsites good for an overnight camp or a longer stay off-peak, but perhaps think of Lake Pamamaroo and the unmarked bush sites at busier times or for longer stays. The campsites around number 30 are a bit quieter.

River transport

In the 1840s, as the Darling was being settled, the horse or bullock teams moved at the speed of about 60 km per week. A trip by dray from the Darling region to Adelaide could take eight or nine weeks. In 1859 Francis Cadell navigated the Darling in his steamship, the *Albury*, as far as Mt Murchinson, just north of Wilcannia. Other steamships had already travelled part of the way up the Darling, but these did not attract the publicity that characterised Cadell's river navigation business success. Cadell brought supplies and cargo to Mt Murchison station, picked up wool bales and returned to his store at Menindee.

The same year, his great rival, William Randell met him on the return journey in his famous steamship, the *Gemini*. Randell had travelled up the Darling past Bourke on to Brewarrina, becoming the first to navigate a steamer so far inland on this river. On his return journey, Randell picked up more bales of wool from Mt Murchison. By chance, neither of these early trips encountered snags or submerged trees, floods or low waters, all of the problems that were going to plague subsequent riverboat captains.

From then until the 1940s river-boat traffic was common along the Darling. The steamers kept the properties going. They carried passengers, mail, gossip and supplies to the stations, and they bartered shop items for fresh food supplies for the boat staff. The Europeans' outback diet consisted of dried fruit and vegetables, potatoes, flour, sugar, coffee, curry powder and other spices, rice, and lots of caraway seed, raisins and currants, which were probably used to make the damper more palatable. Alcohol was also a basic commodity. Stations opened licensed hotels rather than having to supply endless hospitality free of charge. Some of the steamboats even had a limited alcohol licence. On the return journey down the river, the boats brought the station produce to the markets of the south. Some barges could carry 1500 bales of wool.

As news of successful trips up the Darling appeared in Australian metropolitan newspapers, more settlers and business enterprises were encouraged to venture out to the region. Within a few months most of the runs that had previously been forfeited were taken up again, and shanty pubs and stores appeared along the river bank. Drover Vincent Dowling described a couple of outback shanty pubs in graphic terms in his diary in 1862–3. One, he wrote, was nasty, dirty, miserable and cold with two 'most awfully dirty women' in attendance! Another was dirty, filthy and uncomfortable, and he couldn't imagine how the landlord was permitted to hold a licence!

Over 100 years from the earliest settlement in the 1840s, the Darling River was known to run dry on at least ten occasions. Floods also had hazards, with fast-flowing debris threatening the hulls of the boats. Plans to put a system of locks and weirs up the Darling to make it more reliable as an inland waterway in the 1890s were abandoned at the time because this was too expensive.

The steamers often towed barges of wool down the waterway, stretching 450 metres behind them. Both the steamer and its barge were in danger of being snagged by tree branches from the river-side, or marooned by sandbars as the water level dropped. When this happened, the crew would have to dislodge the boats somehow, or wait until the water levels rose — and that could take months!

River transport north of Wilcannia stopped in the 1930s as weirs prevented boats from navigating the river except during floods. In 1963 the Darling River bridge built south of Pooncarie halted large vessels at that point. Before this a punt brought people and vehicles across the river when it was in flood.

MENINDEE TO WENTWORTH VIA POONCARIE

The road on the east side of the Darling River between Menindee and Pooncarie is a wide 130 km dirt track, pleasant when dry and recently graded, difficult or impassable when wet. From Pooncarie to Wentworth, it is 124 km on smooth bitumen, a treat if you are returning to the south after weeks of outback travel. The countryside between these two river towns is a combination of scrub and barren terrain. The trees vary in size and density, depending on the proximity to the river. You will also see red or pale sand, its colour also depending on the proximity of the river.

You will get a good glimpse of the Darling 57 km south of Menindee. At this point, the river joins the road and provides a break from continuous scrubland. It is one of the few opportunities along the road between Bourke and Wentworth to enjoy a natural view of the river without a surrounding township. Here you can imagine the occasion in 1884 when 16 paddle-steamers were stuck between Menindee and Wentworth for eight months until a sudden two-metre rise in the water level at Wilcannia released them all.

To the north and south of this river-access point, fences close the road in again, and you will see animals, windmills, grids and other evidence of station life in the region. In the distance to the west, the course of the Darling is evident by its substantial tree-line. But views of the river are confined mainly to the banks around Pooncarie.

The stretch of river south of Menindee was known as 'the crooked river' because it was one of the more difficult sections of the river to navigate. Sharp bends and U-bends were hazardous and frustrating — a short distance as the crow flies took hours on the water. Even though we now have no access to this part of the river, any map of the area clearly shows the greater number of bends in the river around here.

South of Pooncarie, the road has been sealed providing a smooth run between this town and Wentworth. A driver who took truckloads of supplies to Pooncarie in the mid-19th century recalled that there were once 49 gates to open and close between the two towns! Now it's a clean ride with few diversions.

POONCARIE

This is an attractive and neat town, with a population of about 60, set on the banks of the Darling. It is no surprise that it has won the Tidy Towns award in the past. The town is a focus for water-based tourist activity. It has good tourist facilities, including a store, a post office, caravan park, a fuel station with a mechanic, golfing, fishing, a race track and an aerodrome. Some of the main streets are named after Robert O'Hara Burke, William Wills, John King and Charles Gray — the leading members of the expedition of 1860–1.

There are two main features in Pooncarie: the river, which comes very close to the main road, and the Pooncarie Telegraph Hotel, which has its foundation in the early 20th century. In 1907 the hotel was described having a bar, three pit toilets, no flywire doors or windows; it also had a bathroom and sixteen rooms. This was at a time when the town was going through a period of growth. It had a butcher, a baker, a blacksmith, a slaughter house, a gift shop, a tea-room, as well as the fundamental businesses of outback towns — hotels and a general store. It also had a dance

Races at Pooncarie

It is not known exactly when the famous Pooncarie races began. The races at Wilcannia were already popular in the 1870s. The races in Pooncarie may have started early in the 1880s, but the earliest evidence that there were races down the river in Pooncarie was in 1885.

Race days were a time of great activity in the river town. For a couple of weeks beforehand, owners brought their horses into the town to stable them at the hotel or in the police paddock by the river. Then the crowd began to gather from the outlying stations and by the time the races began, the town was full.

The first race course was laid out behind the Telegraph Hotel. Prizes at the time were quite substantial, and included 20 sovereigns for one race, another race was for the Maiden Plate. Of course the most lucrative action was probably off-field, as betting was as much a part of the pleasure. The day after the races, when all bets were settled, was as exciting and busy a day in Pooncarie as the race days. In the early 20th century, the Pooncarie races boasted a starting-price bookie, someone who took bets off-course. On one occasion in 1936, the crowds backed an outsider called North Wind because there was a north wind blowing! The bookie took the bets but decided not to ring the bets through to his registered bookmaker contact. After North Wind won, the bookie had to work for three months to pay off his debts!

The races were stopped during World War II, and took off again after that. However in the 1950s the number of registered horses available for the outback racing circuit fell. In order to keep the event going, the gymkhana was started and unregistered horses could join in.

Pooncarie races continue as one of the major outback racing events, drawing large crowds from the region.

hall with a floor that sometimes had to be patched during a dance with boards torn off a beer case.

The current Telegraph Hotel was built slowly over a three-year period and was opened in 1929; the old one was then pulled down. The Telegraph Hotel accommodation includes several rooms with ensuites; the rest are single rooms with shared washing facilities. Prices range from $77 for a double room with ensuite to $30 with shared facilities; both include breakfast. You can also get dinner and snack food here. This is a classic outback riverside motel with a pleasant atmosphere and is the place to call into for any information about services in the area (03 5029 5205).

Across the road from the hotel is a public campsite along the river bank. There are shower and toilet facilities that anyone can use, the showers are coin operated. There is a small fee for camping here, payable at the hotel ($5 per car). However it is a fairly public campsite and it wouldn't be the place to stay if you like seclusion. If you really want to make a camp on the stretch of river near Pooncarie but away from it all, the staff in the hotel or the store would be happy to help you. They will give you the names of the station owners you can contact, and have been known to do the contacting for you. This keeps everyone happy, the station owners don't have people on their properties that they don't know about, and visitors are made to feel welcome. Pooncarie is hectic around peak holiday times, and especially in the first week of October when it holds its famous race meeting and gymkhana.

MUNGO NATIONAL PARK

Lake Mungo is one of several lakes along Willandra Creek. It is a major outback destination for Australian and overseas visitors because of its beautiful scenery and its Aboriginal significance. With archaeological sites associated with over 30,000 years of Aboriginal history and culture, it claims to be the oldest archaeological site open to the public.

The turn-off to the Mungo National Park is 29 km south of Pooncarie. From there, it is 60 km along an unsealed road to the main entrance and Visitor Centre. It is a further 11 km out to the best known feature of the park, the Walls of China. There are no facilities or fuel services out here, so it is important that you carry enough fuel to undertake a round trip of at least 300 km. However, if you want to explore the national park, it is advisable to carry enough fuel for up to 450 km.

The most powerful image of Mungo National Park is the series of sand dunes known as the Walls of China. This long, crescent shaped lunette was formed over tens of thousands of years as wind built up the dunes of sand and silt by the shores of Lake Mungo. When the now dry lakebed was full of water, Aboriginal people lived here, drawing on the rich resources of a vast lake system. When the cooling effects of the Ice Age waned about 15,000 years ago, the lake dried up and has been dry ever since. Aboriginal people continued to live in the area until the arrival of European squatters. The ancient history of the dunes is contained in layers, the most ancient at the base being a pink colour, the middle layers (known as Mungo), are grey-brown, and the more recent layer is grey-green. At sunrise and sunset, the colours on the patterned surface are magnificent golds — a photographer's delight.

Lake Mungo (PHOTO: EWA NARKIEWICZ)

The NSW National Parks and Wildlife Service that manages Mungo National Park has created a series of drives around the park. A short drive near the main entrance takes you up to the

Walls and to the 19th-century Mungo woolshed and other station buildings. The popular drive is about 11 km on a track that runs through low green scrub; this leads directly to the Walls of China. You will come to a bank of sand, and this is the beginning of the wall around the boundary of the dry lake. The dunes are not very high, maybe three to four metres but they seem to look higher in photographs. There is a mixture of surfaces: many have a fragile crust that holds them in place, you may not walk on these; some consist of soft, shifting sand, which you may walk on. The longest drive will take you all the way around the park past the Walls of China and out into the scrubland. This is a 60 km round trip.

All around you are fossils, bones, fireplaces and other archaeological remains but, unless you know what you are looking for, it is very difficult to spot them. Evidence of Aboriginal life from up to 35,000 years ago has been found in the layers of the lunettes, the most ancient in the middle or Mungo layer. Stone tools, kitchen middens, hearths, burial grounds and animal bones have all been located and studied here. Extinct animals including a giant kangaroo and the Tasmanian tiger have been found here.

Boardwalks will take you closer to artefacts and the sand formations. It is difficult to work out what is exceptional and special, so if you are keen to see the archaeological remains and find out more about the history of the lakes, we would highly recommend that you join a tour. (Of course, it is an offence to remove any archaeological artefacts, no matter how common or innocuous they may look).

During autumn, winter and spring school holidays, National Parks discovery guides are on hand to direct and advise you. Of the commercial groups, the award-winning Harry Nanya Tours of Wentworth is one of the major tour operators into Mungo. Aboriginal guides from the Barkindji and other people of the area conduct full-day tours that pick visitors up from their accommodation and take them to the Walls of China. The guides provide insight into Aboriginal heritage in the region and identify archaeological remains in the park. With lunch, the tours cost $55 all inclusive. During the summer months, they also offer a sunset tour when you can watch the colours on the sand change from the pale grey through the pink, red and golden colours associated with outback sunsets.

A useful guide to exploring the park is Allan Fox's beautifully illustrated, and periodically updated, *Guide to Mungo National Park* published by NSW National Parks and Wildlife Service. The guide provides concise explanations of the formation of the landscapes at Mungo. It has clear diagrams describing the development of the layers from the time when the lake was full, about 45,000 years ago, through the period when it was dry, to the arrival of sheep and rabbits in the mid-19th century, and up to today when it became a national park. The guide includes details about the flora and fauna of the park, with diagrams and illustrations so that you can identify what you are looking at.

If you are travelling out to Mungo by yourself, be aware that it is a remote area with no fuel or food supplies and very limited supplies of drinking water. You must be confident about the reliability of your vehicle, work out the fuel capacity and mileage, bring additional supplies, and check the weather forecast. If it rains, you may get stranded out here as the roads become extremely slippery and sometimes impassable. When it is dry, the roads are likely to be corrugated, so be considerate of your nuts and bolts and drive slowly. Try to avoid travelling in the heat of summer, and tell a member of your family or someone reliable about your travel plans.

Good information and other facilities are readily available out here. A visitor centre at the entrance to the park has descriptive displays about Mungo National Park that will help you understand the significance of the park. It is open all of the time and staffed during the busy period. There is currently no entrance fee to the park but camping fees apply: $5.50 per site for two people, $2.20 extra per person to a limit of six people per site. There are two camping grounds, one of which is near the entrance and is nicely laid out with plenty of space, except during the peak holiday periods when there may be 20–30 camping parties here. There is also the Belah Camp campsite at the eastern side of the park, again with facilities but no BBQ, and campfires aren't allowed here.

The shearers' quarters at Mungo National Park are also available for overnight accommodation. There are five rooms, each with bunk beds, and together they sleep up to 23 people. There is a communal kitchen and open fireplace; wood is supplied but you will have to chop it yourself. Here is a chance to meet other travellers; the rangers also sometimes join visitors for a chat. There is a clean shower and toilet block with hot water at the shearers' quarters. Overnight charges for accommodation here are $16.50 per adult and $5.50 per child for the night. Bookings are advisable because the rooms can be fully booked by large parties. It may be difficult to get through to the National Parks and Wildlife Service to make the booking but persevere; it is a long way to drive and find yourself without a place to sleep! As with most shearing quarters accommodation, you must bring your own sleeping bag and pillow (03 5021 8900).

Just outside the park on the Mildura road is the Mungo Lodge (03 5029 7297), a standard motel with a licensed restaurant and an airstrip. As you can imagine, this place is often fully booked, so if you hope to stay there, ring before you leave Pooncarie to find out if they have a vacancy. Once there, it is an excellent starting point for the Park, particularly if you don't want to take a tour. The staff at the lodge are used to providing mud-maps and guidelines to visitors over a drink in the bar! They can direct you to some of the interesting sites so that you can find them yourself. They also have a touring licence and a bus that takes groups out to the Aboriginal archaeological sites in Mungo. There is a fee for this ($25 including lunch) and a tour can take 4–5 hours. Check with the Lodge to find out if a tour coincides with your visit.

Wentworth

Wentworth is a popular river-based holiday town at the edge of irrigated vineyards, (population 1450). In the days when gambling was illegal in Victoria, busloads of people came over the border to play the poker machines in NSW and Wentworth. You will see evidence of this in the large gambling venues. However the town is much quieter now that Victoria has its own supply of poker machines and a casino.

The junction of the Murray and the Darling is the focal point of the town. The park by the junction is on Cadell Street in the western part of town, and is signposted as part of the Wentworth tourist trail. (Visitors arriving from Mildura to the east sometimes confuse the junction of Tuckers Creek and the Darling with the junction of the Murray and the Darling). The junction of the two rivers is a picturesque place with willow trees dipping into the water and green lawns to sit on. There are BBQs, lots of shade and a lovely view and atmosphere. You could fish here and may catch redfin or callop, but will probably catch only carp!

In Wentworth, along the Silver City Highway, there is a small historic park called Fotherby Park where the paddle-steamer *Ruby* sits. It is being restored in a dry dock at community expense and there is great local anticipation about seeing the *Ruby* back on the water and docked by the old wharf across the road. However, it is an expensive process, so the renovation will take time. This is good for visitors like us because, for as long as the renovation is under way, we can see an inland dry dock in operation.

There is an example of a drop-log construction in Fotherby Park. This was actually the first courthouse in Wentworth. It was built in 1863 as the headquarters for the local policeman, Simon McClymont, but because of a need to hold court somewhere, it doubled as a courthouse. It was dismantled from its location in town and rebuilt here to provide a glimpse of pioneering history. Coming from a city environment, it is curious to work out how, in practical terms, early pioneers managed to create town environments in isolated places with minimal infrastructure, few facilities and excessive heat, accompanied by masses of flies. This drop-log cabin is a simple structure, and it is not hard to work out how it was conceived and constructed out here in the 1860s. There are other examples of pioneering life on display, with old wagons and other machinery.

The historic precinct of Wentworth on Beverley Street, on the north side of town, features the imposing historic gaol, with a horse trough and hitching post outside. The gaol was built to replace the three wooden gaol cells, one of which was occupied by the warden. It was opened in 1881 and operated for 46 years. Wentworth was the busiest inland port in NSW at the time. It was a male-dominated society, no doubt with all of the attendant problems of drinking and fighting, and the local settlers — notably the clergy — demanded that a proper gaol be constructed. It is considered to be the first Australian-designed gaol and others, such as Long Bay gaol in Sydney, drew on the design. For visitors, the sunny courtyard belies the violent past associated with any colonial gaol. Although no executions took place here, other forms of violent punishment were used. There are about 1 million bricks in this building, all made from clay dug up from the site and fired in situ. The slate was shipped in from NSW. The 12 cells have 45-centimetre-thick walls; 2 of the cells were for females, the rest for males. The communal areas, such as the kitchen and diningroom, are now part of the shop near the entrance. It sells standard souvenirs such as magnets, teaspoons and tea towels.

Wentworth gaol was decommissioned in 1927, but used once again when some of the cells were opened to hold prisoners following a riot in Mildura in 1962. It was also used in the 1930s as an annexe to Wentworth's secondary school.

Wentworth gaol

Across the road is a folk museum with relics of outback life. It also has a small coffee shop, which makes it easy to spend some time relaxing while exploring the museum. The Harry Mitchell Shop nearby is a well-known supplier of good-quality handmade Aboriginal artefacts such as boomerangs, clap sticks, calico bags and paintings. It is particularly renowned for its didgeridoos, which are exported. The Harry Mitchell Shop is also the base for the Harry Nanya Tours. This operation is Aboriginal owned and operated, and reaches out into the Aboriginal community. It organises apprenticeships for young Aborigines and is linked to an alternative correctional institute called Warakoo Correctional Centre out near Lake Victoria, where young Aboriginal offenders can serve their time and develop skills, including traditional skills, and learn about their heritage. They have a group of artists and craftsmen working for them, and the shop is their outlet.

For us, the Harry Mitchell shop and the Harry Nanya Tours provide a valuable opportunity to have access to Aboriginal culture at the meeting of the rivers. The Harry Nanya Tours cover several major features of the region, including the Mungo National Park, Lake Victoria, and Wentworth tour that takes you out to the Perry Sandhills, 4 km to the west. Most of the tours are day trips; they pick you up from your accommodation in their coach and drop you home, providing lunch along the way. They can be contacted at (03 5027 2076) or through their web site at <www.harrynanyatours.com.au>.

There are seven motels in Wentworth and one hotel with accommodation. Costs are standard with motels ranging in price from $60 to $100 for a double room. There is also the Willow Bend Caravan Park on the shores of the Darling. Cabins with ensuites cost $44 per night, powered sites for $15 per night, and unpowered sites $11. Some are even on the river bank. Further out from Wentworth, about 20 km on the old Renmark Road, is Fort Courage Caravan Park. You may also camp down along the Murray beyond the lock. There are boat ramps, but no facilities. Camping here is free but do make sure you leave your campsite clean. The Wentworth Visitor Information Centre on Darling Street can supply names and phone numbers of accommodation, but don't have a booking service so you must make your own calls. However, outside the peak seasons, it shouldn't be too difficult to get a room here for an overnight stop.

FISHING IN WENTWORTH

The banks of the rivers provide plenty of opportunities to drop a line into one of the two rivers. The quality of the fishing will depend to some extent on which river is running and how clean the water is. You are likely to catch carp, but depending on the flow of the river and the weather, you may be lucky and pick up some redfin, silver perch, Murray cod or catfish. The perch, for instance, like the cooler water.

If you have no gear and are really determined to catch a fish, you should go out with Trevor Brown of U-Hook U-Cook. Trevor will pick you up from your accommodation and take you to places, within a 50 km radius of Mildura, where the fish are running. He supplies tackle, bait, and a NSW inland fishing licence if you don't have one. He also lays on chairs, morning tea and a lunchtime BBQ or salad. He won't take you out if it has been raining for a couple of days, or if it is a total fire-ban day — he finds that people don't enjoy the experience if it is too hot. U-Hook U-Cook has a reputation for bringing visitors to good fishing places where they are likely to catch something — his parties have a 70% success rate! If you or one of your party is a beginner, this is a great opportunity to learn. Trevor is happy to teach you how to hook the bait, cast a line, and even to clean your catch! Non-fishing members of the party can join the group for a small cost to cover travel and lunch. Trevor takes parties of 1–4 people, beginning at 7 am, from Monday to Friday. It costs $45 per adult, $20 per child, and $35 for pensioners (03 5023 7553).

If you want to do it yourself, you can also buy fishing gear and bait, such as worms and shrimps, in Murphy's Deli on Darling Street or at the newsagency nearby. Murphy's Deli also sells fishing licences, and hires out punts with motors for $25 per hour. Have a chat with the staff here about the best place to fish for the time you are there; they may be able to give you some useful advice.

6 Cooper Creek

CUNNAMULLA TO LAKE EYRE

This is a great Australian adventure that will take you to the great waterholes of the Cooper where the air is alive with birds, the creeks are teeming with fish, and the campsites are like no others on earth. There are exciting places to explore with Aboriginal rock carvings and plenty of evidence of the tragic Burke and Wills expedition. Although the Cooper is in remote desert country, it is accessible to everyone without expensive equipment or prior outback experience. The journeys from all directions to the Cooper are great holidays in themselves, and in this chapter we have taken you in from Queensland and past several major crossings of the Cooper as far as Innamincka.

This is not a conventional river trip in that it is impossible to follow the course of Cooper Creek by car. When it is flood, it can expand up to 80 km in width over its floodplains; when it is dry, there may be no sign of it in places. But we couldn't leave it out of this book because Cooper Creek consistently provides excellent river-based holidays. Cooper Creek is formed in Northern Queensland and passes through Channel Country into the Cullyamurra Waterhole near Innamincka. It continues on through the Sturt Stony Desert, crosses the Birdsville Track, and ends up in Lake Eyre North. The explorer Charles Sturt (who named it) wanted to call it a river but couldn't identify a current, so felt obliged to call it a creek. This belies the vastness of the expanse of water in some places, but reflects the fact that, in other places, there is often no sign of water at all. The Birdsville Crossing is a fine example of the extraordinary complexity of this

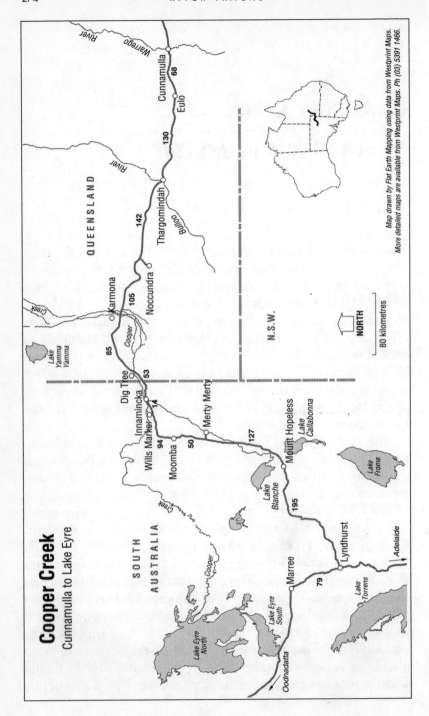

Map drawn by Flat Earth Mapping using data from Westprint Maps.
More detailed maps are available from Westprint Maps. Ph (03) 5391 1466.

NORTH

80 kilometres

Cooper Creek
Cunnamulla to Lake Eyre

QUEENSLAND

N.S.W.

SOUTH
AUSTRALIA

Warrego River

Cunnamulla

Eulo

68

130

Thargomindah

142

Bulloo River

Karmona

105

Noccundra

Cooper Creek

Lake
Yamma Yamma

85

Dig Tree

53

Innamincka

4

Wills Marker

94

Moomba

50

Merty Merty

127

Mount Hopeless

Lake
Callabonna

Lake
Frome

Lake
Blanche

195

Creek

Cooper Creek

Lyndhurst

Adelaide

Marree

79

Lake
Torrens

Lake Eyre
South

Lake Eyre
North

Oodnadatta

river, it can be in full flood one season, then for the next six years there might not even be a trickle!

The trip described in this chapter begins at Cunnamulla in southern Queensland and travels across the Adventure Way, past Thargomindah and on to the first Cooper crossing at Karmona. It then rejoins the Cooper at the famous Dig Tree. The next 80 km is an action-packed river experience along the permanent waterholes. We highly recommend that you camp here for as many nights as you have to spare. From there, we shall direct you briefly to the crossing at Birdsville and then to the Cooper's final destination, Lake Eyre.

As this trip involves a lot of driving in remote country, we have included a section at the beginning of the chapter on preparing your vehicle for an outback trip.

Main route

Cunnamulla — Eulo — Thargomindah — Noccundra — Dig Tree — Innamincka — Minkie Waterhole — Marree — Lake Eyre

Maps

South West Queensland Featuring the Adventure Way, 2nd edition
Innamincka and Coongie Lakes, 4th edition, Westprint Heritage Maps, 2000

Passes

A South Australian Desert Parks Pass is required to camp along Cooper waterholes near Innamincka, and to visit the historic sites at the waterholes. No pass is required for the Queensland section of the trip, including the Dig Tree. The Desert Parks Pass costs $80 for a year. In addition to access to the desert regions, you will receive four excellent Westprint Heritage Maps and an informative handbook about the landscape. Passes are available from agents in South Australia, including the Innamincka Trading Post. For further information and advice about your nearest agent, contact the Department of Environment and Natural Resources on 08 8204 1910.

Distance from starting point

Cunnamulla to Wills Marker (on Minkie Waterhole), 581 km. Wills Marker to Lake Eyre on Oodnadatta Track, 607 km. Lake Eyre to Coober Pedy via William Creek, 285 km.

Maximum distance between supplies

234 km from Noccundra Hotel to Innamincka; 479 km from Innamincka to Lyndhurst via Moomba.

Minimum number of days required in dry conditions

Eight days to include the Cooper on the Oodnadatta Track and return to the bitumen at Coober Pedy.

Best time of year to visit

April to October; note that temperatures during the summer months can reach 47°c in the shade, and may include heavy rain.

Dangers and warnings

There are some blind crests on the single-lane sealed road west of Cunnamulla; drive cautiously over these. The roads west of Jackson Oil Field become impassable immediately after rain. Check weather conditions at Thargomindah prior to leaving. Part of the unsealed road between Jackson Oil Field and the Dig Tree is not distinctive and it is possible to get lost on an unmarked station road. Sections of the unsealed road can be rough with washaways and corrugations if it hasn't been graded for a while. Don't attempt to overtake vehicles through the dust. Slow down to allow oncoming semi-trailers to pass by.

Accommodation and camping

Ideally, this is a trip where the emphasis of accommodation is on bush camping. The large waterholes of the Cooper near Innamincka have some of the finest camping in Australia. There is shade without putting yourself in danger under the limbs of the river red gums, you can be isolated even if it is quite busy — although don't hold us to that during the school holidays! There is swimming and fishing, peace and solitude, and nearby access to a township with supplies, an air-conditioned pub and a hot shower!

Further east, the camping opportunities are also very good. You can experience bush camping beside dry creek beds near the road, or campsite camping.

You can get hotel or motel rooms at Cunnamulla, Eulo, Thargomindah, Noccundra, Innamincka, Lyndhurst and Maree so you needn't camp at all if you don't want to. The rooms in our experience have been fairly basic but adequate and reasonably priced. If you are going to aim for a motel or hotel room in the busy season, ring in advance because this sort of accommodation is limited.

Minimum vehicle requirement

Make sure you have a reliable car in good condition, with excellent tyres and suspension.

The roads

There is a narrow sealed road from Cunnamulla to a point just beyond Jackson Oil Field, about 400 km. From there on, the roads are unsealed and conditions will depend on whether there has been rain or flooding recently, and when the road has last been graded. These roads are impassable when wet. West of Innamincka, the roads are sandy with bulldust and washaways.

Local information and useful telephone numbers

Cunnamulla Visitor Information Centre	07 4655 2481
National Parks Thargomindah	07 4655 3173
Tourism Thargomindah	07 4655 3055
Noccundra Hotel	07 4655 4317
Innamincka Hotel	08 8675 9901
Innamincka Trading Post	08 8675 9900

PREPARATION

Preparing your car for driving on main dirt tracks.

Prepare your car, as you would for any long journey, with a thorough service by a reliable mechanic. Take extra care in checking the tyres and suspension, as these will take more strain on gravel roads than they would on bitumen surfaces.

Checklist

- all engine, gearbox, transfer case, and differential
- oils, change if necessary
- brake fluids, top up or change, if necessary
- fuel filter and pump
- radiator hoses and fittings
- all fan belts
- suspension
- tyres (serviceability and tyre pressure)
- electrical system and fuses
- lights
- battery (serviceability and charge)
- wiper blades and washers
- radiator (serviceability and fluid level).

Suspension

When your car is packed full with passengers and equipment for a fortnight's holiday, the car's suspension will be under stress even as you start out. On the tracks around Cooper Creek, dry creek bed dips and corrugations will put extra strain on your car's suspension. It is essential you check that your car's suspension is in perfect condition. If you have a large party and lots of equipment, you may want to consider upgrading the suspension (there are specialist suspension services in all capital and most major cities).

Tyres

The tyre walls take a battering from the gravel and the gibber stones, and the uneven surface knocks tyres around, so they have to be in excellent condition. Generally, car tyres are of a radial-ply construction and most have only 2-ply walls — the walls are especially vulnerable when over-inflated and hot. Read the various motoring journals and magazine articles to get impartial and up-to-date information about tyres, and be aware of the problems with speed ratings from an insurance point of view. If you can arrange to carry two jacks in your vehicle, we suggest you do so. It will facilitate the task of raising your car high enough so you can get the second jack positioned in the appropriate jacking point. Sometimes this is the only safe way to change a wheel. If you have a portable compressor, you may be able to inflate the flat tyre long enough to lift the car and place the jack into position. Don't forget to pack a sturdy jack plate. It is possible to have punctured tyres repaired at most outback towns.

Trailers

For a large family, it may be necessary to tow a trailer to carry all of your camping needs. There are some excellent off-road trailers available, in a range of prices and quality. A simple domestic trailer can suffice, provided you have it checked thoroughly before you set out. It is essential that the wheel bearings are repacked with the appropriate bearing grease; all nuts and bolts checked for tightness; tyres should be the same size as those on the towing vehicle, and of good quality; and the trailer's suspension checked for serviceability.

Spare parts

At a minimum, you need the following spare parts for the trip along the Cooper:
- a set of radiator hoses and belts
- spare air filter
- fuses to fit your vehicle
- spare tyre (check the tyre pressure before you leave home).

Additional equipment for bush camping along the Cooper

- Cash; EFTPOS is not necessarily available at all points along this route
- fuel funnel, filter and jiggler hose (labelled)
- empty jerry can (metal or plastic; note, petrol must be carried in a metal container)
- water jiggler and water funnel (labelled)
- shovel or spade (preferably with a long handle)
- two jacks, and a jack plate
- snatch strap.

Recovery gear

As a bare minimum, all vehicles should carry a tow-chain or a fabric tow-belt — they take up very little room, but are essential. We also suggest you carry a couple of rated D-shackles in your tool kit.

Tool kit

Your tool kit can be as extensive as you wish, but remember the weight factor. If you have a set of sockets or spanners, ensure that they fit the nuts on your vehicle. Carry the following:
- a set of spanners
- a socket set
- a screwdriver set
- a set of good pliers, including long nose
- a tube of metal glue

- a roll of duct tape
- a small spool of wire
- a patch kit
- metal putty
- your credit card.

If you have any after-market devices fitted to your car, make sure you have the correct tools to fix them if they break down.

Fire extinguisher

We suggest that you carry a fire extinguisher, even though this will meet with some arguments from a few die-hard outback drivers who believe that this device can only be used once, and then what do you do? We have read that you should have a couple of cans of beer handy to spray on a fire, or a pump-up garden spray-can full of water. In general, every vehicle should carry an accessible, fully-charged extinguisher. It should be conveniently ready to hand, and should be the first resource you use in attempting to put out a fire. Make sure that you check it regularly and have it serviced every year.

Packing your car

The rough roads will shake up everything in your vehicle over a period of time. Also, as most visitors to the Cooper are likely to camp, careful arrangement of the vehicle at the start of the trip will make unloading and loading equipment simple and fuss-free at the end of a day's travelling. Here are some tips gathered after many years of outback travelling:
- Pack as much as possible in containers. If you use plastic boxes, make sure that their lids fit well. You can even buy some plastic boxes that fold down flat when empty. Don't use cardboard boxes, as they will eventually fall apart and spill their contents.
- Pack items unlikely to be used frequently in the more remote spots in the car. Then pack other items around them. Keep all heavy items low, and tied down.
- If you have a station wagon or 4WD, consider installing a cargo barrier as a safety measure to prevent your gear from falling forward and injuring a member of your party.

- Everyone travelling in the car should assist with the packing; this will assist with easy unloading and loading.
- Food and containers should be labelled for ready access.
- Be wary of aluminium cans, especially soft drink and beer cans. If you place them loose in your fridge or icebox, expect a mess. In the first place, the paint will rub off and stain your fridge walls, and the contents of the fridge. Secondly, if the can comes into contact with another can or with something sharp, the can will puncture, you will lose the contents and have a dreadful mess at the bottom of your fridge. We pack the cans in threes in containers, and place the middle one in a cloth stubby-cooler. This keeps the cans steady and there is less chance of friction as they are packed in fairly tight. Lids on jars will vibrate loose if you don't ensure that they are very tight when placed back into the fridge or icebox.

Insurance

Before you leave, double-check your cover with your insurance agency. There are two major elements to clarify: firstly, what constitutes an accident in the bush; and secondly, what constitutes a modification to your vehicle.

It is important to note that the policies of individual insurance companies differ. The small print of policies that could make an enormous difference to your claim may change. So put any requests for information in writing to your insurance company and keep their reply. A conversation with the staff in their policy department may also be useful to get a feeling for what they consider an unacceptable risk.

Rollovers, crashing into washaways or hidden dips, being caught in a flash flood or underestimating the depth of a creek are all likely to do considerable damage to your vehicle. Your insurance company is likely to investigate your claim, in these circumstances. If they believe that you took an unnecessary risk, they may reject your claim.

You must inform your insurance company of all modifications you make to your vehicle. It is part of your duty of disclosure to declare in writing any changes you have made that affect the performance of the vehicle. Modifications include dual-battery systems, upgraded suspension, and air differential lockers.

Tyres are problematic when it comes to insurance. The minimum requirements are listed somewhere in the car, perhaps in the handbook in the glove box; the original tyres on a new car comply with that rating. However, those who frequently travel through the outback often change their tyres for some more suited to the gravel and sandy surfaces. Unfortunately, the vehicle manufacturers rate many of these tyres in a category lower than that specified, and this may affect your insurance policy.

Fuel and supplies

This is a remote trip where the intervals between towns are substantial so you have to be careful in planning your fuel and supplies. Most of the track is not sealed and there is no mobile phone coverage. The roads may be cut during wet weather or flooding. It also becomes dangerously hot in summer. Consequently, careful planning is required to ensure a sufficient margin for error. Fuel prices will be slightly higher out here than in the city due to transportation costs. You will need to carry sufficient food, water and fuel to deal with your needs as well as to cater for an emergency. All basic supplies are available at Cunnamulla and Innamincka. Fuel, bottled water and soft drinks are available at several hotels along the way. The cost of food and other supplies will be roughly on a par with city 24-hour convenience stores. The range will be similar.

Even though the greatest distance you will need to travel without access to fuel is 460 km, carry an empty metal jerry can and fill it before you plan to take any exploratory side trips. To estimate your fuel needs, first work out how much fuel your tank holds, how many kilometres per litre your vehicle drives under normal driving conditions, what the greatest distance is between fuel supplies, and then add 30–50 litres for a safe margin.

It is important to bring emergency supplies of food and water just in case an unexpected rain shower closes the road or your car breaks down. Even if you plan to stay and eat in motels or hotels, there are precautions everyone must take to ensure their safety in case something goes wrong. Emergency supplies don't need to be elaborate. High protein snack food such as bread, crackers, unsalted peanuts, small cans of salmon or tuna, canned fruit and other items are easy to carry and won't go off. Avoid salty items or foods with a lot of sugar. Drinkable bore water is available at Innamincka in reasonable quantities. However, it does have a slight mineral taste. It may also exacerbate a delicate stomach condition, though there is nothing dangerous about it. We recommend that you carry about 10 litres of water as emergency supply for each person just in case you are stuck along the unsealed road for a day or two.

There are so many picnic places along this route that, if you take a little care with your lunch food preparation, this can become a highlight of your trip. If you have a chuffer kettle (sometimes known as a volcano kettle) you can boil a kettle of water in minutes by burning twigs or even paper in its central funnel.

A first aid kit, a basic tool kit, a good map, a compass, matches and other basic emergency equipment should be carried in each vehicle along this trip. Although the roads west of Jackson Oil Field are relatively busy, this is remote country and you are better off being able to look after situations if you can. There is access to the flying doctor service at the townships or, in case of dire emergency, via one of the stations.

Weather

Autumn, winter and spring are the best times to travel out here, when temperatures are likely to be in the mid-20s to mid-30s, depending on when you go. It will be cool in the mornings and evenings, and quite warm in the early afternoons.

In the depths of winter, it can be very cold at night and the dew may be heavy, so if you are not using a tent, take a shade tent or a tarpaulin to make a shelter. We prefer a shade tent because when we are in bed we can see the stars and we feel we are sleeping in the open. In these conditions, a sleeping bag and a doona keep us warm.

Rain in the desert is quite dramatic as you will probably see the dark rain clouds coming in from quite a distance. But it is also highly problematic. It can fall at any time of year. Rain makes the roads very slippery and dangerous, and cars travelling on wet unsealed roads cause a lot of damage to the road surface. Road authorities tend to close the roads quickly just after rain starts. There are fines for driving on closed roads if you are not already on them. Information about the weather patterns and recent rain is readily available from all of the local contacts.

The weather along the Cooper is very very hot in summer, 47°c in the shade would be common. This reduces the margin for error to very narrow! You need sophisticated emergency equipment to maintain a safety margin in this weather.

THE ROUTE

Cunnamulla

This is a major country town, 780 km west of Brisbane on the Mitchell Highway (population 1685). Cunnamulla is one of the towns on the Adventure Way, which travels from Toowoomba to Innamincka. Cunnamulla is also the southern gateway to the Matilda Highway, which runs through Queensland to the Gulf of Carpentaria. It is also the last sizeable town, heading west, until you reach Broken Hill in NSW or Hawker in South Australia.

Cunnamulla developed as a 19th-century staging post on the route between the settlements on the coast and the stations of far western Queensland. Thomas Mitchell first mapped the region around the Warrego River during his expedition in 1846. Settlers moved into the area shortly afterwards and the outback stage service, Cobb & Co., set up a station here. This became known as Cunnamulla from the Aboriginal word for the Warrego River meaning 'long stretch of water'. The railroad arrived here from Brisbane in 1898 and established Cunnamulla as an important trading place and centre for Western Queensland agriculture, particularly sheep. It now has the largest wool-loading station on the Queensland rail network.

Long before Mitchell arrived, the Warrego River was the focus of Kunja country. All around the region there are fading signs of Aboriginal life, including wells and trees along the river scarred by people over the centuries to make canoes, shields, weapons and containers. Today the Aboriginal presence in Cunnamulla is very strong. You can learn something more of their culture at the Cunnamulla Visitor Information Centre where there is a display about the town and the region. There is also a shop called the Lost Generation Arts and Crafts shop, which sells local art and craft work. There is a museum in the former Masonic Lodge in John Street that displays tools and implements of the outback. The Cunnamulla Visitor Information Centre is open from 9 am to 4.30 pm, Monday to Friday, and 10 am to 2 pm, Saturday and Sunday from May to November.

As you would expect in a town of this size, Cunnamulla has a comprehensive range of facilities. There is a National Australia Bank, and the post office is a sub-agent for the Commonwealth Bank. There are several grocery stores, service stations, an aero-drome and the hospital. The Warrego also provides good fishing for Murray cod and yellow belly, and the weir is a good picnic and fishing spot.

There are numerous places to stay in Cunnamulla including the Warrego Hotel Motel (07 4655 1737), the Countryway Motor Inn (07 4655 0555) and the Corella Motor Inn (07 4655 1593). There is also the Jack Tonkin Caravan Park that has ensuite cabins as well as campsites (07 4655 1421).

CUNNAMULLA TO THARGOMINDAH

If this is your first venture into the arid regions of Australia, you will experience the joys of desert travel without having to worry about the road surface for 198 km. A strip of bitumen runs through this beautiful country, linking the two towns. Sometimes there are long vistas to the north and south over low scrub, some-times the road is lined by trees. As you get closer to Thargomindah, the trees form two distinctive layers with low mulga and taller acacia trees at the upper level. As you move west, the red sand that is so characteristic of central Australia begins to appear.

This apparently inhospitable country once easily supported several groups of Aboriginal people, including the Kunja and, fur-ther west, the Budjari people. It has extensive lake systems with

Kunja Aborigines of Cunnamulla

Cunnamulla is the largest town in Kunja country and we are fortunate to have a wonderful account of the people's lives and traditions in Hazel McKellar's book, *Matya-Mundu*. She describes sites where the Kunja people used to meet, such as a men's place where initiation ceremonies took place. The last two Kunja men to be initiated talked of the feast of lizards that were caught and specially cooked for them by the old men to provide them with strength and stamina to carry them though several weeks of initiation rites. The women's place was a waterhole where women went to dance, have meetings and give birth. Young women were initiated here. One ceremony involved the young women lying on a bed of leaves on heated ground while the older women danced and sang around the group. These ceremonies were reputed to have a calming effect.

When tribal life broke down with the arrival of the Europeans, many of the Kunja made camp at a former meeting place called Dinnenbooroo, later known as Tinnenburra, a station camp. This is now to the west of the road between Cunnamulla and Bourke. Here, for many years, the Kunja managed to continue their traditional practices. It was a stable environment, with plenty of employment for men and women. The older people received rations of flour, sugar, tea and tobacco from the government. In the meantime, the older people maintained their traditions, with rain dances still being practiced well into the 1920s. They taught the young men about their history and ways, and they tried against all odds to maintain tribal law concerning carefully controlled marriages.

The stable life of the camp collapsed in the 1930s when the effects of the depression were felt on the large stations and the land was broken into smaller holdings. The Kunja people were dispersed. Some went to Eulo and Cunnamulla, some went south to Enngonia. Some of the people were sent by government officials to Aboriginal reserves. Gradually, families with no incomes congregated on the outskirts of the towns in reserves. Conditions were poor and the infant mortality rate was high. An ABC Four Corners television program in 1969 drew attention to the lives of Aboriginal people in the area and there was a positive response from the federal and state government. Houses were built and flats constructed to rent to Aboriginal people. By 1976 all of the people were living in the town and the reserve was closed.

several permanent water supplies, all supporting animal and plant life. The Aboriginal people knew the character of the land, and developed strict tribal laws to maintain the balance of tribal harmony, food and water resources and medicines. Times of drought and flooding were anticipated, and they would only use as much as was required. Female animals were only killed at times of plenty, and young animals were seldom or ever killed. Nests of emu or duck eggs were never emptied. Small fish were thrown back. When the various signs of drought or flooding appeared (such as the gidgee tree not flowering), the group moved around far more to ensure that food and medicinal plants were not over-harvested.

Yet despite the rich resources and their evolved customs, the Budjari people barely survived white settlement. Many moved to the huge stations to work when access to their traditional country was closed off. The flu epidemic in 1919 took a heavy toll out on the stations. The last fluent speaker of Budjari died in Eulo in the 1950s.

Today, the only activity you are likely to see through the plains are animals grazing near the road, and oncoming vehicles. Both can be hazardous if you are not vigilant or if you drive too fast. Horses, feral goats, kangaroos and other wildlife close to the road can suddenly dart out into the path of your vehicle. Be particularly cautious near crests on the road and at dusk. Oncoming traffic may also cause a problem, particularly at crests. Slow down and be prepared to move out onto the soft gravel shoulder. The dangers here are loss of control of your car if you are going too fast, or a stone being kicked up by an oncoming vehicle and smashing your windscreen. As a courtesy to truck drivers, particularly those with several trailers, move onto the soft shoulder and give them the entire road.

Eulo

Eulo is situated on the Paroo River and, although it only has a population of 60, it seems larger than this. Eulo is the home of a date farm and winery, opals, the yapunyah tree and lizard racing! Two features dominate the place. The smaller of the two is the Eulo Queen Hotel, famous because of the stories about Isobel Richardson, the extraordinary woman the pub was named after.

Aboriginal rock carvings, Cooper Creek (PHOTO: GARRY TICKNER)

Cullyamurra waterhole, Cooper Creek (PHOTO: GARRY TICKNER)

Fallen red gums in the Barmah State Park (Photo: Bill Bachman)

The other noticeable feature in town is the giant lizard head that stands at the top of a long rectangular corral. Inside the corral is an unusual wooden grandstand — this is the home of Australia's premier lizard racing event.

Lizard racetrack grandstand, Eulo

Every year, in late August or early September, the lizard races of Eulo draw the locals together in a great social event that provides an opportunity for some entertaining betting, and raises money for the Royal Flying Doctor Service. The races have been an annual event for about 40 years. Shingleback lizards were the first to race; these can be found on any Eulo property. Now the lizards — shinglebacks or bearded dragons — are collected from the bush, tagged, recorded and the place where they were taken from identified by a coloured marker so that they can be returned after the race. Everyone is welcome to watch the fun and join in the betting if they wish.

The date farm on the western outskirts of the town is worth

visiting. Here Ian and Nan Pike make a wide range of products from dates. These include date wine, spreads and toppings, as well as unusual products such as date moisturising cream and soaps. The Pikes are happy to show visitors the processes involved in turning dates into these products.

There are two places you can stay in Eulo. The Yapunyah Caravan Park (07 4655 4945) has one on-site van as well as powered and unpowered sites, and the Eulo Queen Hotel has cabins and basic rooms (07 4655 4867). Opposite the Eulo Queen Hotel are the shire offices where you can find clean toilets and a public shower.

MUD SPRINGS

There are several mud springs signposted on the south side of the road, 7 km west of Eulo. The piles of mud formed by the springs are about 3 metres high. Now extinct, they began to dry up as more and more water was drained from the artesian basin for agricultural use in the outback over the past 100 years. The ground in the surrounding area is wet and sludgy. Further away from the springs, the ground is crusty with mineral salts deposited from the artesian water. These mud springs are a bit dull compared to live mud springs such as those along the Oodnadatta Track. But they are diverting enough to be a place to stop and stretch your legs.

LEOPARDWOOD MINES

One of the few tourist attractions listed along this stretch of road is Leopardwood mines. This is a private operation where, for a fee of around $5, you can fossick in the Black Gate Opal Field or just have a tour of the area from Mick Sawicki who has been living out here for over 30 years. You can also camp at Leopardswood mines and make dinner in the quirky kitchen. The kitchen reminded us of a cottage kitchen complete with range, except that it is wide-open with only a roof to keep you dry. On the down side, the camping area had the foulest washing facilities we have seen in the outback. Access to Leopardswood mines is signposted 44 km west of Carpet Springs.

The Eulo Queen

The romantic name of the hotel in Eulo comes from the nickname of a celebrated hotel owner in pioneer days. The Eulo Queen was Isobel Richardson, born in Mauritius in 1850. She was the illegitimate daughter of an army captain and was educated in England before she migrated to Australia as a teenager. At the age of 17 she married an engineer who died soon afterwards. She worked as a governess and, at age 21, she married a station manager who brought her to outback Queensland.

With her husband, they took up a licence of a shanty hotel in Eulo in the 1880s in opposition to an existing hotel. There she became a well-known and colourful character. She was reputedly short, plump and very beautiful with flawless skin. She wore the latest fashions and fabulous jewellery. She was known for her toughness, as well as for some kindness. She gave lavish parties to wealthy graziers and opal miners.

Her name apparently came from an incident one evening when a drunk was causing trouble in her hotel. She challenged him, declaring 'I am the queen of Eulo, now get out of here!'

The Eulo Queen bought opals from miners, and by 1889 she had made a good deal of money with which she purchased another hotel in Eulo where she had a stately gambling room. She and her husband expanded their businesses from there, adding a store, another hotel and a butcher shop.

She was always on the fringes of the law and landed in court numerous times. She lost some of her fortune in the 1890s but survived nevertheless. Her husband died in 1902. A year later she married one of her staff who was aged 29; she gave her age as 35! Her disregard for licensing laws landed her in trouble with the law so often that the heavy fines began to eat into her resources; then her two hotels burnt down. By the end of World War I, she was broke and drinking heavily. She attempted suicide in 1922 and left Eulo shortly afterwards, a destitute woman. The Eulo Queen died in a mental home in Toowoomba at the age of 79. The hotel that now carries her name was established about 40 years ago.

LAKE BINDEGOLLY

This is such a beautiful place that it is probably worth travelling from coastal regions simply to sit in the atmosphere of Lake Bindegolly. Realistically, it would be an ideal day trip if you were staying in Thargomindah for a few days because the camping is not great. It is situated 80 km west of Eulo and is well signposted. However you cannot miss it because of the abundance of wildlife, difference in the terrain and tree cover, and glimpses of water. It is close to the traditional home of several different groups of Aboriginal people and was a popular place for gatherings. Research indicates that the Aboriginal people were living around here at least 1700 years ago.

Lake Bindegolly is in a 14,000 hectare national park and there is a sensitively laid out rest area and information display. The lake itself is one of the network of freshwater and salt water lakes, called Dynevor, that forms after good rain in its catchment area. On average it is empty one year in ten, but the surrounding area will remain lush even if the lake is empty.

Several walks have been laid out to allow visitors to get a sense of the place. The paths are lined by lignum, samphire plant and acacias which dominate the water side. There is plenty of bird life with up to 60 species in the area, depending on the amount of water and the season of the year. Black swans, cormorants, teal, duck and pelicans are the most common birds you will see here. The walks vary in length from a pleasant 2.5 km stroll to a seat where you can watch the bird life quietly, to a vigorous 9 km circuit. Be sure to bring a good supply of drinking water and a hat on these walks, even if it is a cool day.

There is a camping ground on the south side of the road and to the east of the bridge. The entrance is signposted and it is 2.2 km along a reasonable stock route on the east side of the lake. Conventional vehicles with confident drivers will have no problem managing this track. The bush campsites, which are not specifically marked, are in a large open grassy patch with no shelter. There is a fence between the camping ground and the lake. There is no firewood, so use gas for cooking. There is plenty of space but because it is flat and there are few trees, you will hear the sounds of other campers if there is anyone else there. But it is a good place for an overnight stop or for keen birdwatchers. So it is likely that fellow-campers, if there are any at all, will respect your privacy.

Aborigines of South-West Queensland

Hazel McKellar has recorded the lives of the Aboriginal groups that lived in the country that now surrounds the road between Cunnamulla and Jackson Oil Fields. Several distinct groups lived along here: the Kunja lived in the eastern section around the Warrego River, the Budjari lived roughly between Thargomindah and Eulo, and the Kullilla centred on the magnificent Grey Range to the east of Thargomindah. The waterways provided a rich source of life.

The groups were related to each other and shared many customs and beliefs. Hazel McKellar has provided information on some of their laws and customs. Families tended to have two or three children, ensuring that the land could sustain the population. Birth control was available through a special drink made from the juices of a vine that grew around the lakes after the wet season. During difficult times marriages were arranged to avoid child-bearing.

Other customs were designed to prevent the influences of evil spirits or other negative influences. When someone died, smoke was used to cleanse places and keep evil spirits away. Smoke from special bushes was used on newborn babies to protect them from evil spirits. Evil spirits were also detected in certain winds and rain. Ceremonies with chanting and other customs were used to negate the impact of these spirits.

There were also laws designed to destroy anything that might have a bad effect on the environment or the group. Fire was used to clear the ground and promote new growth. Boning and poisoning were used on individuals who threatened the harmony of the group. Even whirly winds that contained evil influences could be destroyed by ceremonies.

Thargomindah

Thargomindah is a small, neat town set in the heart of the oil country, 198 km west of Cunnamulla. It has an air of prosperity, no doubt benefiting from being the headquarters of the large oil-rich shire of Bulloo. It has all basic facilities, including excellent café lattes in the post office coffee shop. The town is set on the Bulloo River where there is good fishing access. Much of the town's water supply comes directly from the steaming artesian bore outlet on the outskirts of town, so if you stay in one of the motels, you will notice a strong mineral smell permeating the bathroom after you have had your shower!

The river and the artesian bore outlet have both given the town its history. When this area of Queensland was being opened up by explorers and pastoralists in the mid-19th century, the crossing on the Bulloo River became a focal point for activity. The town was first settled in 1864 and gazetted ten years later. In 1893 the bore was opened and a constant supply of water guaranteed. By that stage, Thargomindah was a busy outback town with its own newspaper. When the bore water was tapped for hydroelectric power in the 1890s, the *Bulletin* magazine announced that Thargomindah was one of the three great centres of electricity in the world after London and Paris!

Hydro-electricity continued to be used in Thargomindah until 1951. The bore is still there and pumping out hot water for the town. In national terms, it is not a particularly fine example of a bore outlet but if you haven't seen one close up before, take a look at this one. The smell, the build-up of minerals around the hot pipes, and the unusual vegetation in the water stream are worth looking at. The romance of water coming from far beneath the earth's surface adds to the experience. The disconcerting issue of waste water pouring out into the ground, as if it is an endless supply, is being addressed nationally.

Driving around the town, the evidence of prosperity is all around you as evidenced by the swimming pool, the school, the hospital, the large municipal buildings, neat gardens, good roads, and the gangs of men in bright orange overalls who maintain roads and other public areas. The Thargomindah Hospital has a regular morning clinic with a weekly visit from the flying doctor. The airstrip has a fuel depot making this a popular outback stopover for people flying around Australia in their own planes.

There are a few tourist spots to visit in the town, the best of which is Bulloo Built, Vonda and Terry's craft shop at the old hospital. Vonda and Terry create unique wooden objects out of discarded wood from the region. They gather wood from abandoned shearing sheds and homesteads, and make household objects — mirrors, picture frames, furniture, boxes and other pieces, small and large. They decorate them with the discarded paraphernalia of outback station life such as shearers' combs and wrought-iron lacework. Their signature 'Bulloo Built' is on much of their work, but they will remove it on the spot if you don't want it there.

The other good reason for visiting Vonda and Terry is to look at the old Thargomindah Hospital. They have restored the hospital as their home and have gone to a lot of trouble to collect period furniture, such as original outback hospital beds. They don't do tours officially, it depends on time and other commitments. But even looking at the old hospital from the outside and chatting to them will give you a sense of the history of the place.

The bricks used to build the hospital were handmade by the creek and feature animal footprints. Vonda has gathered information about life at the hospital. Unlike some missionary hospitals, the nursing staff here weren't on a limited contract but stayed until a replacement arrived or until they had to get out. The hospital had a ward for eight beds, a surgery, a dispensary and two rooms for staff. Patients often didn't make the long trip to the hospital until they were desperate. It was not an easy posting.

There is a small museum in Thargomindah in a neat house known as the Historic House. Displays celebrating Thargomindah's 135 years of history have been erected. Information about regional transport as well as newspaper extracts will give you a flavour of life in the past. Having travelled to this place from the east or west in the comfort of contemporary vehicles, this display will help you to envisage the hardships faced by European settlers in the early years.

There are good travel facilities here. The Oasis Hotel has a nice restaurant attached to it where you can get dinner, a welcome retreat after a long drive (07 4655 3155). There is a bar attached to the other Bulloo River Hotel/Motel which is also welcoming (07 4655 3125). And there is a caravan park where visitors can camp or place their caravans, but there is no on-site accommodation (07 4655 3198).

The supermarket at the Shell Station is well stocked. In the usual outback way, you can get hot food, mechanical repairs, fuel, fishing gear and bait, and some basic auto supplies. The station has EFTPOS and takes the usual cards.

There are good fishing opportunities in the Bulloo River. Bait is available in town and local information should be sought. At this stage there are no official camping areas around the river, although people do camp there. It is preferred that visitors camp in the caravan park.

The early bridge built for the transport company, Cobb & Co., is visible from the modern bridge over the Bulloo. The walks along the river are beautiful and peaceful, with lots of wildlife, cranes, pelicans and ducks.

The river floods periodically, sometimes three times a year. This may have nothing to do with local weather but may be flood water from further north. If the creek is flooded and you are stuck, there is a flood truck that will ferry you and your vehicle across the floods for a fee of about $20.

Medicine and childbirth in Aboriginal communities in south-western Queensland

The Aboriginal people had a great knowledge of the medicinal properties of plants in their area. The dogwood bush was used for coughs and colds. The leopardwood tree was used for sores on the body, eyes could be treated with sandalwood, and there was a vine that grew around water holes that could be used for birth control.

When a woman was pregnant, she was treated specially. She was given particular food to eat and looked after by the older women in a special place. For childbirth, she was cared for in a secluded place by the women. The umbilical cord was cut with a mussel shell kept for that purpose. After the birth, the woman squatted over warm coals to heal and relieve the pain.

The mother and baby returned to the general camp after about a week. In the meantime, the elders would have worked out the newborn's future marital relationships. This was a complicated procedure designed to ensure healthy children and harmonious relations in the group and between neighbouring groups. The child's marriage would be arranged while it was still tiny. Breaches of the marital rules were treated severely because they could lead to fighting and warfare, and threaten the viability of the group. This complex social system was destroyed by European settlement.

THARGOMINDAH TO NOCCUNDRA

The road between Thargomindah and the Noccundra turn-off is exceptionally beautiful in places. It runs through what was traditionally Kullilla country, a place with water holes and quarry sites, none of which you will see from the road. The road itself is a narrow strip of bitumen that snakes its way through the plains and over the Grey Range. The terrain between Thargomindah and the Grey Range is mostly flat scrubland broken by lines of trees marking out the usually dry creek beds. As you leave Thargomindah, there is a wetlands area to the north of the road. The vegetation in the vicinity is thicker with more animals, such as kangaroos and feral goats. There are also signs of station life, including windmills and fences. Some of the last elders of the Kullilla group made an annual trip to a secret spot near here. A photo of some of these men was taken in 1913 and is one of the few of the people in their traditional setting.

From the hill tops (altitude 190 metres), there are magnificent views into the distance. The mulga and scrub are low enough not to impede the vistas around you.

West 112 km from Thargomindah are termite mounds, some about 70 centimetres tall. If you haven't seen these close up in the past, here is a good opportunity to see a small version of a phenomenon that is common in the north and west of Australia. Termites create the mounds by secreting a substance that was used as a natural cement base by miners and settlers in the Northern Territory in the past. They crushed the mounds and mixed them with water; when it hardened it created solid floors in their huts.

The one hazard to be aware of on this stretch of road is the potential danger of the crests — they will impede your view of oncoming vehicles. The road is only a single lane, so you won't be able to see another vehicle coming over the crest on the other side; this can lead to a high-speed head-on collision if you are not careful. So at crests, slow down and be prepared to straddle the gravel shoulder if required. Don't assume that everyone carries a brightly coloured dune flag on their roof-rack or attached to their aerial, although it is recommended for this terrain. Also if you stop on a crest to take a photo, pull right in off the road.

Noccundra

The turn-off to Noccundra is clearly sign posted at 122 km from

Thargomindah. Nockatunga Station is to the east of this junction through mulga, red sand and stony ground. The township is 20 km south of the main road on a sealed and smooth road. It consists primarily of a low sandstone building with a monument to the bizarre Andrew Hume expedition on the neat front lawn. The Noccundra Hotel was built in 1882 and its age is reflected in the low, crooked door frames and uneven floor.

In the usual way, the entrance to the outback pub is intimidating. You walk from the bright light of the countryside into the dark and unknown interior. The main bar is the first room you walk into so don't be put off if four or five pairs of eyes look you up and down while your own eyes are still adjusting. The atmosphere is warm and family-like and there are plenty of cosy corners, information leaflets and memorabilia to explore. During the day they serve pub food; in the evening they serve a set dinner menu with a wine list. There is an open fire which would be most welcoming on a winter's evening.

The Hotel has several recreational rooms arranged for family parties. They have created a lovely day lounge with Nintendo and TV for kids who want an electronic diversion from the joys of outback travel. There is also a tennis court for more active travellers. Accommodation is motel style (07 4655 4317).

One of our favourite outback pastimes is to read the visitors' book, when one is available, and the Noccundra Hotel visitors' book is a good one! Reading through the inscriptions, one can imagine the lively evenings spent here in the company of the lads from the oil fields who have names like Chucky, Snakey, and The Grog Monster!

The other major feature of Noccundra is the long waterhole of the Cooper within 'cooee' distance of the hotel. There are some great bush camping sites by the creek which you are most welcome to take advantage of. Here you can fish for yellow belly and perhaps even bass. It won't be difficult to locate a good campsite along this creek. Ask Jill and Mac in the hotel for advice or simply drive along the creek line until you find a site that suits you. The proximity to the hotel is good for people who aren't quite sure of their surroundings and haven't become used to picking good spots in the bush. You can also book in for dinner in the evenings, and use the spacious showers and loos by the hotel for

Andrew Hume expedition

Andrew Hume's expedition was one of the odder tales of exploration in 19th century Australia. Born in England in 1832, Hume (no relation to Hamilton Hume) was raised in rural NSW where he made great friends with the local Aboriginal people. When his family were very sick, both he and his mother recovered, thanks to the help and expert advice they received from the Aboriginal people. From an early age, Hume spent much of his time in the bush; by the age of 18 he had journeyed beyond the mountains of NSW as far as Queensland. He then began a life working as a bush man, making his way as a station hand but preferring the company of Aboriginal people.

Hume claimed to have crossed Australia from east to west in the 1860s but there are serious doubts as to whether he actually did that, although few doubted his knowledge of the outback. After one outback trip in 1866, he was returning to Sydney via Baradine, a settlement with two shanty pubs. Hume began drinking heavily in one pub, sharing stories with other travellers. Over a period of about a week, he drank, gambled and then ran out of money. He teamed up with an older man and while still drunk the pair of them held up the pub he had been drinking in for the previous week. He only asked for goods rather than money. In the course of this he boasted that he was related to some notorious bushrangers. This was at a time when bushrangers were causing great tension in the outback.

Hume was arrested shortly afterwards and given a harsh sentence of ten years' hard labour. Shortly afterwards he said that on his travels he had met a man in the outback who he claimed was a survivor of the famous and tragic Ludwig Leichhardt expedition. Leichhardt's expedition had vanished after setting off in 1848 and had remained the subject of romantic speculation in the coastal cities ever since.

Hume's story struck a chord and after five years in prison, he was released to go and find this survivor. As one modern writer suggested, he had to be admired for talking his way out of prison!

Hume teamed up with Timothy O'Hea, an Irish man who had been awarded the Victoria Cross, and Lewis Thompson, a piano tuner. The three set off from NSW in 1874 and passed through Cunnamulla, Thargomindah and Nockatunga Station. They were aiming for Cooper Creek. Disregarding the warnings from the staff at Nockatunga about poor travelling conditions, the trio continued on their journey. Nine days after leaving the station, Thompson was found staggering along a track towards the homestead on his horse;

he was so weak from hunger and thirst that he could barely stand. The party had been overly optimistic about water supplies along the way and hadn't taken their fill when they could. When they did run out of water, they couldn't find their way back to the previous supply. They had split up to search for it and Thompson had found his way back to help. Hume's body was found by a search party shortly afterwards, O'Hea was never located but there was little doubt but that he had perished also.

a fee ($2). For those like us who like isolation, there is so much space that you are likely to find a secluded spot — except perhaps in the busy periods during July and the school holidays.

NOCCUNDRA TO THE DIG TREE

As you leave Noccundra, you will enter the true outback. The sealed road ends 80 km west of the Noccundra turn-off and you won't see bitumen again for several hundred kilometres. You will also meet the Cooper for the first time at Karmona. The scenery along this 214 km track is spectacular.

Insolbergs and spinifex are two noteworthy and distinctive natural features along this track. The insolbergs are flat-topped plateaus of residual rock against which erosion on the plain can be measured. None of the flat-topped insolbergs are close to the road, most are some distance away on the horizon. It is difficult to gauge either how high they are, or how far away they are from the road as there are no other features around to assist in measurement. It is likely that they are perhaps 1–200 metres high, and the closest would be at least several kilometres away. We would not dream of venturing across the scrub to try and reach one, it would damage the scrub and potentially puncture our tyres. The insolbergs form part of the landscape, rather than features to be explored.

The fields of spinifex are bedded in the classical red soil of the Australian centre. In several places along this route, the land to the north and south of the road is covered by spinifex blowing gently in the breeze like fields of yellow wheat. This reminded us of so much of the terrain along the Canning Stock Route in

Western Australia. If you have never come across this common
Australian plant, take the opportunity to take a closer look.
Spinifex grows in clumps with a dense dark base clinging lightly
to the sandy ground. From this, the tall grass sprouts. It is common in the central and western districts of Australia; Aborigines
used it in their firestick farming process. By burning it, they fer-
tilised the ground, trapped animals and reseeded the plants.

However, don't attempt to walk through the spinifex. The
sharp tips of the grass stings, scratches and even attaches itself to
your shins. It was known to early explorers as 'wait a while'! The
sting is vicious and the feeling lasts for some time. Another note
of warning, spinifex burns very easily and if you drive through it,
it is likely to gather under your car and could cause a fire. When
we drove down the Canning Stock Route, we had to set up a camp
in the middle of spinifex because there was nowhere else to go.
We cleared a wide space around the campfire and parked the car
upwind and facing out towards the track, in case we had to move
the car quickly. You won't need to make a camp in the spinifex
here, but be aware of its highly flammable nature.

Away from the spinifex, you will spend most of your time driving through vast, magnificent plains that are often stony and
covered with low muted green scrub stretching out to the horizon, interrupted occasionally by a tree-lined creek. We camped
off the road once, under a crescent of trees with red peeling bark.
The sunrise over the flat plain made the trees glow red. It was
beautiful to watch from the snug warmth of our sleeping bags.

There are several hazards that you need to be aware of driving
along this road. The bitumen ends 80 km after the Noccundra
turn-off, past Jackson Oil Field. From there on, the quality of the
dirt track will depend on recent weather and when the track was
last graded. When it is dry, the worst you will experience is bulldust, corrugations and washaways. These are particularly hazardous for vehicles with low clearance — but we have passed caravans being pulled along here and they seem to get through!
When it is wet, it is likely to be closed, so it is important to check
the weather reports at Cunnamulla, Thargomindah or
Innamincka before you set out.

The other hazard is the lack of signposting and the potential
confusion about the direction of the road after heavy rain. In our

experience, the Queensland road people in the region are not as efficient as the NSW road authorities in erecting signposts. The road direction may vary due to weather conditions as alternative routes are found to get around boggy sections. Watch your trip-meter, note distances from unmarked junctions, and monitor points of no return in terms of your fuel consumption. There are not many signposts to aid you along this section, but also there are many unmarked station tracks and oil roads that may not appear on the maps.

About 40 km west of the Cooper, near Karmona, are several small clay pans, each no more than about 100 metres in length along the road. However, immediately after rain, these would be impassible and quite boggy for a period of time after wet weather. Up-to-date information about flood warnings along the Cooper are available on the internet at the Australian Bureau of Meteorology site at <www.bom.gov.au>.

On the positive side, the road between the Dig Tree and Noccundra is heavily used, (it is the main route to Queensland from Innamincka), so there will always be some activity unless the road is closed due to rain. If you find yourself in difficulty, stay with your vehicle. Outback travellers — whether tourists or locals — tend to be generous with their assistance if you need help. At the very least, someone with radio contact can talk to Innamincka or, in cases of great emergency, a nearby station.

Aboriginal hunting techniques

Much of the country you will be passing through on the way to the Dig Tree was the traditional ground of the Wangkumara people. They had several different ways of hunting, depending on the char-acter of the animal. All hunting required great skill and knowledge, and these were passed on through the generations.

Similar techniques were used for hunting emus and kangaroos. A decoy was used to attract the attention of the animal. For the emu, the decoy covered himself in mud to disguise his body odour and used coolibah leaves as camouflage. He would then whistle to attract the inquisitive big bird. The rest of the hunting party would wait to attack the emu with nulla-nullas, spears and axes. The flesh of one emu could feed a family for several days.

THE COOPER AT KARMONA

The major feature on the road between the Noccundra and the Dig Tree is the Cooper. About 105 km west of the Noccundra turn-off, the Cooper crosses the road with many creek channels and a large waterhole. There is a sealed bridge over the waterhole but the rest of the road is not sealed and when the Cooper is in flood, this may affect the quality of the track. Access issues aside, this is a beautiful location. Around the waterhole and through the surrounding wetlands, gum trees swarm with bird life, including ibis, hawks, eagles, swallows, ducks, scrub hens, heron, egret, magpies and finch. This is an oasis of activity, although the camping along here isn't great.

The Goondabinda Waterhole is marked on maps and is on Karmona Station. However, because of problems with thoughtless campers and other visitors, the station management has closed off this waterhole to visitors and a sign declares that camping, shooting and fishing are prohibited. You can certainly stroll along the track, over the bridge, and enjoy the environment. However, keep your fishing until you get to the Dig Tree, and your camping to another point along the track.

The turn-off to the Dig Tree, 190 km after the Noccundra turn-off, is at a crossroads and clearly signposted. The 14 km drive down to the historic tree passes the entrance to Nappa Merrie station. This is the home of a pioneering story of the mid-19th century that comes straight out of the pages of a *Boy's Own* magazine. The Dig Tree is on Nappa Merrie property but the station management allow visitors access to the area that was the focus of the Burke and Wills expedition base camp in 1860–1. Thousands of tourists visit the tree every year in buses and cars. This has placed a strain on the fragile environment and, in order to protect and preserve the tree and the area, Nappa Merrie charges a $10 fee per vehicle to get into the tree area. It is based on an honesty system.

The Dig Tree

This famous coolibah tree stands in an idyllic place by one of the permanent waterholes of the Cooper. It is the focal point of the

The Nappa Merrie story

In 1872, 20-year-old John Conrick left the settled districts of Victoria with several friends and 1600 cattle, following in the wake of the explorers to stake a claim in the recently charted country. He established a cattle and sheep station on Cooper Creek, close to the Dig Tree, which he called Nappa Merrie. Unpredictable weather, dust storms, flooding, and resentful Wangkumara people all threatened his enterprise. The Wangkumara gave him two months to move on, but he dug in, living in a rude hut by himself. The Wangkumara then mounted an ambush on Conrick, during which his dogs attacked one man savagely. Conrick called the dogs off and, instead of shooting the man as he lay injured (apparently some settlers would have done so!), he directed him to shelter until his people could pick him up safely. This influenced his relationship with the Wangkumara; he gained their trust and many eventually worked for him as stockmen.

Thirteen years later, he brought his wife Agnes up to the Creek also. She was a young, lively, musical woman from a Victorian family. Around them, settlers came and went, many unable to cope with the intense heat, the loneliness, the financial pressures, the floods and droughts, and the ever-present antagonism with the Aboriginal people. Conrick organised races at Innamincka and promoted communication to the region. He never overstocked the land, and monitored flood and drought conditions to avoid the heavy losses others suffered in the district. The reputation of the animals from Nappa Merrie survived long after the death of John Conrick. In 1951 when the Nappa Merrie cattle were brought into an auction ring, the butchers rose in spontaneous applause!

On the family side, the Conrick household was not such a happy one. Agnes' life in Nappa Merrie was very difficult. As her husband spent much of his time around the extensive station, she was by herself in the stone house on the top of the sand hill by the creek. There was little or no female company in the area, and her husband would not allow any of the men to associate with her. There, in isolation, she had several miscarriages and raised four children. Two of the births were in Nappa Merrie, two were in cities where she received medical attention. In 1892, eight years after moving to the outback, Agnes left the Cooper. Conrick lived on with three of his sons. He died in 1926. His sons took over managing the properties, again maintaining the high standards in difficult conditions. The last of the Conrick shares in the station were sold in 1960. By then the property was a total of about 3000 square miles.

Helen Tolcher, the source of so much published information about the development of Innamincka, has written a terrific account of this extraordinary man and life around the Cooper. The book is called *Conrick of Nappa Merrie* and is usually available in the Innamincka store.

fateful Burke and Wills expedition, and an evocative symbol of the pressures and tragedies of 19th-century exploration. The expedition set up a base camp in the clearing by the tree in December 1860. They spent a few weeks here before dividing the party.

Like every other historic site along Cooper Creek, the Dig Tree seems to be in the middle of nowhere. In fact, in the early 19th century this was close to one of the principal crossing points along the creek used by Aboriginal people. You can camp here and, if there is no one around, it is a beautiful location with relatively shallow waters surrounded by bushy lignum. You can fish in the Cooper for yellow belly and silver bream. Nearby, another tree is blazed with an image of Burke; this was done in the 1890s by a local station worker. But be aware that this is a popular tourist site and your isolation may be broken by a large tour group arriving in a bus.

THE DIG TREE TO INNAMINCKA

Shortly after you rejoin the main road to Innamincka, about 5 km along the road, you will reach the Burke and Wills Bridge over the creek. The 200 metre bridge is an extraordinary sight, principally because its straight line looks incongruous in this part of the world. It was opened in 1992 to provide access over the unpredictable creek for traffic travelling to and from Queensland. It seems to be a popular camping spot with easy access to the water but expect traffic from sunrise to sunset, with many of the drivers taking pleasure in feeling bitumen under their tyres — even for a short stretch!

From the bridge, the 53 km road to Innamincka runs across stony gibber plains with occasional sandy relief. Some of the stones seem to be quite sharp and excellent tyres are necessary for

Burke and Wills expedition at the Dig Tree

In December after Burke, Wills, John King and Charles Grey set off for the Gulf of Carpentaria, the remainder of the party dug in to protect themselves and their supplies from the heat and a plague of native rats. Led by William Brahe, the base party was instructed to stay there for three months — longer if possible.

Initially Brahe's group relaxed in the environment, then the heat and poor food resources began to take their toll. Day after day, as the temperature reached 43°c in the shade, the party grew weak. Initially, the Aboriginal people of the Cooper gave them gifts of fish, nets and native foods, but the Europeans didn't know how to respond in kind. So the people helped themselves to the expedition's equipment and, in response, the Europeans built a stockade to protect their supplies and cut off communication. Consequently their diet was reduced to what they had brought with them, rice, sugar, tea, damper, meat and biscuits, augmented occasionally by ducks or fish.

By April, there was still no sign of Burke and Wills and several members of the base camp were ill. They were relying on William Wright from Menindee to arrive with back-up provisions and stores as Burke had arranged, but there was no sign of him either. So on 21 April, Brahe packaged some provisions for the four explorers, buried them in the ground, marked a tree with instructions to dig, and left — possibly only eight hours before Burke and Wills returned to the base camp.

En route Brahe met Wright at Bulloo on his way up to the Cooper. The pair returned to the Dig Tree to see if there was any sign of Burke, but only spent 15 minutes there. Neither spotted the marks that Burke and his party had left after their visit there late on 21 April, nor did they find Burke's note in the buried cache. Brahe and Wright made their way back to Menindee.

this trip. It is a lovely drive with fabulous views at times down to the creek line and beyond into the desolate plains. This is the one part of the Cooper where you get a continuous sense of the creek as you drive along the road. In fact, it is probably one of the finest stretches of outback creek line in the country. West of the bridge, 36 km, a deep red sand dune joins the road from the south. Expanses of red sand are a rarity in this region and it is well worth getting out of your car to experience the feeling of the fine red sand under your feet. But wear shoes when you are climbing up the dune because some nasty burrs lurk in the sand, particularly near the base.

CULLYAMURRA WATERHOLE

Cullyamurra Waterhole is a treasure and the highlight of the trip along into Cooper country. Access is well signposted and you will see the track about 47 km west of the bridge. This is the primary destination for many visitors who come to Innamincka. The word 'waterhole' is misleading as it suggests a small lagoon. In fact this is a huge expanse of water that will surprise you: it is several kilometres long and roughly 200 metres wide. It is surrounded by huge river red gums and the creek flows through it, providing a continuous stretch of permanent water. You must have a South Australian Desert Parks Pass to camp here.

Cullyamurra Waterhole is home to fish and turtles, and is alive with birdlife including pelicans, budgies, and many varieties of parrot. It is also the location of some of the best camping on any river in this book, with bush campsites marked out at reasonable intervals over several kilometres along the waterhole. The vehicle track is well defined and the campsites by the high creek banks are about 100 metres off the main track. The campsites are natural clearings surrounded by river red gums, mulgas and other smaller gum trees. They provide shade but also create danger; pick the location of your bedding carefully to avoid overhanging branches. Then sleep under the stars, be woken by the corellas and enjoy extraordinary sunrises, sunsets, and the moon over the water.

There are several pit loos near campsites along Cullyamurra because this is such a popular camping place. There is no loose wood so you will have to use a gas cooker. If you don't mind proximity to other campers, pick a site near the beginning of the strip. If you want isolation, keep travelling along the vehicle track and before you get to the carpark at the end, about 15 km along the winding track, you are bound to find a good, relatively secluded site by the creek.

The death of Burke and Wills

The small exploration party had made camp at the end of Minkie Waterhole (by Wills Memorial) for a number of weeks after they had lost contact with the Aborigines who had supplied them with fish, fat native rats and other foods. They had virtually exhausted their own supplies of food, they had few clothes because of a fire, and were becoming so weak that they feared they would not survive until a search party arrived. They had also weakened themselves in attempts to reach the settled areas now in the southern reaches of the Strzelecki track. All the three Europeans ate was nardoo, a local plant that the Aborigines cooked but the visitors ate raw, which is actually poisonous.

By the end of June 1861, Burke, Wills and King realised their only hope of survival was to try and make amends with the Yantruwanta people who had shown them great kindness until Burke had alienated them. But Wills was too weak to leave the camp so Burke and King left him with a week's supply of nardoo, water and firewood and walked east along the creek. Two days later at Cullymara waterhole, Burke died. King struggled back up the Creek, keeping an eye out for Yantruwanta people on the way. The weather would have been fairly cool but walking along the creek line with its many indents and soft sand would have been exhausting. When he got back to their camp, he found Wills dead also. King buried him before tracking the Aboriginal people once more.

BURKE'S MEMORIAL

The memorial to Robert O'Hara Burke is situated under the trees at the western end of the Cullyamurra Waterhole. This memorial marks the point where Burke died at the end of June 1861. Burke and King had left Wills at the Minkie Waterhole, a trek of about 24 km to the west. They walked most of that on the first day; the following day Burke was too ill to walk much at all. He asked King to put a revolver in his hand and not to bury him when he died. King followed his orders and left Burke under the trees. When Howitt and his party found King in September 1861, the explorer brought them to the site. The rescue party buried him there, but later his remains were disinterred for a huge funeral ceremony in Melbourne.

The access track to the memorial is well identified and the

concrete memorial itself is about 200 metres to the east of the car park across a soft sandy track. The memorial is surrounded by a metal rail, yet it is easy to miss because it blends into the landscape. The memorial is not on the creek bank but about 70 metres in from it under the trees. On the one hand it is so difficult to imagine how a group of men could die of starvation at a creek that had so much food in it and in the air around it. They had a large stock of fish hooks and plenty of weapons. On the other hand, when we stay here for a week or two around Christmas with good food, refrigeration and the option to go into an air-conditioned hotel or car, we find the terrain and weather very debilitating — and we are on holiday with choices! The peacefulness and beauty of this place are evocative of both the heroism and tragedy of the tale of Burke and Wills.

ABORIGINAL ROCK CARVINGS

Another highlight of a trip along the Cooper is a chance to visit some Aboriginal rock carvings in a place virtually unaffected by European settlement. The rock carvings are situated at the eastern end of Cullyamurra Waterhole where the creek narrows into a channel. They were made by an ancient people, a long time before the 19th century. An entire crescent of rocks is covered in carvings. The red markings in the dark rock are distinct once your eye becomes accustomed to the difference between man-made marks and natural marks. The symbolism of the carvings is unknown. Suggestions of turtles, moon and sun, and other objects seem to fit the shapes. But as the late camp host, John Coates, once said to us, the people who made the carvings are long gone and with them their secrets — so we'll never know.

This is a very striking place and truly a magical moment on the Cooper. A few times in outback Australia we have felt a strong spiritual presence. When we have visited these rock carvings, we have got this sense again. We were pleased to read in Stanbury and Clegg's *Field Guide to Aboriginal Engravings* that they believe that there is invariably a feeling of presence, atmosphere or tension around the sites of rock engravings. This has certainly been our experience. The location itself is peaceful and quiet. The crescent shape gives the area a structure so it is a bit like visiting a holy place of any culture. Up high in the rocks behind the carvings is a small oval shape surrounded by boulders that seems like a man-made meeting place. From the sunken floor of the space, you can see far out across the plain to the north of the Cooper, but it would be difficult for anyone to see you.

To get to the carvings, drive to the end of the track along Cullyamurra. It is about 18 km and ends in a car park. From there the rock carvings are a 1.5 km walk along the waterhole, past three major rock outcrops. A vague walking track follows the creek bank but it is easy to miss the carvings if you don't know what you are looking for. Stay by the water and look out for the crescent of rocks near the point where the creek narrows to a channel. Take water, a sun hat and sunscreen before you head off down the creek bank. It is a long walk along a rough track and, even in winter, can become quite hot and dehydrating. The best time for viewing the engravings is when the sun is low in the sky so that the light casts a shadow in the grooves.

Innamincka

The tiny township of Innamincka is visible first by its communications mast on the horizon. From whichever angle we approach Innamincka, this is what we look for to tell us we are about to arrive. As you come in from the high gibber plain, you will see some postcard views of the town with the creek beyond. The town is set on a large dusty space with four main buildings: the hotel, the store, the National Parks and Wildlife office in the old hospital, and the ablution block with a solar-powered telephone booth outside. Several other buildings are dotted around the outskirts of the settlement, and that's it.

Yet this town provides a comprehensive range of outback visitor services and makes the outback region readily accessible. You can get fuel, food supplies, groceries, basic first aid equipment, camera film, basic car repairs, and information. You can have a shower, wash clothes, hire a canoe, join the weekly BBQ in the hotel on a Sunday night, or stay in the motel. Considering the remote location of Innamincka, food and other groceries are not outrageously priced, with costs on a par with city convenience stores.

Aboriginal rock engravings

Stanbury and Clegg provide an overview of Aboriginal rock carvings in their *Field Guide to Aboriginal Engravings*. Aboriginal rock engravings were made by abrading, cutting, hitting or drilling the rock with tools made of stone, shells or wood. One method was to create a series of holes, then connect them to form a line. When the engravings were first made, they would have been sharp with strong contrast between the new engraving and the dark stone and possible lichen around it. Over the years weathering has reduced their clarity, the grooves have become shallower and the brightness of the newly scraped rock has faded. In some cases it would appear that Aboriginal people sometimes worked over the engravings long after they were first engraved. This may have been part of a ceremony.

Aboriginal rock engravings contain a direct tie for Aboriginal people to their ancestors and their land. They are the only record of a people — their ceremonies, customs and traditions — that died a long time ago. Generally, Australian Aboriginal rock engravings depict gods, animals, people, weapons or hunting tools. Some may have had sacred significance, some were connected with secret sites, and some connected with initiations or other ceremonies. They may have been made to illustrate a story or a song, or as a teaching aid.

The engravings in Cooper Creek were made by a people who have long gone and we have no way of knowing for sure what the images were intended to depict or what their purpose was. They are not very distinct but once you begin to work out what you are looking at, a great number of carvings will become clearer. Some shapes seem obvious, but even if we can decipher a turtle or an emu, we can never know the full meaning.

The Innamincka Hotel is a friendly environment that welcomes families, although from the outside it looks as intimidating and rugged as any outback pub. As your eyes adjust to the interior of the hotel after the bright lights, and the lads propping up the bar have lost interest in you, get yourself a drink and a snack, and enjoy the displays around the bar.

The hotel is probably the best source of information on fishing in the region as visitors drop in to tell their tales of what they have caught and, if you are lucky, what bait they have used. The fishing in the waterholes is excellent, with plenty of easy access on the muddy banks. You will catch yellow belly and silver bream here, and occasionally hook a turtle which you should release as gently as possible. You can get bait in the Innamincka store.

INNAMINCKA TOWN COMMON

On the western edge of the town, there is a long strip of shady ground along the channel between the Minkie and Cullyamurra Waterholes that is referred to as the Town Common. This is a good place to set up camp and is not as public as its name would suggest. Access to the water side resembles a dirt bike track you might see in a city suburb. The undulating dusty ground is sparsely covered with trees that provide the only shade and privacy. But down by the creek it is actually very pleasant with wide, flat camping spaces shaded by river red gums. At this point, the creek is narrow and the vegetation lush, there is a strong almost alien greenness about it. The banks are low and access to the water for swimming and fishing is easy.

John and Catherine fishing at Cooper Creek

This is the ideal place to camp if you are passing through Innamincka and are not inclined to venture out onto one of the major waterholes. It is perfect for people in conventional vehicles who may be a bit concerned about driving through bulldust to get to the more isolated campsites. It is also great for reluctant campers who like access to a hotel, an ablution block and cold beers! The township is a short walk away depending on exactly where you camp. There are pit loos but, as you would expect, no wood. There is a $5 donation per vehicle or motorcycle for camping overnight here, payable at the store in the town. Of course with its easy convenience, it may become pretty busy, especially during school holidays. By the way, take note of local flood warnings — caravans have been washed away from here.

INNAMINCKA TO WILLS MEMORIAL

The tracks to the west of Innamincka township are soft, sandy, and fairly narrow. There is likely to be a lot of bulldust depending on recent weather conditions. The track is graded occasionally, but as this isn't an arterial track, maintenance is not a major priority. Vehicles with high clearance will have no problem here but drive carefully, taking all bends cautiously. It is possible to lose your grip on a sandy corner and end up in the trees. There may also be oncoming vehicles and rapid swerving on these tracks is risky. But taken slowly, this road is no problem. It also follows the Cooper to more magnificent permanent waterholes, historic sites, and great picnic and camping areas. This is a great day trip if you are camping at Innamincka or Cullyamurra Waterhole.

SKI BEACH AND POLICEMAN'S POINT

These two popular campsites are at the eastern end of Minkie Waterhole, but you must have a South Australian Desert Parks Pass to camp here. Both camps are at a narrow part of the creek and the banks are low to the water, providing good swimming and fishing access. The camping areas themselves are relatively small so only camp here if you don't mind other people camping near you. This campsite is ideally suited to family groups because of the water access and the pit loos.

Both Ski Beach and Policeman's Point are signposted from the main track and the access track is likely to have considerable bull-dust on it. This will make it uncomfortable for conventional vehicles with low access. The turn-off to Ski Beach is 6 km west of Innamincka and the access track is 2 km long. Policeman's Point turn-off is 4 km west of Innamincka and its access track is 1.5 km long.

KINGS MARKER

Kings Marker on Minkie Waterhole reputedly identifies the location where John King was found by the rescue party in September 1861, three months after his companions had died. A search party led by Alfred Howitt began at the exploration party's depot on the Cooper and then headed west where they found evidence of the explorers. One of their party also met a group of Aborigines, amongst whom was one man wearing a European hat. As the rescuer approached him, the man fell on his knees in prayer and identified himself as John King.

Kings Marker is situated on a low bank on Minkie Waterhole. The turn-off is 7 km west of Innamincka, and the marker is 1.5 km off the main road. The direction of the track may vary, there may be several tracks to bring you around washaways and deep bulldust, but all should lead you towards the water and the marker. The marker is the remains of a tree that was damaged in a windstorm in 1987. The tree was engraved as recently as 1947.

We don't recommend that you camp too close to the marker because a lot of day-trippers visit the spot. To the west of the marker is a kilometre or so of terrific campsites. An obvious track leads to plenty of natural bush campsites, each about 100 metres off the track and in the shade of trees by the creek. You need a Desert Parks Pass to camp here and you will need to use gas because there is little or no fire wood. This is a good area for people who like some isolation, although it is likely that during busy times there will be other campers within earshot of you.

WILLS MEMORIAL

A stone cairn under the great river gums by Minkie Waterhole identifies the location of Wills' death in June 1861. It is a partic-

ularly beautiful spot at a point where the creek narrows towards
its western channel and the water drifts around the small islands
covered in rich green vegetation of grasses and trees. It is an isolated place with only the sounds of corellas, budgies, crows and
flies breaking the silence. In the hotter part of the day, when the
birds are at their quietest, there is virtually no sound at all. This
is where Wills died alone of malnutrition and exhaustion.

The location of the Wills' death place was carefully noted in
the records of the expedition search party but few visitors to the
area would have known where to find it until 1973. Then the leg-
endary Innamincka character, Mike Steel, took it upon himself to
honour Wills' memory by erecting the sandstone and quartz cairn
with the help of his Red Rover Tour group. There is a second
marker in the car park area. The elegant metal says simply 'Wills
died in creek, 1861'.

The rescue of King

After the death of Burke and Wills, King had managed to locate the
Yantruwantra people who took pity on him after seeing the dead
body of Burke. They cared for him, taking him with them when they
moved camp, feeding him fish and other food. In return, King shot
crows and promised them gifts when the rescue party arrived. He
was very weak when Howitt found him so the rescue party remained
at the creek for nine days.

During this time the group reburied Wills, whose remains had
been disturbed by dingos. They also buried Burke in a Union Jack.
Before they left, Howitt gave the Aborigines gifts to thank them for
caring for King. King got back to Melbourne in November but, as a
junior assistant to the two gentlemen explorers, he was not given a
noisy hero's welcome. The great sacrifice of Burke and Wills dominated the conversation, and King, like any good soldier, was considered as having shown appropriate endurance.

King died of tuberculosis in 1872 at the age of 31. He never fully
recovered from the privations of the expedition.

The quality of the track on the access to Wills' Memorial will
vary depending on recent weather. The turn-off, 14 km west of
Innamincka, is signposted. The track down to the mark travels

through a pale, sandy plain sometimes surrounded by low red dunes. The trees thicken as you approach the creek. A speed sign suggests you do 40 km, any more would be risky anyway. Close to the creek, the track forks; the eastern track leads to the camp ground by the creek. The other fork leads to Wills' Memorial. There is a maze of vehicle tracks around the marker but they all lead to the creek bank. You don't need a Desert Parks Pass to visit the marker but you do need one to camp.

The Wills Memorial camping area is 200 metres from the fork. It is a small exposed spot with little protection from a strong breeze or hot sun, nevertheless the camp will give you magnificent views towards the east over the creek. This is guaranteed to provide spectacular sunrises on clear days. The bank is steep so the site is not recommended for those with small children; the floor of the creek will be muddy and will probably get deep very quickly.

MINKIE WATERHOLE TO LAKE EYRE

When you leave Minkie Waterhole, you will probably be leaving the Cooper completely. From here to where the creek reaches its final destination in Lake Eyre North, there is a very good chance that there will be no sign of it. It only flows west of here during periods of great flood, and this may only be once every six or seven years. If you want to visit the place where the Cooper crosses the Birdsville Track, or look at Lake Eyre from the Oodnadatta Track, you will be embarking on several great desert tracks and we shall describe briefly how to reach these places. However, each of the tracks deserve entire chapters to themselves and we recommend that you read about them in *Desert Tracks* (Lothian Books 1998) before you head out that way.

The quickest way to Lake Eyre from Wills Marker is to continue along the dusty track to Moomba, then head down the Strzelecki Track to Lyndhurst. This is a total of 480 km from Innamincka, and there is no fuel supply between the two towns. The 81 km track between the Wills Marker turn-off and the Moomba Gas Plant is rough and sandy with bulldust and washaways, so drive carefully.

The junction with Walkers Crossing track is 50 km after the

Wills Marker turn-off. The Walkers Crossing track travels through station country before reaching the Birdsville Track. You need permission to travel on this road from the National Parks and Wildlife ranger in Innamincka. If you do get permission you need to have good outback experience as the track is not clearly marked and is very confusing in places because of the gas roads, and station tracks. Approximately 70 km after the junction, you will come to a bridge over the Cooper known as Walkers Crossing. This short bridge was erected to ensure access for Moomba Oil and Gas Field vehicles at times when there was water in the Cooper. It was named after one of the gas field staff.

The rough track from Minkie to Lyndhurst joins the well-maintained road that carries the traffic from Moomba to the south. From here it is 7 km to the Moomba Gas Plant, which is closed completely to visitors, then 365 km along the Strzelecki Track to Lyndhurst. The Moomba Oil and Gas Fields' authorities maintain this track but if there is any sign of rain, they close the road immediately. The Strzelecki Track is a popular route for South Australians taking fishing holidays at the Cooper water-holes.

There are several good diversions along the road. The natural environment of Yaningurie Waterhole is 107 km from Moomba Gas Plant, and a good place for a picnic and a swim. Montecollina Bore is 51 km further south. This is a man-made waterhole with an artesian bore water outlet pouring into it. Close to the outlet, there is a delicious warm-water swim. It is not a good place to camp because so many people have camped there before you, and unfortunately it is not a particularly clean area.

Lyndhurst is another tiny settlement with a roadhouse with fuel, and the friendly Elsewhere Hotel. You can get snacks and meals in the hotel. It also has hotel-style accommodation with a number of family rooms (08 8675 7781).

From Lyndhurst it is 79 km north to the railway town of Marree. This is the point at which the Oodnadatta Track and the Birdsville Track take off. Marree is always interesting, with its railway carriage sitting stranded in the centre of town, and the 1880 hotel dominating the street. Accommodation is available in the wonderful 19th-century Marree Hotel, 08 8675 8344.

You can get some views out over Lake Eyre from the

Oodnadatta Track, 82 km west of Marree. The lake is likely to be dry, or have puddles of salty water in it. The edge of the lake is obvious enough because the saltbush grows close to the muddy lakebed. From a car, this is as close to the final destination of the Cooper as you will get. The drives up to William Creek and out to Coober Pedy, or on to Oodnadatta, are some of the busiest outback tracks in terms of diversions and things to see and explore. This was close to the original route of the Ghan Railway and there are many relics of that along the way.

If you want to look at the Cooper crossing along the Birdsville Track, head directly north of Marree for 148 km, past Lake Harry and Etadunna homestead. The creek bed on the track is 5 km wide and, when dry, is a beautiful drive over crunchy stones and past great gum trees inhabited by noisy corellas. When it is in flood, you will need to get a ferry across the creek; the flood track travels behind Etadunna Homestead and is signposted. If you want to see images of the Cooper in flood, find a copy of the 1954 film 'Back of Beyond', staring the Birdsville Track mailman, Tom Kruse. When the movie was filmed, the Cooper was in flood and Kruse had to transport everything across the water on a small ferry.

ALTERNATIVE ROUTE OUT OF INNAMINCKA

The most popular way of leaving the Cooper is via Tibooburra and Cameron Corner through spectacular red sand dunes. This is the route most visitors from Victoria or New South Wales use to get to and from the Cooper and it is one of our favourite drives. The longest stretch without fuel is between Cameron Corner and Innamincka; this is 245 km. The route is well signposted and well used.

EQUIPMENT CHECKLISTS

In the settled areas along the rivers, there are plenty of shops, cafés and restaurants, places to stay, toilets and public showers. The following checklist is designed for travellers who prefer to be self-sufficient and who plan to do some bush camping. Items marked with an asterisk (*) are discussed on pages 322–30.

CAR TRAVELLING KIT

- Large bottle of water per person
- Toilet roll and matches in plastic bag* (see Toilet paper)
- Moist towellettes
- Towel
- Soap
- Garbage container
- Torch

PERSONAL TRAVELLING KIT

- Large hat
- Sunglasses
- Sunscreen
- Insect repellent
- Personal toiletries
- Towels
- Toilet rolls
- Changes of clothes
- Plastic bags for dirty clothes
- Boots or strong shoes*
- Sandals or light shoes
- Gardening gloves* (see Gloves)
- Pillow*
- Torch
- Matches
- Credit/EFTPOS card or sufficient cash
- Fly veil*
- Clothes detergent
- Thongs*

FIRST AID KIT

- ❏ Variety of bandages for cuts
- ❏ Variety of bandages for limb injuries
- ❏ Sling
- ❏ Splint
- ❏ Butterfly sutures
- ❏ Surgical tape
- ❏ Safety pins
- ❏ Cotton swabs
- ❏ Gauze
- ❏ Non-stick bandages
- ❏ Sting ointment
- ❏ Burn gel
- ❏ Antiseptic cream
- ❏ Antiseptic powder
- ❏ Paracetamol or asprin
- ❏ Magnoplasm
- ❏ Gastrolyte
- ❏ Scissors
- ❏ Eye wash
- ❏ Disposable rubber gloves* (see Gloves)
- ❏ An easy guide to first aid (see pp. 336–40)
- ❏ A supply of your own medicines

FOR SLEEPING UNDER THE STARS OR IN A TENT

- ❏ Large tarpaulin, or smaller tarpaulin and ground sheet* (see Tarpaulin)
- ❏ Tent pegs
- ❏ Tie-down ropes
- ❏ Lump hammer
- ❏ Mattress*
- ❏ Sleeping bag, and additional doona in winter
- ❏ Pillows*
- ❏ Tent, pegs and poles*
- ❏ Shade tents* (see Tents)
- ❏ Fly spray
- ❏ Mosquito coils
- ❏ Portable toilet and appropriate chemicals
- ❏ Portable solar shower
- ❏ Bucket
- ❏ Swag*

FOR MEAL PREPARATION AND COOKING

see also pp. 341–8.

- ❏ Water containers
- ❏ Gas cooker and cylinder*
- ❏ Matches*
- ❏ Gas lamp with mantles and gas cylinder; or fluoro light with battery-charge
- ❏ Connection; or kerosene lamp and bottle of
kerosene* (see Lighting)
- ❏ Camp oven* (see Cooking equipment)
- ❏ Saucepans* (see Cooking equipment)
- ❏ Frying pan* (see Cooking equipment)
- ❏ Jaffle iron
- ❏ Pie dish

- ❏ Barbeque plate
- ❏ Wire rack (for camp oven)
- ❏ Wire mesh (for sieving charcoal)
- ❏ Chuffer kettle
- ❏ Billy* (see Cooking equipment)
- ❏ Iron hooks (for hanging pots, etc., over fire)
- ❏ Esky or cold box* (see Refrigeration)
- ❏ Plates
- ❏ Mugs*
- ❏ Plastic glasses
- ❏ Bowls
- ❏ Cutlery
- ❏ Chopping boards
- ❏ Box of disposable gloves* (see Gloves)
- ❏ Chopping knives
- ❏ Sharpening stone
- ❏ Long-handled tongs
- ❏ Toasting fork
- ❏ Can/bottle opener
- ❏ Vegetable peeler
- ❏ Egg lifter
- ❏ Soup ladle
- ❏ Whisk
- ❏ Mixing bowl
- ❏ Measuring jug
- ❏ Corkscrew
- ❏ Washing-up gloves* (see Gloves)
- ❏ Washing-up detergent
- ❏ Washing-up cloth/brush
- ❏ Pot scourers
- ❏ Teatowels
- ❏ Kitchen cloths/sponges
- ❏ Garbage bags* (see plastic bags)
- ❏ Clothesline
- ❏ Clothes pegs
- ❏ Basin for heating water
- ❏ Table
- ❏ Folding chairs
- ❏ Plastic bags*
- ❏ Kitchen paper
- ❏ Bottle sealers
- ❏ Plastic containers with sealing lids
- ❏ Aluminium foil
- ❏ Shovel
- ❏ Lifters
- ❏ Gardening gloves* (see Gloves)
- ❏ Axe or tomahawk

LEISURE EQUIPMENT

- ❏ Camera and accessories
- ❏ Film
- ❏ Binoculars in case
- ❏ Books
- ❏ Music or books on tape
- ❏ Writing paper, pen, envelopes
- ❏ Drawing materials and paper
- ❏ Cards
- ❏ Board games
- ❏ Musical instruments
- ❏ Cricket, football and other sports gear
- ❏ Fishing gear
- ❏ Swimsuit, flippers, floaties, and other equipment

NOTES ON EQUIPMENT

Boots or strong shoes; sandals and thongs

Although it may be hot, thongs and other light shoes may not be safe in some circumstances. When you are making a bush camp, going for walks, or collecting firewood, wearing shoes or boots with thick soles will allow you to walk about with the confidence that a sharp stick or burr is not going to penetrate your footwear. Boots will allow you to use your foot to break up larger sticks without scratching or injuring your foot.

Thongs and sandals do have a role to play. They are useful in the public showers, both to protect your feet and to speed up the drying process, or if you take your shoes off when travelling and need to get out of the car for a few minutes. Be careful when using them at night — it's easy to stub a toe or stand on a sharp burr.

Cooking equipment

Cast-iron Dutch or camp ovens are available in outback stores. Get one to suit the size of your party. Dry it properly after use, and oil it before storing it back home. Carry it in a canvas or heavy plastic bag, as the base will become dirty very quickly.

Cast-iron frying pans with wooden handles are also available from camping stores. They have a very thick base that allows you to cook on an open fire without burning everything immediately.

Billies are available in camping stores. If you can, get one with a metal holder on the lid, other holders are going to burn and break off sooner or later. This is not a major problem, a hook made from a wire coat-hanger can be used to lift the lid.

Use saucepans with heavy bases for cooking rice, pasta, beans, etc., over hot coals. If you are cooking just on gas, you will only need a couple of standard saucepans, and perhaps a standard frying pan.

Fly veil

Flies can be bad in the bush, particularly if you are in cattle country in hotter regions. The flies appear at dawn and remain until dusk. They are very persistent in their efforts to get to the moisture in your eyes, nose, ears and lips.

A fly veil or net will keep them away from your face and, if they can't get at your face, you are unlikely to notice them on the rest of your body — unless you are preparing food. A standard fly net that hangs over your hat, or a very light, thin veil worn in the same way works very well. The holes or gauze should be large enough to give you complete vision but small enough to keep the flies out.

If you are preparing food and do not have a shade tent, you may have to ask one of your party to waft a plate or teatowel over the food-preparation area to keep the flies away.

Gas cooker and cylinder

These are essential items of your camping equipment because wood is so limited in the bush. A simple two-burner stove with a small barbecue plate is adequate for most cooking needs, and can be used in all weathers.

Gloves

Gardening gloves are vital for your comfort on a camping trip, and they should be kept in a handy place in your car so that you can reach them as soon as you pull into a camp. The gloves make collecting and breaking wood manageable — without them, you will get splinters in your hands, or you may accidentally wrap your hand around a bull-ant or other insect with a painful sting. Take spare pairs.

Disposable surgical/rubber gloves are useful when you are preparing food. Sometimes it may not be possible to clean your hands thoroughly enough to handle raw food, particularly meat. Alternatively, you may need to open things or get access to items while you are cooking that would necessitate washing your hands thoroughly again.

Some cooking processes — such as basting vegetables in oil and spices, or preparing pastry — are quite messy, so wearing gloves makes it more convenient.

We keep a box in the car in case we might need them to prepare lunches or snacks; they are also an essential part of our first
aid kit.

Washing-up gloves make the task of washing up easier. Often
you will use straight boiling water rather than diluting it with
additional cold water. Washing-up gloves make this bearable.
Some of the items you will be handling will be very grubby — the
bases of your cooking pots, for example, will be black with charcoal and ash. In addition, the amount of water you can use for
cleaning the items is limited, consequently the water becomes
greasy very quickly. Use whatever water you have for cleaning the
pots, then rinse them in clean hot water.

Lighting

While a torch may provide sufficient light on a short trip, if you
plan to set up camp and cook, bring some means of lighting up a
large part of the camp. A **gas lamp** attached to a cylinder of LPG
or propane, is very bright and energy efficient. However, it will
make a lot of noise, and the glass surrounding the mantle can
break easily — a spot of rain on a hot lamp will crack it. If you use
a gas lamp, bring a supply of mantles, as they tend to disintegrate
very easily.

We use a **rechargeable fluorescent lamp** instead of a gas
lamp. Modern lamps are made of heavy-duty materials, and throw
off a strong light. They can be recharged using your vehicle's cig-
arette lighter socket as you drive along.

There are also some excellent 12-volt fluoro lights, which
work directly off the car batteries. On the downside, they attract
insects and this can be quite irritating, so we tend to turn them off
after cooking our meals and eat by the light of our kerosene
lanterns.

A **kerosene hurricane lamp** gives off a very gentle light.
These lamps are very cheap and available in most camping, dis-
posal and hardware stores. The glass shades break easily, but you
can avoid this by carrying them, well packed, in a rigid box. They
create a cosy atmosphere when suspended from the trees around
your camp, they don't make a lot of noise and they don't attract

as many bugs as the bright fluoro lights. Kerosene and methylated spirits (to start your lamp) are readily obtainable in outback shops and roadhouses.

A **kerosene tilly lamp** gives off a very strong light, but it is noisy and needs to be pumped up every now and again. It consumes kerosene very quickly and the mantles break easily, but it is a reasonable alternative to gas.

The repair kit of some cars now includes a portable lamp that can be plugged into the car's battery system, and attaches magnetically to the body of the car. It can provide good light. We have a table set up at the back of our vehicle, and use this light to prepare food.

Each car should have a reasonably large torch that is kept in a handy place. If there are more than two people in your party, you may find it useful to have a torch each. All members of the party, particularly children, should be encouraged to carry a torch at night, as it is easy to be disorientated in the dark or to fall on uneven ground. Give them their own colourful torch each.

Matches

Each vehicle should carry several boxes of matches, indeed, in remote areas each adult member of the party should have a box of matches in their personal kit for burning toilet paper after use.

Green waterproof matches are available, but can be very difficult to light. The long standard matches are probably easier to use in a campfire situation than the shorter ones, although standard matches are perfectly adequate. Keep matches in a dry place or inside a plastic bag.

Mattresses

Various camping mattresses are currently available. If comfort is important to you, a self-inflating thermal mattress is ideal. When it is inflated, it has enough air to be comfortable, even on rough ground, and it also insulates you from ground chill. It doesn't need a pump, and it rolls up neatly to about the size of a pillow.

An ordinary air-inflatable mattress won't give the same level of comfort if it punctures. There will be nothing between you and the ground, except the thin outer layers of the mattress, which will provide no insulation and certainly no comfort.

Foam mattresses are fairly comfortable, and provide some insulation from ground chill. They are cheap and light enough to carry on a roof rack, but take up a disproportionate amount of space.

The high-density camping mats of the sort often used by hikers and cyclists take up very little space, but unless you are used to sleeping on these you might find them very uncomfortable. They have the advantage of giving you insulation from ground chill.

We are very conscious of our comfort level, so we use a combination of a high-density foam mattress and a self-inflating mattress for complete luxury.

Mugs

After tolerating plastic and enamel mugs for a few years, we welcomed the present from a friend of a set of insulated mugs. They have become an essential item in our bush kitchen. Insulated mugs are available from large hardware stores. The brand we use has a lid, and keeps tea or coffee hot for up to 30 minutes. It also keeps liquids icy cold.

Plastic bags

Take a variety of plastic bags for garbage, opened containers, collections of loose objects, and other uses.

Good quality heavy-duty bags with a tie are required for your garbage, both to control the rubbish in your campsite and to carry the bag safely for a distance to a dump. Much of the rubbish will be cans and bottles, so the stronger the bag the better.

Smaller garbage bags are useful for car rubbish, and for hanging in a kitchen area or by a bed. Supermarket bags usually suffice.

Plastic bags are also useful for wrapping around billies and other pots to protect other items from being marked by charcoal and ash that inevitably cover the outside of the cooking pots.

Pillows and pillowcases

If you are planning to camp or stay in cabins, take several pillows. They contribute to your comfort and act as padding for your equipment when you are in transit. Extra pillowcases are recommended, as the cases can become quite grubby, and it is refreshing to have a clean pillowcase at least once during a trip.

Refrigeration

A good-quality **Esky** and **block ice** will keep food frozen for several days in the winter. Open the Esky as little as possible. Indeed, if you have the space, also take a smaller, daytime Esky that you open and close for drinks and lunch.

It is quite difficult to buy block ice; usually the only ice widely available in the outback is party ice. This melts quickly and you may find yourself spending a lot of money on ice. Before you leave the city, freeze nearly-full plastic bottles of water and put them in your Esky. When they thaw, you will have an additional supply of drinking water.

Freezer packs contain chemicals, which work when agitated by breaking one chemical into another. These can be handy if you have the space, but they are quite expensive, can only be used once, and obviously cannot be drunk. You also have a chemical that needs to be disposed of somewhere.

There are numerous brands of **car fridge/freezers** on the market and they all have their advantages and disadvantages, but they are not cheap. We had a three-in-one, gas/electric/battery fridge, but it only worked if it was kept exactly level, and it had no insulation. We lost our perishable food on that trip. We then purchased an Australian-made 73-litre Autofridge by Quirk. It runs from the car battery, and has worked perfectly for us in all conditions, including 50°c temperatures. It even freezes bottles of water, and we then use them in the day-Esky.

Swag

If you are going to go bush camping frequently, you may want to consider buying a swag. They vary in price and size, and are obtainable from most camping stores. Swags are canvas envelopes into which you put your mattress and other bedding. You will be protected from the ground and from rain by the canvas.

Chose your swag with care. Swags can be airless, and very hot. Some swags don't unzip to the end of the bed. Some don't include flyscreens. If you are in a warm area, you may want to be able to fold back the top canvas cover but have a flyscreen over you. Our double swag — a Royal-dual — is fitted with a built-in fly net that zips closed over us. The top layer of canvas can be folded back to the end of the bed. This keeps us cool and also keeps the insects out. But beware, if any part of your body comes into contact with the fly net, you can still be bitten by mosquitoes!

If it is raining and you need to cover your head with the canvas, swags can be very dark and claustrophobic. Raise the canvas about one metre over your head with the short poles that may be provided with the swag. Even when the canvas is raised, it can be stuffy and dark, but you will stay dry, even in heavy rain. If we are expecting rain and are sleeping in our swag, we also erect a 'hutchie' over it so that we don't have to sleep with the dark canvas over our heads.

Tarpaulin

A tarpaulin is useful in any circumstances, including wet and cold weather. Your tarpaulin should measure about 2 metres x 4 metres in order to provide ground cover or overhead cover as required.

A 'hutchie' (a military term that refers to a very simple lean-to) made from a tarpaulin of this size will sleep two or three people comfortably. One version of the hutchie involves tying a rope from tree to tree, placing the tarp over it, and securing the tarp with tent pegs.

For a simpler version attach the tarp to the car by sliding the edge over the tops of the two doors on one side of the car, and close the doors firmly. Pull the tarp out about 1.5m to create a triangular lean-to, fix the corners with tent pegs, then fold the remainder back under towards the car as a ground sheet. For extra height, use short tent poles or stick to raise the outer corners of the tarp, and hold these in place with octopus straps and tent pegs.

If you are travelling with more than two people and you are likely to need overhead cover, you will probably need two tarpaulins, one for either side of the vehicle.

The light-blue plastic tarpaulins available from most service stations are perfectly adequate for this purpose. You will need several tent pegs and two tie-down ropes or octopus straps for each hutchie. It is convenient, but not essential, to have two tent poles for each hutchie as well.

Tents

The type of tent you purchase is a matter of personal choice and finance. If the weather is likely to be windy or wet, bell tents are ideal because you can sit and stand inside them comfortably. Small two-person tents are perfectly adequate for an overnight stop, and would be cosy in poor weather.

If you plan to camp in places as far away from other campers as possible, you may choose not to sleep in a conventional tent. In these circumstances we frequently use shade tents on our travels in the outback. The standard shade tent is large (4 x 4 x 3 metres high), with a plastic roof and walls of light mosquito netting. Consequently, a breeze flows through, and if you sleep in the tent you will have a clear view of the night sky through the sides of the tent. On a night with a full moon, you may even need eyeshades!

Shade tents are essential if you are going to camp for several days in an area where there are lots of flies and/or mosquitoes. You can use it to prepare and eat your meals in comfort. Equally, at night, if the shade tent is used as a bedroom, you will sleep comfortably in the knowledge that mosquitoes will not bother you.

Shade tents are either relatively cheap (about $110) or very expensive (about $800). There are two difficulties with the cheap tents: the zips don't last, and the poles tend to be clumsy to erect. We have overcome the problem of the inadequate zips by sewing up one side and having a heavy-duty zip sewn into the other side. We use two people to support the poles when erecting the tents.

For comfort, place a large tarpaulin on the ground of the sleeping shade tent. At night, if ants bother you, use fly spray around

the edges of the tarpaulin to discourage their passage towards
your sleeping bag.

Toilet paper

It is essential that you do not simply discard toilet tissue in the
bush — it takes a long time to break down and is very unsightly.
We recommend that you keep a roll of toilet paper in a small plastic bag, together with a box of matches and a pack of moist towellettes. In the bush, dispose of used tissue by burning carefully
or, if you are travelling, by storing them in a sealed plastic bag and
getting rid of the tissue at the next toilet. Calculate your needs
before you leave home, and then add an extra roll or two.

Water containers

Water containers should not be too large because if one leaks, or
is tipped over or contaminated accidentally, you will lose all of the
water. You will find that 20-litre containers are fairly standard.
However, you may find this heavy. If you are about to purchase
containers, buy two 10-litre containers instead of one 20-litre
container. Self-inflating containers are good because they don't
take up much room, but when they are empty they can be easily
punctured.

HAZARDS AND EMERGENCIES

If your vehicle or the track brings you to a halt on one of the remote unsealed tracks that we describe in the book:

- Don't panic! This will not change the emergency.
- Be flexible, and think laterally.
- Boil a billy and have a cup of tea while you assess the situation.
- If you are on any one of the tracks we describe in this book, someone will pass sooner or later.
- Avoid alcohol, as it will dehydrate you.
- Stay with the vehicle, unless you know that you are within walking distance of help, and you have companions fit enough to walk the distance, and you know exactly where you have to go. If you are not sure of this, you should all stay with your car.
- If it looks like you are going to have an extended stay, erect a tarpaulin for shelter, and relax.

ANIMALS

We do not recommend driving after dark when travelling in the outback. In the southern states most roads are fenced, but kangaroos and other animals still present problems. If you hit a large kangaroo or other animals at speed, there is a chance of the animal coming over the bonnet, through the windscreen and landing in your lap.

If you have no choice but to travel after dusk and before dawn, drive slowly, and have as many of your party as possible employed as spotters. We usually allocate the passenger in the front seat to the left-hand side of the vehicle, any back seat passenger is allocated the right-hand side, while the driver concentrates on the road straight ahead. If an animal appears, then the driver immediately slows to a walking speed until past the animal.

If an animal is hit or run over, it is the responsibility of the vehicle's occupants to ensure that the animal does not suffer. It is not a task for the squeamish, but there is nothing worse than allowing an animal to die slowly and in pain. The blade end of a shovel will suffice to put the animal out of misery. You should be guided by your conscience when deciding whether to report the accidental killing of domestic stock to station owners.

SNAKES

In all the years we have been camping in the outback we have seen just one tiger snake near our campsites, and one or two on the roads while we have been driving. They are not commonly seen. If you are lucky enough to see a snake, look at it from a safe distance and allow it to move away. You should not attempt to chase it or bother it, as it may attack you if provoked. If you do find one in your camp, watch it closely, back away to a distance of about 10 metres, and throw stones or sticks near it to encourage it to move off. If necessary, move your campsite.

Snakes usually bite if they are surprised, provoked, cornered or stood on. Most bites are ankle to knee-high. You can do several things to prevent snake bite:
- Be wary about walking through high grass, especially on creek, billabong or river banks. If you have to walk through this sort of ground, do so with a lot of noise. Wear boots if you can, and stomp hard on the ground as you walk. The vibrations from your movement should alert any snake in your path and give it time to get away. A stick pushed ahead of you and waved through the grass will have a similar effect.
- Never put your hand into a hole in the ground or in fallen timber. Apart from snakes, there could be spiders or scorpions in the hole.
- Take care during the early morning, as snakes are likely to be sunning themselves at this time. They may be sluggish until their body temperature is warm, but don't count on them not to bite if provoked.

Hazard	Signs	Danger	How to deal with it
Car dust on unsealed roads	Obvious	Loss of vision on the track ahead	If the vehicle is ahead of you, don't overtake until it is clear to do so. Be patient, but, if you must pass, make sure the other vehicle is aware of your intention to overtake. Use your lights and horn to alert the driver of your presence. If the vehicle is on-coming, slow down and, if necessary, prepare to stop as far to the left-hand side of the road as possible. You cannot be sure that some idiot will not overtake through the dust cloud.
Corrugations on unsealed roads	Wave patterns on the track ahead	Damage to shock absorbers, dislodging of load; excessive and frequent vibrations will damage your car and its components	Slow down to a point where the corrugations are not bone-jarring, and allow your shock absorbers to cool by stopping frequently. For example, if the corrugations are rough and you have a full car, take a break every 30 minutes or so.
Dead animals/ road kill	Obvious most of the time. Occasionally, dead animals on the road will be indicated by the presence of birds, such as eagles, hawks and crows.	Depends on the animal: carcasses of large road kill animals, such as cows and horses, can cause massive front-end damage and injury to vehicle occupants if hit at speed. Small animal bones can penetrate tyres.	Avoid them wherever possible and slow down until you have safely passed the carcass. It's also a good idea to close all air-intake vents and close your car windows to stop the smell from getting in your car.

(continued)

Hazard	Signs	Danger	How to deal with it
		Also, be aware that carrion eaters may wait until the last minute to fly/ bolt away.	
Floods	Usually very obvious, but occasionally signposts will indicate in advance that there is water across the road	Bogging, water flooding the vehicle. If you are crossing a creek or river, your car could be washed away, and the occupants injured or drowned.	Never cross a flooded creek without first checking the speed and depth of the water. If practicable, walk the crossing to check for underwater obstacles, and to determine if the bottom is solid or soft. Wrap a tarpaulin across the bonnet of your car and under the engine. This will assist in keeping the engine from water-logging. If the water depth and speed is low enough to allow you to ford it safely, enter the water slowly, and maintain a constant speed following the path you have previously chosen. If the water is spread all over the track and the surface is unsealed, your best bet is to back track and find another route. It is definitely not worth the risk of attempting to forge a way through and ending up bogged for an extended period. It is stress-ful, hard work to have to dig your-self out of one bog after another.
Road trains on unsealed roads or on narrow sealed roads	Obvious	Dust, with resultant loss of vision. The sheer size and number of trailers can result in buffeting, and subsequent loss of steering control.	Get off the road if possible by slowing or even stopping completely. Allow the train to pass unhindered. Never overtake through a road train's dust. Wait until the dust has settled before resuming your trip. If you are caught behind a road train, pull over, boil the billy, have a cup of tea and relax.

Hazard	Signs	Danger	How to deal with it
Roads not on the map in remote areas	Unidentifiable intersection	Losing your direction, with the resultant danger of being stranded	Note your trip-meter reading, the time, and any noticeable feature. Be prepared to return to your last-known starting point, and wait for other vehicles to provide advice on direction.
Stones and passing traffic	Oncoming vehicles on a stony road that don't slow down	Windscreen damage; injury to vehicle occupants	Move as far to the left of the road as possible. Slow down, even stop. Flash your lights at oncoming traffic to encourage them to travel slowly. If you are stationary, stay in the vehicle. If out of the car, get behind it and use it for protection from flying stones.

MEDICAL EMERGENCIES

If you plan to go bush camping or travel out to Cooper Creek, we recommend that at least one member of your party has some recent first aid training. There are several very good courses available from such bodies as the Red Cross and the St John Ambulance. We also highly recommend that you carry a reliable and clear first aid book. Probably the best guide to first aid measures available is the current *Australian Red Cross First Aid Manual*. Other excellent books are *Australian First Aid: An Authorised Manual of St John Ambulance Australia*, and Jennifer Brown and Tony Walker's *Royal Children's Hospital Safety & First Aid Book* (Lothian Books 1996).

Of course, every party must have a good first aid kit that can deal with all basic medical emergencies. Our kit has a comprehensive collection of bandages, dressings, ointment, tapes, powders and creams, all in small containers and arranged in a neat plastic fishing tackle box. We have added our favourite creams and ointments. In our equipment list we recommend items that should be included in any first aid kit for bush travel to remote regions.

It is important to refer to a first aid book for comprehensive information about symptoms and treatment. Here we have included some basic information about some of the medical emergencies that you may encounter. Stings, scratches, burns and stomach complaints are far more likely to occur than snake bites and heat exhaustion, but we have listed all these here for people who are unsure about venturing into the bush for the first time.

THE NATURE OF THE EMERGENCY AND HOW TO DEAL WITH IT

Burns

Pour cold water on the burn, and then use a water-soluble burn gel such as Burnaid. **Never apply creams or ointment to burns.** Gels are okay. If blisters form, do not burst them.

Burrs

Wash the infected area gently and then remove the burr, if possible. Some burrs have hooked spines that can break off in the skin and the area will quickly become infected. Put Magnoplasm on a pad, such as an Elastoplast strip, and secure this over the entry area to draw out the burr's spine. Avoid burrs by wearing sturdy footwear — we have seen burrs big enough to penetrate a thong and a foot!

Diarrhoea

Diarrhoea can be very dehydrating for young children, so make sure that they continue to drink fluids, preferably town or bottled drinking water mixed with Gastroltye rather than bore water.

Don't give anti-diarrhoeal medicine such as Lomotil. It is better to have a rest day and to allow nature to take its course, drinking only boiled water between doses of Gastrolyte, and avoiding dairy products.

Check that your group's camp hygiene is of a very high standard. If diarrhoea remains a problem, make sure everyone avoids drinking bore water.

Drowning or near drowning

If one of your party gets into difficulty in water, you may need to apply expired air resuscitation (EAR) or cardiopulmonary resuscitation (CPR). All basic first aid manuals will describe these procedures and the circumstances where each is necessary. But a manual cannot prepare you for these skills nearly as well as a basic first aid course. Do take precautions on any river trip and exercise common sense.

Eye injuries

Smoke or small foreign objects, such as bugs or twigs, are common sources of problems with eyes in the bush. Wash the eye by pouring cold water over it — use your drinking water to ensure that it is clean. This could take 20 minutes or so.

If a foreign object is embedded, do not use water to flush the eye. Instead, pad and bandage both eyes and seek medical assistance.

Heat exhaustion

Cool the person slowly by loosening their clothing, give them water to drink and sponge with cool water. Lie the person down in a cool place with good air circulation and fan, if necessary.

Insect bites

For most minor insect bites an application of a proprietary medicine, such as Stingose, will help to reduce the discomfort and itch. Refer to the table below, which details the actions that you should take, depending on the nature of the bite.

Identified Creature	Cold Pack	Pressure immobilisation	Reassure	Medical Attention
ANT	✔		✔	
BEE	✔		✔	
Allergy to bee		✔	✔	✔
CENTIPEDE	✔		✔	children
SCORPION	✔		✔	children
SNAKE (ALL)		✔	✔	✔

Identified Creature	Cold Pack	Pressure immobilisation	Reassure	Medical Attention
SPIDERS:				
Funnel-web spider		✔	✔	✔
All other spiders	✔		✔	✔
TICK		✔	✔	✔
WASP	✔		✔	
Allergy to wasp		✔	✔	✔

Lacerations and haemorrhage

Apply direct pressure and elevate the wound — combined dressings are ideal for this. Treat for shock if necessary. If the injury is severe, seek local medical assistance.

Limb injuries

Where it is obvious that bones are broken, immobilise the limb with well-padded splints, and bandage firmly into place. Treat for shock, and seek medical assistance as soon as possible.

Do not move anyone with back or neck injuries without medical advice. Call for assistance, using whatever means you have available, such as your HF radio. The Royal Flying Doctor Service will give you instructions regarding what actions you should take.

Shock

Shock can be recognised by pale, cool, sweaty skin, weak and rapid pulse, altered conscious state, discomfort, nausea, thirst, history of injury or illness that has resulted in a loss of any body fluid, bleeding, vomiting, diarrhoea, burns, internal injuries or fractures. Follow first aid procedures to maintain airway, breathing and circulation, control normal body temperature and minimise fluid loss. **Seek urgent medical assistance — SHOCK CAN KILL!**

Snake bite

Wrap a broad, heavy, smooth crepe bandage immediately over the snake bite. Wrap a second bandage from the toes to the groin, if the bite is on the leg. If the bite is on a hand or arm, bandage as far as the armpit if possible. Each wrap of bandage should cover half to two-thirds of the previous wrap. Splint to avoid movement of the affected limb. Treat for shock.

Identify the snake if possible, but don't endanger others or yourself in the process. **Seek medical assistance as soon as possible.**

Sprains and strains

In the event of sprains or strains, apply ice-packs for up to ten minutes, with a short break between applications for the first few hours. Do not apply heat or heat rubs for at least three days. If you have any doubts about the injury, treat as a fracture.

Sunburn

If you adhere to the 'Slip, Slop, Slap' regime, sunburn should not be a problem. However, even when sitting in the shade you can still be exposed to reflected UV rays. Frequent application of 15+ sunscreen is a must.

If a member of your party is suffering from sunburn, and you have ice or icy water, put this into a towel and gently pat the burnt areas. Then apply a burn gel such as Burnaid, give plenty of liquids to drink, and keep the person in the shade. Don't apply calamine lotion. If blisters form, try not to break them.

COOKING IN THE BUSH
HINTS AND TIPS

Food and wine are part of the attraction of the waterways, and there are plenty of places to eat along the river tracks. However, there are also many opportunities for fun and easy bush cookery. The following are tips based on our experience.

Menu planning

- You can have a wide range of meals in the bush, from simple barbecues to rich casseroles.
- Anything you can cook on a gas or electric ring at home can be cooked in the bush on gas, but it will be slower.
- After a long drive, select a simple meal that cooks quickly and uses few utensils, such as jaffles or a barbecue.
- Invite older children and teenagers to plan a meal and co-ordinate its preparation from start to finish.
- At least once on the trip, after a short drive or a day relaxing in camp, try an elaborate, wood-cooked meal with some of it cooked under coals in an underground pit.
- Plan your menu around your refrigeration, using perishable food early in the trip. We usually have baked fish early on because it takes up so much room in the fridge, and we prefer not to freeze it before leaving.
- Marinating meats and basting vegetables will provide flavour, and ensure that the food does not dry out. Food can be put into a marinade earlier in the day, but check that the container seals well!

- If you are driving for much of the holiday and plan to cook your own food along the way, you could pre-cook a casserole, curry or bolognese sauce that can be heated up very simply in a saucepan on gas.
- When travelling all day, put some thought into lunches because they are a very important part of the trip. When travelling with children, we often schedule to have lunch on a long stretch of road between features to add our own diversion from the track.
- Root vegetables — such as potatoes, pumpkin, sweet potatoes, onions — last very well on a long trip. Wrap them individually in paper to extend their shelf-life. Take note of restrictions on carrying fresh fruit and vegetables into the quarantine areas along the Murray River (see pp. 22–3 for quarantine information).
- Use cans of peas, mushrooms, carrots and other vegetables to add substance to a casserole later in the trip. Add the water in the can to the casserole. Dried vegetables are also very useful.
- When we set up camp for a number of days, we hang the vegetables up in a large net bag to let air flow around them.

Gas cookery

- Use a gas cooker when possible, because wood can be scarce.
- Keep most of your meals simple and quick, to save on gas.
- Bring one or two conventional saucepans for cooking on the gas rings.
- Large gas cylinders, such as the 9 kg variety, are very heavy. We carry a 2 kg gas cylinder and fill it up at the larger service stations. Make sure your bottle has been recently inspected and stamped by an authorised inspection service, or the roadhouse managers won't fill it.
- Use a windshield on your stove if you have one, otherwise choose a sheltered spot so you don't waste the heat.
- Use a chuffer or volcano kettle to boil water quickly and save on gas.
- Ensure that all adults and teenagers in the party know how to turn the gas stove on and off. Incorrectly tightened knobs could cost you gas.

- We use a double adaptor on our gas cylinder so that we can run the cooker and the gas lamp from the same outlet.

Wood cookery

- Firewood can be limited, so keep wood cookery to a minimum.
- Wood in the semi-arid country is very dense, and you won't need much to cook a meal on.
- Always use gardening gloves when handling wood.
- For safety, draw a circle around the fire as a line beyond which children should not go.
- Big blazing campfires, particularly when you are cooking, are a waste of firewood. The food will either undercook and dry out quickly, or overcook and burn. It is almost impossible to control the heat. Even vigorous basting or adding lots of liquid to casseroles will not help. Most campfire cooking is best carried out when the wood has burnt down to glowing embers or coals. Enough heat is generated by a couple of shovelfuls of hot coals, replenished several times, to cook a covered casserole slowly and thoroughly (see pp. 345–8).
- Vegetables in foil cooked on coals underground are very difficult to burn (see pp. 345–6).

Food preparation

- If there are a lot of flies around, prepare the meal inside a shade tent or wait until sunset. Alternatively, roster your family to waft a small leafy branch or fan over the person preparing the food to keep flies at bay.
- Keep cooked and uncooked meats separate, and if possible use separate boards and knives or wash them thoroughly during food preparations.
- Chop vegetables that are to be cooked together into even-sized pieces.

Utensils

- When planning your menu, work out how many saucepans or pots and kitchen tools you may need.

- Two chopping boards, one large knife and one small sharp knife will always be useful.
- Standard, long-handled barbecue equipment is important to protect your hands from the heat of a fire.
- Ideally use a lightweight metal plate and a grid on legs for cooking your barbecue.
- A stainless-steel billy resists denting, and will not rust. A chuffer or volcano kettle will boil water in five minutes by burning leaves and twigs in the central cavity.
- A cast-iron Dutch oven or bedourie oven can be used for most of your campfire cooking, including roasts, casseroles, soups, pasta, etc. If you want to make bread, the bedourie is the preferable shape. Its lid can double as a frying pan, also it will not crack like a cast-iron Dutch oven if dropped.
- Have a good pair of oven mitts or pot-holders and a pair of steel lifters in your kitchen kit.

Refrigeration

For information on refrigeration, see page 327.

Rubbish and camping in remote areas

- Keep glass bottles to a minimum, and take all empties with you until you find an authorised dumping site.
- Burn cans to clean them out, allow them to cool, and then squash them before putting them in your rubbish container.
- Vegetable and fruit peelings should be disposed of in the fire, or in an authorised dump. Never throw peelings away — there is a chance you could introduce unwanted plants into the bush.
- Burn all paper, cork, and cardboard rubbish, but be mindful of the threat of bushfires from flying embers. Watch the wind, and have someone on stand-by to put out spot fires should they occur. If it is too windy, store materials until the next safe opportunity to burn them.
- Use heavy-duty plastic bags for your rubbish, even doubling them inside one another if you have to carry them for a distance.
- You will find designated rubbish dumps near most major country centres.

Preparing the campfire

LIGHTING THE FIRE

Use a designated fireplace if one has been provided; in most national parks and state parks this will be the case. If you have to make your own fire:

- Dig a trench and mound up the soil or sand downwind of the fire, as you don't want sand or dust blowing into your food while it is cooking
- Place a handful of dry grass or leaves into the trench or fireplace first, and progressively add twigs and then branches. Light the fire. Once your fire is burning well, add thicker branches. Dry bush timber can generate a tremendous amount of heat that can be controlled more easily if allowed to burn down to coals.
- If you want to cook food underground, dig a shallow trench about 1 metre long beside the fireplace.

HOW TO COOK FOOD UNDERGROUND

Cooking underground is an ideal method for cooking meats and fish, and is absolutely perfect for cooking vegetables:

- Cut vegetables into large chunks and wrap them securely in aluminium foil. We would cut an average-sized potato in three, baste in oil and spices, and wrap all three segments together in two layers of foil.
- If you are cooking fish, fill the fish with your favourite fillings, and wrap the fish in several layers of foil.
- Shovel a layer of hot coals into the trench, leaving the remaining coals in the original fire.
- Count the number of foil parcels so you don't miss any later, then place them into the trench, laying them carefully on the glowing coals. Put a couple of shovel-loads of coal over them.
- Quickly fill in the trench with your reserved soil or sand. In this ground-oven, your food will cook thoroughly.

When you are ready to leave your camp, fill in the trench and self-made fireplace with clean soil or sand, and tramp them down. Leave no unsightly mounds to indicate your presence. Any charcoal should be buried.

A ROAST

A really delicious meal that should be cooked in a campfire during a long-stay camp is:

* Roast scotch fillet of beef, chicken, a lamb leg, or a piece of roasting pork (it's up to you)
* Roast potatoes, pumpkin, sweet potatoes, swedes and carrots
* Canned peas, drained, or fresh beans
* A rich sauce that is simple to prepare.

1. Prepare the meat as you would at home, ensuring that you oil it thoroughly. Place it on a wire rack in a hot Dutch oven.
2. Cover and place the oven over a bed of coals. Set this up by simply placing a shovel full of coals from the fire onto the ground beside the fireplace. A trench is not required unless there is a wind, then a windbreak of some sort would be a good idea. Place some coals on the oven lid.
3. Check the meat after half an hour and adjust the quantity of coals on the lid if it is burning or cooking too slowly. Too many coals and the meat will burn, too few and the meat will take too long to cook.
4. Peel the potatoes, swedes and carrots, and wash the skins on the pumpkin. Cut the vegetables into even-sized pieces. In a bowl, lightly coat the pieces with some oil and mixed herbs and then make aluminum foil parcels consisting of a sample of each vegetable or individual pieces. Fold the edges of the foil over several times to dust-proof the food as far as possible. Parcels of green beans are delicious cooked this way too.
5. Place the parcels on a bed of coals in the trench. Count the number of parcels so you don't miss any later. Cover them with a layer of glowing coals, and another layer of soil or sand, and leave for about 40 minutes. When cooked, use a shovel to turn the sand cover of the trench and use a heat-proof glove to retrieve the parcels of cooked vegetables.
6. Open the parcels carefully to avoid introducing any dust or ash. The vegetables will be slightly smoky, flavoursome, juicy, fluffy and will cook perfectly without any danger of burning.
7. Remove the meat from the Dutch oven, taking care not to allow any dust into it. If the meat hasn't burnt, take some of the juices from the Dutch oven, and pour them into a small

saucepan. For ease, cook up a packet sauce and pour immediately over the meal.
8. Serve without hesitation — food in the bush gets cold quickly.

VEGIE BURGERS

Any leftover vegetables and meat can be combined the next day with flour, eggs, herbs and spices into patties, and cooked in an oiled pan or on a barbecue plate. The patties are delicious hot, or served cold as a lunchtime snack.

CURRIES AND CASSEROLES

Bush curries and casseroles are filling and delicious meals. Eat them when they are hot, then use leftovers as fillings in jaffles or pies. The base of the casserole may be beef, chicken, lamb, sausage, vegetables, or fish (although fish requires a different technique — you will need to cook the fish pieces separately and then combine with curried vegetables). For meat casseroles or curries, follow these steps:
1. Cut the meat into even-sized pieces and toss them in a plastic bag with flour, mixed herbs, or spices.
2. Place a liberal amount of good vegetable oil into the Dutch oven and sit it on a bed of coals away from the fire. Then add the dry herbs and spices (or curry mixture, if that is what you plan to make). Add coarsely chopped onions, a clove of crushed garlic, and fry until soft. Do not attempt to cook a casserole on flaming wood.
3. Place the meat little by little into the oven, and brown each piece. Ensure that you seal the meat before adding any liquid. The burnt bits on the bottom and sides of the oven add to the flavour of the stew or curry.
4. If you are making a sausage casserole or curry, give the sausages a longer browning time than other meats. Bacon pieces in a casserole add a new set of flavours too.
5. Add a cup or two of water, a cup of red wine, a can of tomatoes with their juice, and a dash of vinegar or lemon juice. Cook for ten minutes and then add washed potatoes and carrots and mushrooms (leave the vegetables in largish pieces), salt and

pepper to taste, and add some more water to cover the lot. Put the lid on and put the oven on some fresh coals. Place some coals on the lid also.

6. Cook for another 20 minutes, then check the liquid level. By now there should be a thickish sauce around the meat and vegetables. Give it a stir, taste it so that you can adjust the seasoning, and then put the lid back on and cook for another 20 minutes or so. Add fresh hot coals to the base or lid if required. The slower and longer the cooking the better, except that the vegetables will disintegrate if you cook them for too long.

7. If you are having a curry, you may wish to cook some rice. Rice is a bit of a problem to cook on an open fire, gas is definitely the easiest way to cook it. But, with some care, it can be done over hot coals. We use the absorption method, and find that we use more water than we would at home. Instead of two cups of water for one cup of rice, try three cups of water for one of rice. Then watch it closely! Don't bother putting coals on top of the oven, a few coals underneath is sufficient. Besides, you are going to have to take the lid off frequently to ensure that the water hasn't boiled away.

PIES

The camp oven is very good for cooking both savoury and sweet pies. Use your normal piecrust pastry for the savoury varieties and a sweet shortcrust for fruit pies. Packet pastry mixes are excellent value and easy to use in the bush.

When you are cooking the pie in the Dutch oven, put a metal grid or several stones underneath your pie dish so that it does not come into contact with the base of the oven. This will help to prevent it burning. Monitor the progress of the pie carefully so that you can adjust the coals to achieve a golden crust.

CAMPSITE READING

* *

The following is a list of well-written and gripping stories that we recommend for campsite reading along the tracks. Our main source of information on Aboriginal history was *The Encyclopaedia of Aboriginal Australia*, edited by David Horton (Aboriginal Studies Press 1994).

Burke and Wills: from Melbourne to Myth, Tim Bonyhady (David Ell Press 1991)

Innamincka, Elizabeth Burchill (Hodder and Stoughton 1960)

Henry Lawson: A Stranger on the Darling, Robyn Burrows and Alan Barton (Angus and Robertson 1996)

Lament for the Barkindji: The Vanished Tribes of the Darling River Region, B. Hardy (Rigby 1976)

Conquest of the Ngarrindjeri, G. Jenkin (Rigby 1979)

Menindee: First Town on the River Darling, Sandra J. Maiden, (Sunnyland Press, n.d.)

Matya-Mundu: A History of the Aboriginal People of South West Queensland, Hazel McKellar (Cunnamulla Australian Native Welfare Association 1984)

Cooper's Creek, Alan Moorehead (Penguin 1988)

Mystery of the Leichhardt Survivor: The Story of the Men Who Fought to Solve It, Les Perrin (self-published 1991)

Drought or Deluge: Man in the Cooper's Creek Region, Helen Tolcher (Melbourne University Press 1986)

Conrick of Nappa Merrie: A Pioneer of Cooper Creek Helen Tolcher (1997)

INDEX